COMPLETE
HORSE
CARE
MANUAL

COLIN VOGEL

Penguin Random House

ORIGINAL EDITION (1995)
Project Editor Louise Pritchard
Project Art Editor Gurinder Purewall
Editor Katie John
Design Assistant Darren Hill
Production Hilary Stephens
Managing Art Editor Nigel Duffield
Senior Managing Editor Josephine Buchanan
Senior Managing Art Editor Lynne Brown
Editorial Consultant Gig Lees
Photography Andy Crawford and Kit Houghton

SECOND EDITION (2003)
Senior Editors Pip Morgan, Simon Tuite
Senior Art Editors Edward Kinsey, Joanne Doran
US Editor Christine Heilman
Managing Editor Deirdre Headon
Managing Art Editor Lee Griffiths
DTP Designer Louise Waller
Picture Researcher Juliet Duff
Production Manager Lauren Britton
Production Controller Heather Hughes

THIS EDITION
Senior Editor Paula Regan
Senior Art Editor Gadi Farfour
Production Editor Luca Frassinetti
Production Controller Mandy Inness

Photographed at
Wellington Riding, Heckfield, Hampshire, England

First American Edition, 1995
This revised edition published in 2011
Published in the United States by
DK Publishing
1450 Broadway, Suite 801
New York, NY 10018, USA

15 17 16
026—179999—Feb/2011

Published in Great Britain by Dorling Kindersley Limited.

A catalog record for this book is available from the
Library of Congress.

ISBN: 978-0-7566-7160-0

Color reproduction by Colourscan, Singapore

Printed and Bound in China

**A WORLD OF IDEAS:
SEE ALL THERE IS TO KNOW**

www.dk.com

CONTENTS

Introduction

INTRODUCTION

THE DOMESTIC HORSE has always occupied an important place in human life. At first, domesticated horses probably had two roles, the slower, "cold-blooded" forest horses as beasts of burden and the faster, "warm-blooded" plains horses as a means of travel. Today, horses are no longer used in battle, the tractor has largely taken over in agriculture, and the gasoline engine is the main means of transportation. Yet horses are still held in high esteem. People have bred them selectively to suit their needs or their concept of beauty. Several different types of horses and a large number of breeds are now recognized internationally.

Being in control of your horse

The relationship you build up with a horse must be based on respect, not on fear and pain. Until that relationship is established, you must convince the animal that you are in control. Once you show uncertainty, it will start to act up and test you. Your horse is probably bigger and certainly stronger than you. At over 1,000 lb (500 kg), the average riding horse is six times heavier than an average man, so you cannot dominate it with strength. The horse must do what you ask because it wants to, or expects to, not because it is afraid of you.

Communicating with each other

A horse cannot be expected to understand exactly what you want it to do the first time it is asked. It will, however, know when it has done something right if you show that you are pleased. Communication should be a two-way process. Try to understand what your horse is saying to you, too, by learning its body language. Horses are not really intelligent; most are not problem-solvers, but they learn quickly. They have no concept of morality, so they learn what humans consider to be bad behavior just as easily as good behavior—if they are allowed to. You must be particularly careful not to allow a horse to learn that it can get what it wants through undesirable behavior. For example, don't let it learn that if it threatens to bite you, you will allow it to have its own way.

Considering the horse's needs

When you agree to care for a horse, you take on the responsibility of providing it with everything it needs. To do this properly, you should understand how the horses live in the wild. You will then be better able to provide an environment for your horse that is as close to natural as possible. You must know a little about the horse's structure and how its body systems work, learn to recognize signs of ill health, and know how to deal with injury or disease. You must also use equipment and tack so that it does not hurt the horse. If the horse is happy in its home and in its work, it will be more willing and able to do what you ask of it, and the two of you will enjoy a mutually beneficial relationship.

CHAPTER **ONE**

LOOKING AT THE HORSE

WE HAVE APPRECIATED THE HORSE'S BEAUTY OF

FORM AND MOVEMENT SINCE THE STONE AGE,

YET WE DID NOT KNOW HOW A HORSE MOVED:

GREEK ARTISTS DEPICTED A GALLOPING HORSE

WITH ITS FRONT AND BACK LEGS EXTENDED TOGETHER.

BUT EADWEARD MUYBRIDGE'S PIONEERING

PHOTOGRAPHS SHOWED US EXACTLY HOW A

HORSE MOVES. EVEN TODAY, MOST PEOPLE KNOW

LITTLE OF THE HORSE'S ORIGINS—ITS ANATOMY,

BODY SYSTEMS, AND NATURAL BEHAVIOR ARE ALL

ADAPTED FOR A LIFE AS A WILD HERD ANIMAL AND

DICTATE HOW IT SHOULD BE CARED FOR.

DEVELOPMENT OF THE HORSE

The modern horse (*Equus caballus*) has been 60 million years in the making. That is how long it has taken its earliest ancestor, *Eohippus*, to evolve into the family Equidae. This family includes the zebra, the donkey, and the domestic horse, as well as the less well-known wild asses of Africa and Asia, and Przewalski's wild horse. It is thought that the immediate ancestors of the modern horse were three primitive types of horses. From these, two pony types and two horse types possibly developed; these, in turn, were the foundation of all modern types and breeds.

ANCIENT AND MODERN

MODERN HORSE

EOHIPPUS

Small ancestor
Eohippus was much smaller than the modern horse—only about 14 in (35 cm) at the shoulder. Instead of having one toe protected by a hoof, as a modern horse has, it had a pad with four toes on the forefeet and three on the hind feet.

THREE PRIMITIVE TYPES

Forest horse (*left*)
An important ancestor of some modern breeds was the Forest Horse of northern Europe. It lived in woodland, where galloping speed was not important. It had large hooves to spread its weight on wet ground, and thick hair to protect it. It may have looked like this modern French Poitevin, which lives on marshes.

Przewalski's horse (*above*)
Przewalski's horse is the only true survivor of the three early types of horse. In prehistoric times, it lived on the steppes of central Asia and Europe. It has coarse features and a tufted tail—more like an ass than a modern horse. Small numbers have been bred in captivity since 1902, and selected groups are now being used to increase the wild herds.

Tarpan (*right*)
The Tarpan has influenced many breeds. We are probably indebted to it, via the Arab, for the refined look of our modern horse's head. The original Tarpan is extinct, but attempts are being made to recreate it, as shown here. It evolved in semi-desert conditions in Europe and Asia and had a fine physique, necessary for traveling long distances in search of food.

DESCENDANTS OF FOUR BASIC TYPES

EXMOOR PONY
HEIGHT: 12.2–12.3 HH
(127–129 CM)

Highland
Pony Type 2 lived in northern Europe and Asia. It was adapted to be resistant to cold and was heavily built. The Highland pony is thought to be a descendant.

HIGHLAND PONY
HEIGHT: UP TO
14.2 HH (147 CM)

Exmoor
The Exmoor, possibly the oldest breed in Great Britain, is believed to be similar to Pony Type 1. This type lived in northwest Europe. It had a thick coat and bushy mane and tail to protect it against cold and wet.

Akhal-Teke
Horse Type 3 was a tough horse that lived mainly in the deserts of central Asia. Its fine coat and slender build helped it to lose heat. The Akhal-Teke is probably a descendant.

AKHAL-TEKE
HEIGHT: 15.2 HH
(157 CM)

PERCHERON
HEIGHT: 16.2 HH
(168 CM)

Percheron
One of the largest modern horse breeds, the Percheron is actually descended from the delicate Arab, which in turn is thought to derive mainly from Horse Type 4. This was a fine-boned desert horse that lived in western Asia.

TYPES OF HORSE

A breed is a distinct genetic entity. If one member of a breed mates with another, all their offspring will be similar to them in appearance. Humans have helped to fix horse breeds by mating selected animals and crossing their descendants to reinforce the horses' best features. Today, recognized members of a breed are entered in an official stud book. Horses that are not any specific breed may be described as a certain type. Types have a set of physical characteristics that happen to help them perform specific functions. Horses of the same type do not breed true when they are mated to each other, which means that their offspring will not necessarily have all the same characteristics.

Show pony

A miscellany of breeds can be mixed together to produce the show pony. Most often the mixture contains Thoroughbred blood and pony breeds. Some ponies have more Thoroughbred in them than others and are used primarily for showing rather than for casual riding. By definition, a pony is under 14.2 hh (147 cm); in competitions, they are grouped in classes according to height—for example, 12.2 hh (127 cm) and under.

Well-muscled hindquarters for withstanding a variety of activities

Refined, "appealing" head

"Clean" legs with short cannons and flat, hard joints

The head is carried extended rather than flexed

Quarter horse

This is claimed to be the most popular horse in the world. It was bred to sprint over a distance of a quarter-mile, and so has heavy, muscular quarters. It grows up to 14.3—16 hh (150—163 cm) high. Famous for working with cattle, the quarter horse can turn tightly. It has short cannons and its fetlocks slope at 45°. The head is carried extended rather than flexed.

Short cannons

The fetlocks slope at 45°

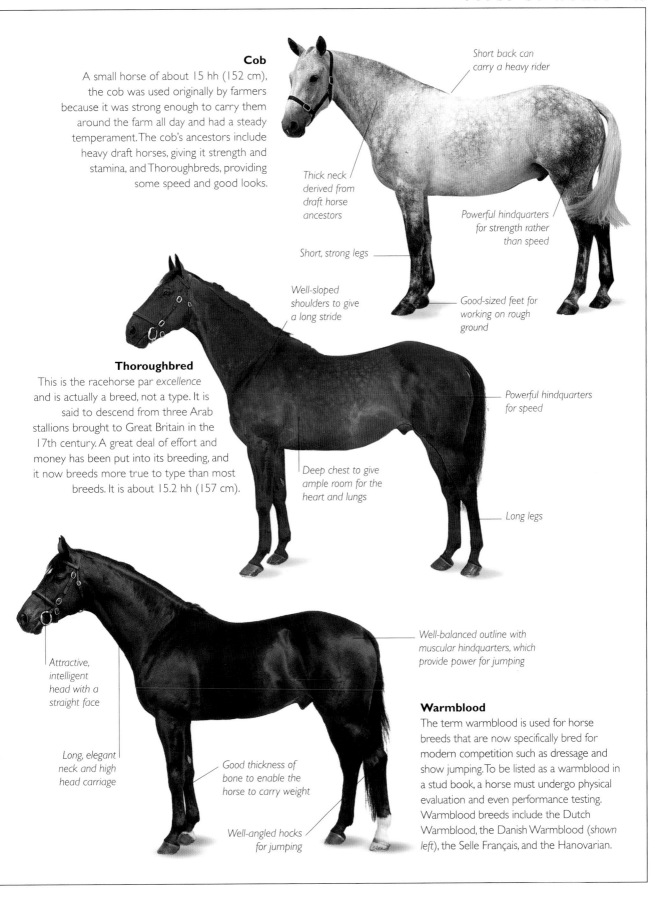

Cob

A small horse of about 15 hh (152 cm), the cob was used originally by farmers because it was strong enough to carry them around the farm all day and had a steady temperament. The cob's ancestors include heavy draft horses, giving it strength and stamina, and Thoroughbreds, providing some speed and good looks.

Short back can carry a heavy rider

Thick neck derived from draft horse ancestors

Powerful hindquarters for strength rather than speed

Short, strong legs

Good-sized feet for working on rough ground

Well-sloped shoulders to give a long stride

Thoroughbred

This is the racehorse par *excellence* and is actually a breed, not a type. It is said to descend from three Arab stallions brought to Great Britain in the 17th century. A great deal of effort and money has been put into its breeding, and it now breeds more true to type than most breeds. It is about 15.2 hh (157 cm).

Powerful hindquarters for speed

Deep chest to give ample room for the heart and lungs

Long legs

Well-balanced outline with muscular hindquarters, which provide power for jumping

Attractive, intelligent head with a straight face

Long, elegant neck and high head carriage

Good thickness of bone to enable the horse to carry weight

Well-angled hocks for jumping

Warmblood

The term warmblood is used for horse breeds that are now specifically bred for modern competition such as dressage and show jumping. To be listed as a warmblood in a stud book, a horse must undergo physical evaluation and even performance testing. Warmblood breeds include the Dutch Warmblood, the Danish Warmblood (*shown left*), the Selle Français, and the Hanovarian.

COLORS AND MARKINGS

The coat of early horses was probably a certain color to provide camouflage in the wild and allow the horse to blend into its background and so hide from predators. A sandy-colored coat still provides Przewalski's horse (*see p. 10*) with a good camouflage in its desert home. Most of the colors we see today have been developed by humans through selective breeding. Some colors are dominant over others; a foal will be the dominant color if only one of its parents is that color. Other colors are recessive; only if both parents are that color is the foal likely to be, too. The order of dominance of the main colors to each other is gray, bay, brown, then black. Chestnut is recessive.

DORSAL STRIPE

A dark stripe along a horse's back is called a dorsal stripe, or list. Early horses had one, and the mark can be seen today on some dark-skinned horses.

BASIC COAT COLORS

First impression
The color of a horse is one of the first things used to describe it. Important factors in determining this color are not only the color of the horse's body, but also the color of the skin, mane and tail, and extremities of the legs.

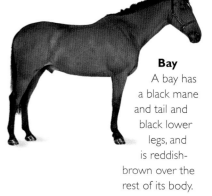

Bay
A bay has a black mane and tail and black lower legs, and is reddish-brown over the rest of its body.

Dun
A dun varies from mouse-colored to sand-colored with a dark skin. It usually has a black mane, tail, and legs.

Chestnut
This is a reddish-brown horse with a similar-colored mane and tail.

Brown
A horse with a black mane, tail, and legs, and a mixture of brown and black hairs over the rest of its body.

Palomino
A gold-colored horse with a much paler, sometimes almost white, mane and tail.

Roan
Roans have white hairs mixed with black (blue roan, *left*), bay (red roan), or chestnut (strawberry roan).

Gray
Gray horses vary from white to dark gray and can be plain, dappled (right), or flea-bitten. All have black skin.

Spotted
Brown or black spots, confined to a "blanket" on the rump or spread over the whole body.

Pinto
The coat has large areas of brown or black and white. A horse of this coloring is also known as a paint.

LEG MARKINGS

Extents of white

When describing the white markings on a horse's leg, it is best to refer to the top limit of the white. White areas are susceptible to infections because the skin, which has no pigment, is delicate.

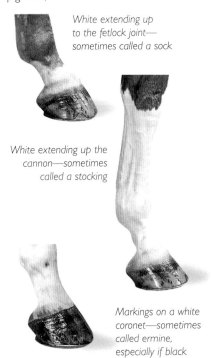

White extending up to the fetlock joint—sometimes called a sock

White extending up the cannon—sometimes called a stocking

Markings on a white coronet—sometimes called ermine, especially if black

FACE MARKINGS

Names

White markings on the face can be a star (any white marking between or above the eyes), a snip (a white mark between the nostrils), a stripe (a narrow, vertical white mark), a blaze (a wide mark down the nose), or a freckled stripe. These markings are often the inspiration for horses' names.

STAR

SNIP

STRIPE

BLAZE

FRECKLED STRIPE

HOOVES

DARK HORN

PALE HORN

MIXED HORN

Horn variety

The hoof may have dark, pigmented horn, creamy, pale horn, or both. If both colors are present, the boundary is always a vertical one, with particular areas of the coronary band always producing the same color horn. All horn is the same hardness.

EYES

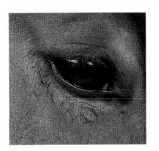

PIGMENTED IRIS

WALLEYE

Pigment variety

The majority of horses have a brown-pigmented iris in both eyes. Irises with no pigment, or with a tinge of blue, are called walleyes. These can make a horse look a bit wild, but are no indication of character. The horse can see perfectly well.

PHYSICAL FEATURES

The relationship between the structure and function of a horse is referred to as its "conformation." The ideal conformation looks good and also works efficiently. In the wild, a horse must be able to move easily in its particular environment to find food and water, and escape quickly from danger for its survival. Humans can support and protect a domestic horse with boots and bandages, but it is more likely to perform well without strain or injury if it has a good conformation.

POINTS OF THE HORSE

Good conformation

A horse should have "clean," symmetrical limbs that enable it to gallop at speed without the joints being jarred. A deep chest is necessary to contain the heart and lungs, and powerful hindquarters are needed for propulsion. Its head should be in proportion to the rest of its body, and its neck should be well set into powerful, sloping shoulders.

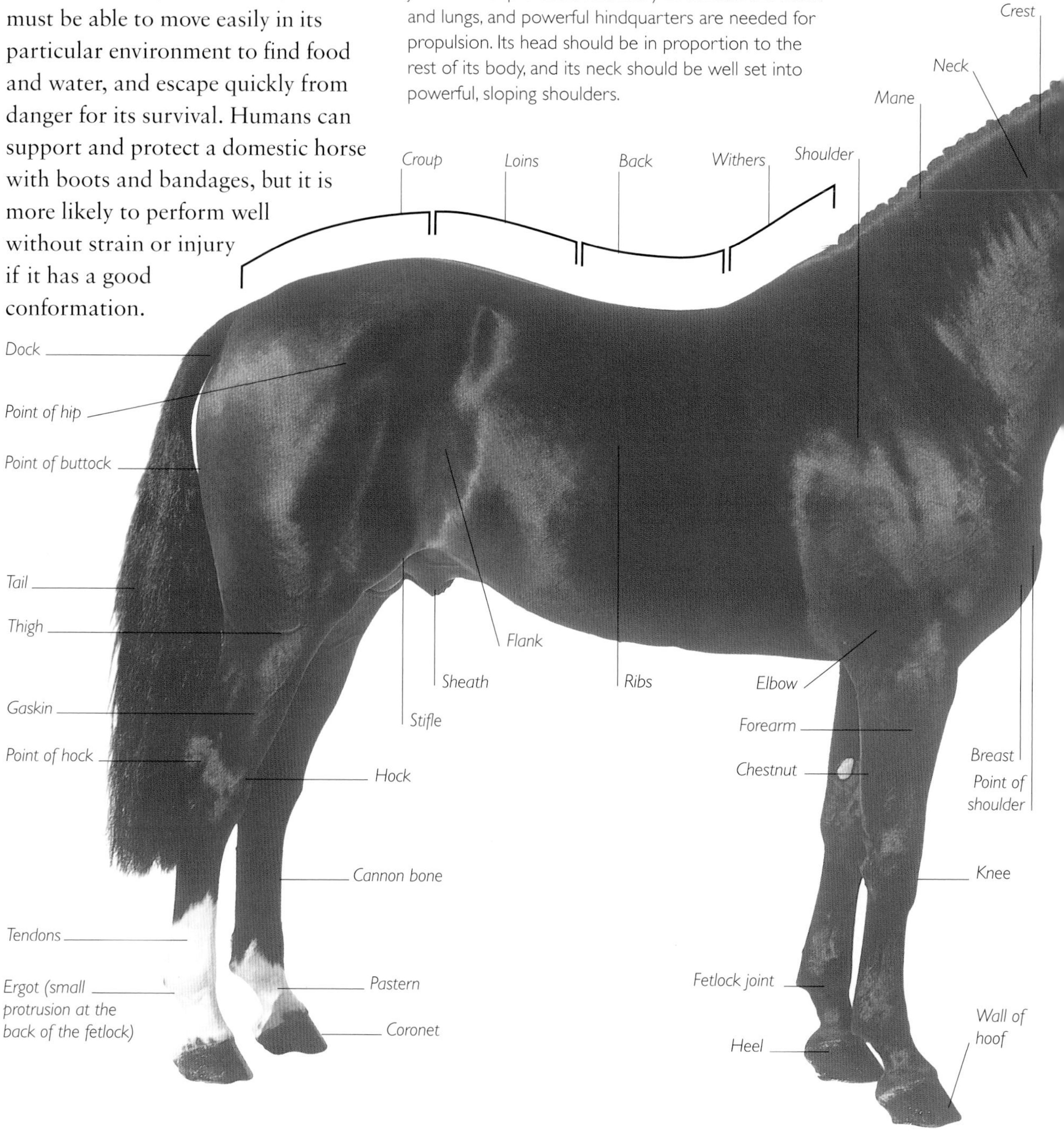

Crest

Neck

Mane

Croup

Loins

Back

Withers

Shoulder

Dock

Point of hip

Point of buttock

Tail

Thigh

Gaskin

Point of hock

Hock

Flank

Sheath

Stifle

Ribs

Elbow

Forearm

Chestnut

Breast

Point of shoulder

Cannon bone

Knee

Tendons

Ergot (small protrusion at the back of the fetlock)

Pastern

Coronet

Fetlock joint

Heel

Wall of hoof

SKELETON

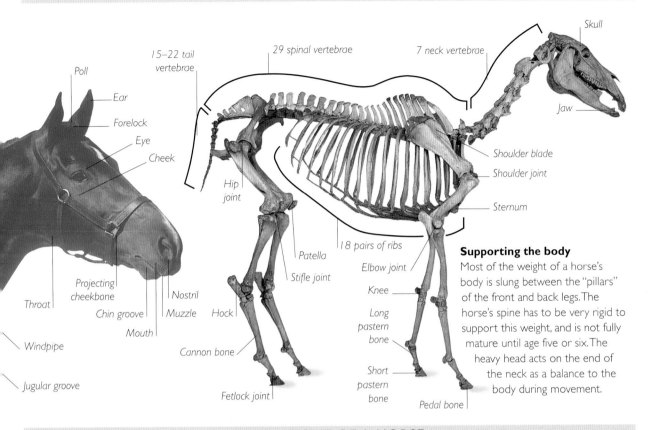

Poll

Ear

Forelock

Eye

Cheek

15–22 tail vertebrae

29 spinal vertebrae

7 neck vertebrae

Skull

Jaw

Shoulder blade

Shoulder joint

Sternum

Hip joint

18 pairs of ribs

Patella

Stifle joint

Elbow joint

Knee

Long pastern bone

Short pastern bone

Pedal bone

Projecting cheekbone

Throat

Chin groove

Nostril

Muzzle

Mouth

Hock

Cannon bone

Windpipe

Jugular groove

Fetlock joint

Supporting the body

Most of the weight of a horse's body is slung between the "pillars" of the front and back legs. The horse's spine has to be very rigid to support this weight, and is not fully mature until age five or six. The heavy head acts on the end of the neck as a balance to the body during movement.

THE HEIGHT OF A HORSE

HANDS AND INCHES

METERS AND CENTIMETERS

Measure at the highest point of the withers when the horse is standing square—ideally with no shoes on

It is useful to know a horse's height as part of its description and as a size guide for buying tack and clothing. Horses are also grouped by height at horse shows. Height is often given in hands and inches. Originally, a hand was the width of a man's hand, but it was standardized to 4 in (10 cm). Height may now also be given in centimeters.

LEGS AND JOINTS

The main components of the leg are the bones, muscles, tendons, and ligaments. In the horse's leg, there are no muscles below the knee and hock; long tendons link the muscles to the foot and lower leg to allow movement. The legs often undergo great stress; for example, at certain moments when the horse is galloping, its whole weight is carried by only one leg (*see p. 22*), and severe tension is put on the tendons at the back of the cannon bone. Good conformation helps prevent abnormal strains from developing and causing injury.

STRUCTURE

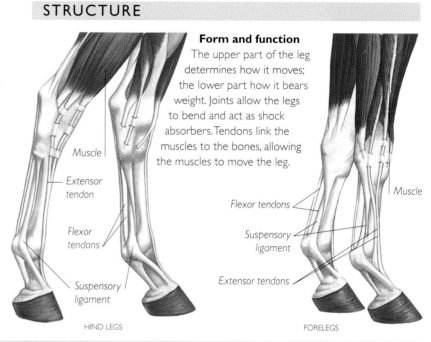

Form and function
The upper part of the leg determines how it moves; the lower part how it bears weight. Joints allow the legs to bend and act as shock absorbers. Tendons link the muscles to the bones, allowing the muscles to move the leg.

Muscle

Extensor tendon

Flexor tendons

Suspensory ligament

HIND LEGS

Flexor tendons

Suspensory ligament

Extensor tendons

Muscle

FORELEGS

COMPARISONS

Legs to suit the horse
Although the leg joints of all horses have the same anatomy, they have adapted over the centuries to the role that their particular breed has to fulfill. As a general rule, thin legs are lighter and better for speed, and are more easily moved. Large joints have a greater surface area over which to spread the weight of a heavy horse. Small joints on a large horse, or vice versa, result in problems.

Well-angled hock to absorb the impact of the foot hitting the ground

LIGHT HORSE (ARAB)

Fine joint for speed

Relatively upright hocks typical of modern draft horses

HEAVY HORSE (ARDENNAIS)

Joints are large for weight-bearing

Agility is important, so the leg joints are fine

PONY (SHETLAND)

Despite the pony's small size, the knee is suitable for speed

GOOD CONFORMATION

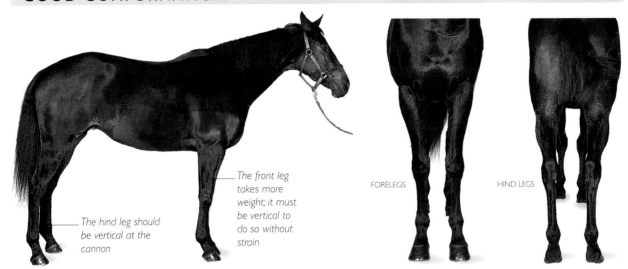

The hind leg should be vertical at the cannon

The front leg takes more weight; it must be vertical to do so without strain

FORELEGS

HIND LEGS

Important features

It is difficult to find a horse with legs that are perfect in all respects, but the better they are, the less likely they are to have problems. The horse should be able to stand foursquare, with the hind legs exactly behind the forelegs. Each pair of legs should match, with joints the same size and both legs truly vertical. Seen from the side, the legs should be straight, apart from the angle at the hock. The feet should not turn either in or out, and there should be no swelling or puffiness around the joints and tendons.

BAD CONFORMATION

Forelegs

Conformational defects prevent the horse's weight from being evenly supported all the way down the leg. Instead, extra stress is put on certain areas. If a horse is over at the knee or back at the knee, its weight is shifted backwards onto the vulnerable heel region. Toes turned in or out put unequal strain on one side of the fetlock, pastern, and foot.

OVER AT THE KNEE (TOO FAR FORWARD)

BACK AT THE KNEE (TOO FAR BACK)

PIGEON-TOED (TOES TURNED IN)

SPLAY-FOOTED (TOES TURNED OUT)

Hind legs

If the hocks are too far under the horse, the muscles exert their maximum effort too early in the stride. If the hocks are too far out behind, then the maximum effort comes too late to achieve proper propulsion. Cow hocks and bowed hocks weaken the propulsive force of the hind legs because the horse's legs tend to bend more, rather than stay straight.

HOCKS TOO FAR UNDER THE BODY

HOCKS TOO FAR BEHIND THE BODY

COW HOCKS (TURNED IN)

BOWED HOCKS (TURNED OUT)

FEET AND HOOVES

The horse's hoof is a variation on a claw or human fingernail. The rigid wall forms a broken circle, with the flexible heel region across the open arc. This allows the hoof to change shape slightly with the stresses of weight-bearing. The horse's weight is actually suspended from the sloping hoof walls rather than supported by the soles. Although hind feet differ slightly in shape from front feet (they are more diamond-shaped than round), they are otherwise identical in structure.

STRUCTURE

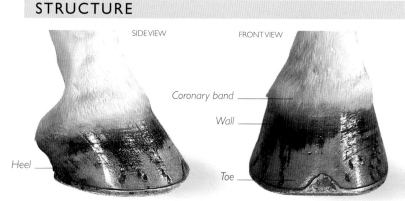

SIDE VIEW

FRONT VIEW

Coronary band

Wall

Heel

Toe

Bulb of heel

Bars provide support for the heel area

Seat of corn

Frog has a rubbery consistency and helps to minimize slipping

Cleft of frog

Sole is concave, which helps the foot to grip the ground

Point of frog

White line is where the horn and sole join

The outer surface
The horn of the hoof is made up of a protein called keratin. It is formed by the cells of the coronary band in tubular structures that run vertically down the hoof wall. A healthy hoof has a smooth surface, without any horizontal ridges or vertical cracks.

The underside
The horn of the sole should be hard, not soft and flaky. The sole should be slightly concave, with the majority of it level with the wall of the trimmed feet. Contrary to popular belief, the frog does not play a role in blood circulation in the foot—it acts more as a spring, absorbing the percussion (shock of impact) as the foot hits the ground.

HOW THE HOOF GROWS

The hoof wall grows separately from the sole, the two types of horn meeting as a white line. The wall grows downward from the coronet, taking 9–12 months to reach the ground at the toe but only 6 months at the heel. Variations in nutrition or blood supply to the coronet cause uneven growth, giving rise to ridges in the wall. Overgrown hooves will splay at the toes and sink at the heels, resulting in abnormal stresses in the foot as a whole.

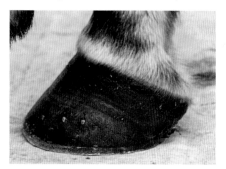

NORMAL HOOF

GRASS RINGS ON A HOOF

Internal structure

The weight of the horse's body is transmitted down the straight column of bones that make up the pastern. That weight is suspended from the hoof wall by the laminae. The navicular bone and the deep flexor tendon that lies over it and holds it in place are particularly susceptible to abnormal stresses.

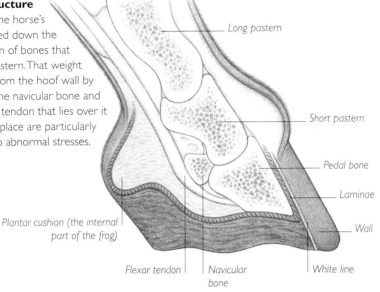

Long pastern

Short pastern

Pedal bone

Laminae

Wall

Plantar cushion (the internal part of the frog)

Flexor tendon

Navicular bone

White line

Close-up of laminae

The laminae link the pedal bone to the hoof wall. They consist of thousands of tiny interlocking leaves or fingers of bone and hoof, separated only by a thin network of blood vessels and nerves.

A BALANCED FOOT

Why symmetry is important

Every time a foot hits the ground, the impact sends shock waves up the leg. If the foot is not balanced—that is, not properly shaped to send shock waves up the pastern parallel to the bones—then abnormal stresses will be placed on the tendons, joints, and bones of the leg. Few horses have perfect feet, but proper care can prevent flaws from becoming problems.

Front view

Line A is an imaginary line down the front of the leg. It should divide the hoof equally. Line B, across the coronary band, should be parallel to line C, across the bottom of the hoof. This foot shape means that shock waves are sent evenly up the middle of the leg, rather than to one side.

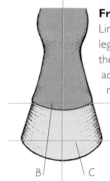

B   C

A

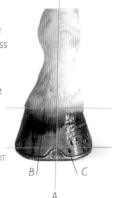

SLIGHTLY LOPSIDED FOOT

B   C

A

Correct proportions

Line D goes from the heel–wall junction to the center of the toe, and line E goes across the widest part of the sole. These lines should be of equal length. If D is longer than E, the toe is too long; this puts extra pressure on the heel region.

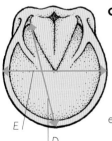

E

D

FOOT WITH A LONG TOE

E

D is slightly longer than E

D

Side view

On the side view of a leg, an imaginary line F runs down the center of the pastern. It should be parallel to line G, running up the front of the wall. If the lines converge or diverge, the horse is said to have a broken hoof/pastern axis.

F   G

F meets the ground about halfway along the sole

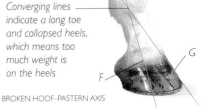

Converging lines indicate a long toe and collapsed heels, which means too much weight is on the heels

G

F

BROKEN HOOF–PASTERN AXIS

GAITS AND MOVEMENT

The horse did not evolve for prolonged periods of movement. It spends most of its day grazing, and usually only when it needs to move to new pastures does it travel any distance. It is rare for a wild horse to walk or trot for more than five to 10 minutes without stopping. By trotting for ten minutes, a horse can cover quite a distance, certainly far enough for it to reach a new grazing area. Fear will stimulate a horse to gallop away from danger, but it cannot keep galloping for long, and it is not necessary for it to do so. After a few minutes, the horse will either have escaped the danger, such as a predator, or succumbed to it.

OTHER GAITS

Certain breeds, particularly in North and South America, have been bred for other gaits apart from those shown on the right. One such gait is the running walk, a smooth, four-beat, lateral gait, also known as the Paso. The horse performing this gait (below) is a Paso Fino.

WALKING

Four-beat gait
At the walk, the horse has three feet on the ground and only one in the air at any time. It places each foot on the ground in turn; first a hind leg, followed by the foreleg on the same side, then the other hind leg and finally the remaining foreleg.

TROTTING

Two-beat gait
At the trot, opposite forefeet and hind feet hit the ground together in turn to give a two-beat gait. The fact that only one forefoot or hind foot is bearing weight at any one time makes this the best gait to use to detect lameness (see p. 136).

CANTERING

Three-beat gait
At the canter, two diagonal feet hit the ground together while the other two feet hit the ground separately. This makes a three-beat gait. One forefoot is followed by the opposite hind foot, then the other two feet together. At some points, no feet are on the ground.

GALLOPING

Four-beat gait
This follows the same pattern as the canter, but the paired limbs do not hit the ground together. The hind limb lands slightly before the paired forelimb, making a four-beat gait. In the gallop and the canter, a horse can change the leading foreleg.

LEFT **Strong bonds** In the wild horses live in small family groups or larger herds. Even domesticated horses communicate with each other and can form very strong bonds with other horses.

RIGHT **A horse's eyes** Because its eyes are on the side of its head, a horse has a very wide field of vision. This gives it the ability to watch out for danger from many directions, even when it has its head down while grazing.

BELOW **Running horse** The way a horse trots and canters is not only graceful to look at, it is also a very efficient way of covering the ground. If, however, the horse does have to stand and fight, those long legs are powerful weapons.

TEETH AND JAWS

A horse relies heavily on its teeth. Its digestive juices cannot break down the cellulose in grass, so this is done by bacteria in its colon. But the teeth must first break down the herbage to a thick "soup," or the bacteria cannot work on it, the horse will get no nourishment from it, and the fibrous material may become wedged in the intestines. The lack of functional teeth is one of the major reasons why a horse may not live to an old age in the wild. The molar teeth are pushed farther out of the jaw with age, while their grinding surfaces are worn away. Because the upper jaw is wider than the lower jaw, this tends to produce sharp enamel points on the outside edge of the upper molars and the inside edge of the lower molars.

DIFFERENT TEETH

Function of the teeth

The horse's upper and lower jaw are basically mirror images of each other in terms of teeth. Each has six incisor teeth (three on each side). These are the teeth that cut food. In the adult horse, there are six premolar and six molar teeth (three of each on each side). These are the teeth that chew food. In a young horse, the back three molars are not present. In male horses, there may be one canine tooth on each side. These have no function.

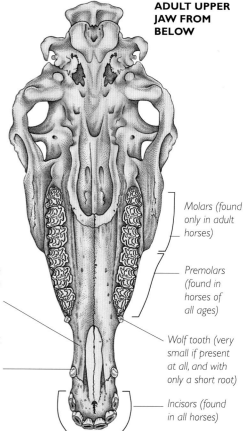

ADULT UPPER JAW FROM BELOW

Molars (found only in adult horses)

Premolars (found in horses of all ages)

Wolf tooth (very small if present at all, and with only a short root)

Incisors (found in all horses)

Diastema (the space where the bit conveniently fits—also known as the bars of the mouth)

Canine tooth (not usually present in mares)

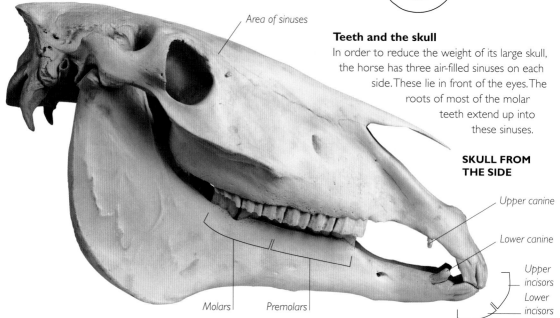

Area of sinuses

Teeth and the skull

In order to reduce the weight of its large skull, the horse has three air-filled sinuses on each side. These lie in front of the eyes. The roots of most of the molar teeth extend up into these sinuses.

SKULL FROM THE SIDE

Upper canine

Lower canine

Upper incisors

Lower incisors

Molars

Premolars

THE INCISORS

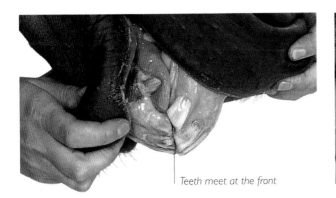

Teeth meet at the front

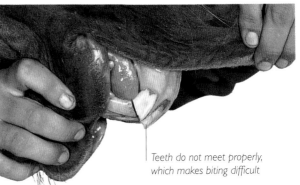

Teeth do not meet properly, which makes biting difficult

Teeth that meet
The incisor teeth must meet their counterparts in the opposite jaw if they are to cut properly. This is especially important for horses in the wild, because if they cannot cut grass, they cannot get any food. Domestic horses can have food cut up for them.

Teeth that do not meet
In some horses, the upper jaw is longer than the lower jaw, preventing the teeth from meeting and causing the upper teeth to be in front of the lower teeth. A horse with this problem is called parrot-mouthed. When, more rarely, the lower jaw is longer, the horse is called sow-mouthed.

TEETH AS AN INDICATOR OF AGE

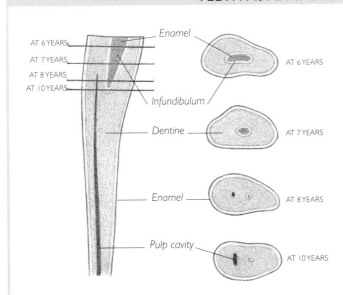

AT 6 YEARS
AT 7 YEARS
AT 8 YEARS
AT 10 YEARS
Enamel
Infundibulum
Dentine — AT 7 YEARS
Enamel — AT 8 YEARS
Pulp cavity — AT 10 YEARS
AT 6 YEARS

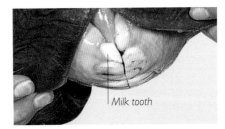

Milk tooth

THE STRAIGHT TEETH OF A FOUR-YEAR-OLD HORSE

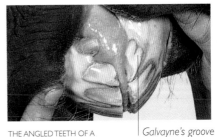

THE ANGLED TEETH OF A 20-YEAR-OLD HORSE

Galvayne's groove

Wear of the surface of the teeth
A horse's teeth can be used as a means of estimating its age, although the estimate can be only approximate. The cutting surface of the incisor teeth becomes worn down with age, revealing a different cross-section as it does so. This can help in estimating age up to eight years. From then on, the horse will be officially referred to as "aged." The older a horse is, the more angled its front teeth will be. At about the age of 10, a mark known as Galvayne's groove appears at the top of the upper corner incisors. It gradually grows to the bottom, then starts to disappear from the top.

Temporary and permanent teeth
A foal has a set of milk teeth, which are gradually replaced by permanent teeth—all of them usually by the age of five. A horse's bones are mature at the same age. The number of milk teeth present is therefore a guide to how much work a horse should do.

BODY SYSTEMS

As the horse evolved, its body systems adapted for its particular needs. For example, as a grazing animal, its digestive system had to digest cellulose, so the large colon became a reservoir for bacterial fermentation. As a "fight or flight" animal, the horse's muscles sometimes needed extra oxygen suddenly, so the spleen developed to store red blood cells and push them into the blood on demand.

RESPIRATION AND CIRCULATION

Working together

The respiratory and circulatory functions are inextricably interrelated. There is no point in extracting oxygen from the air breathed in, which is the role of the respiratory system, unless that oxygen can be delivered to the body cells, which is the role of the circulatory system. The underlying principle is that gases move from where they are in a high concentration to where they are in a low concentration. Oxygen from the air passes through the walls of the lungs into the blood, which is pumped around the body by the heart. At the same time, carbon dioxide passes from the blood into the lungs and is breathed out.

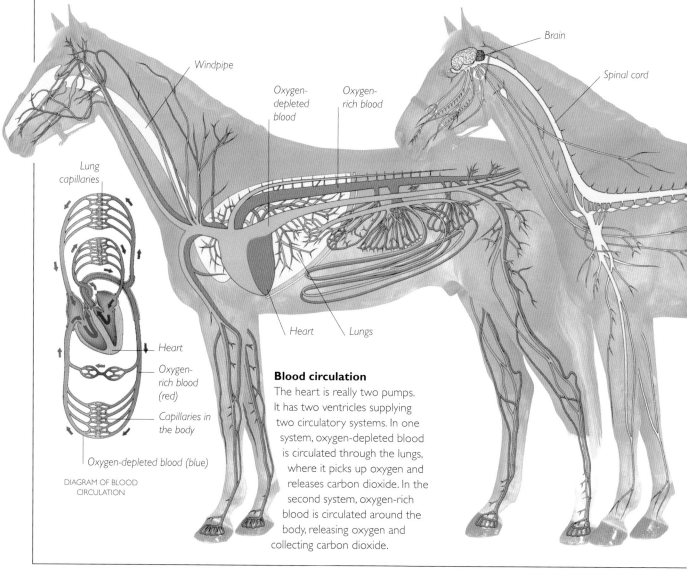

Windpipe

Oxygen-depleted blood

Oxygen-rich blood

Brain

Spinal cord

Lung capillaries

Heart

Oxygen-rich blood (red)

Capillaries in the body

Oxygen-depleted blood (blue)

DIAGRAM OF BLOOD CIRCULATION

Heart

Lungs

Blood circulation

The heart is really two pumps. It has two ventricles supplying two circulatory systems. In one system, oxygen-depleted blood is circulated through the lungs, where it picks up oxygen and releases carbon dioxide. In the second system, oxygen-rich blood is circulated around the body, releasing oxygen and collecting carbon dioxide.

NERVOUS SYSTEM

Instructing the body
The nervous system coordinates all the activities of the body. It receives information via the senses, decides what action is needed, and then sends instructions to the relevant system to achieve that end. Most of the nervous system's work is automatic.

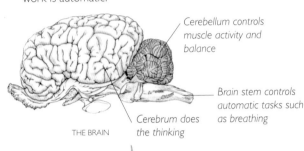

Cerebellum controls muscle activity and balance

Brain stem controls automatic tasks such as breathing

Cerebrum does the thinking

THE BRAIN

Esophagus (gullet)

Signaling network
A network of sensory nerves throughout the body sends information to the spinal cord. Vital reflex responses, such as to heat from a flame, are triggered from the spinal cord, but most signals pass up to the brain. Instructions for action run back down the cord.

DIGESTIVE SYSTEM

The process of digestion
The horse needs only a small stomach because food passes quickly to the small intestine for digestion. Undigested fiber passes to the cecum and the large colon to be broken down. Fluid is absorbed into the blood, and the solid remains of the food are expelled as manure.

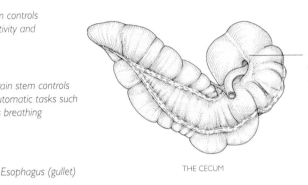

Products of digestion are absorbed into the blood from the caecum

THE CECUM

Stomach *Small intestine* *Small colon* *Position of cecum (dotted line)*

Rectum

Liver *Spleen* *Large colon*

Fiber breakdown
Horses eat much cellulose, or fiber. This has to be broken down by bacteria that live in the large colon. There are several types of bacteria, each adapted for a certain type of fiber. If the horse's food changes, the bacteria change. The long digestive tract has two 180° bends where food can easily get stuck and cause colic.

THE HEALTHY HORSE

A healthy horse is one whose natural physical capabilities are not restricted by accident or disease. In the wild, there is a sharp distinction between healthy and unhealthy horses. The healthy ones survive and the unhealthy ones succumb to predators and diseases. Among domestic horses, this distinction is much more blurred; even very sick horses may survive, thanks to veterinary care. Do not confuse health with fitness; a healthy horse is not necessarily a fit one. A fit horse's performance is not restricted by fatigue, while there are many healthy horses that are easily tired by exercise. A healthy horse should be neither too fat nor too thin (*see p. 125*). The former problem in particular can lead to health problems in horses, just as it does in humans. Old horses tend to be more susceptible to disease, so you must watch them carefully to spot even the slightest variation from their normal healthy appearance or behavior. Beware of attributing any potential symptom to "just old age."

Temperature, pulse rate, and respiration rate
These are important signs of health or illness. Learn what your horse's rates are by measuring them when you know the horse is healthy (*see p. 45*). The normal levels in a healthy horse at rest are: Temperature: 101–101.5°F (38.3–38.6°C); Pulse rate: 30–50 beats per minute; Respiratory rate: 8–16 breaths per minute.

Tail
The tail should not be clamped down between the legs, nor held to one side as the horse trots away. It should be clean, without rubbed patches on the dock, which might indicate worms or sweet itch (*see p. 147*).

CAPILLARY REFILL TIME

Pressing on the gum creates a white area as blood is pushed out of the capillaries

A simple way to assess your horse's circulation is to press hard with a finger on the soft tissue of its gum. When you remove the finger, it should not take more than four seconds for the white area now visible to regain its normal pink color. This is known as the capillary refill time.

Droppings and urine
A healthy horse's droppings form balls that break as they hit the ground. They contain no fibrous lumps or whole cereal grains and are produced 6–10 times every 24 hours. The urine has a strong odor and is dark yellow and cloudy.

Ears

A horse's ears should be alert and follow you around, just like another pair of eyes. The sense of hearing is just as valuable to a horse as its sight.

Eyes

The eyes should be bright, with no discharge. It is normal for there to be cauliflower-shaped black bodies hanging from the top of the iris. These bodies are called the *corpora nigra*. The membrane around the eye and inside the eyelid should be salmon pink.

Mouth and nostrils

Most horses have fixed eating habits, and they do not change their behavior unless something is wrong. They should not drop food out of the mouth while eating—a sign of dental problems (*see p. 147*). The nostrils should not be flared while the horse is at rest, and there should be no discharge.

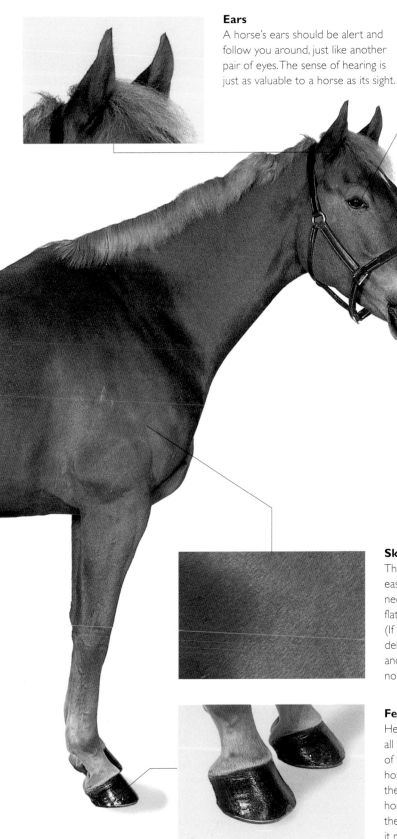

Skin and coat

The skin should be supple and move easily. If you pick up a fold of skin over the neck and then release it, the fold should flatten out again almost immediately. (If it stays raised, the horse is probably dehydrated.) The coat should be smooth and shiny rather than "staring" (dull), with no loose hair unless the horse is shedding.

Feet

Healthy horses are happy to take weight on all four feet, although they take 60 percent of their weight on their front feet. Many horses habitually rest a hind foot more than the others. The hooves should not have any horizontal grooves or vertical cracks, and the horn must not be broken or split where it meets the ground.

EQUINE SENSES

Horses in the wild rely on their senses—sight, hearing, touch, smell, and taste—for survival. Sight and sound warn of danger, and taste and smell identify safe or bad food. Domestication has dulled their response to some of these stimuli—for example, they may not run away every time they see a car—but their senses are just as acute as ever. When they react to something we haven't noticed, it is often put down to a "sixth sense." In fact, it is really the horse's extremely sharp senses processing the information that we have missed.

SIGHT

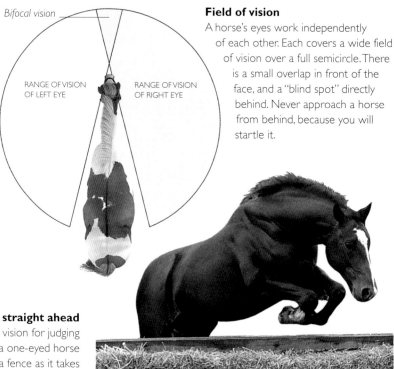

Bifocal vision

RANGE OF VISION OF LEFT EYE

RANGE OF VISION OF RIGHT EYE

Field of vision
A horse's eyes work independently of each other. Each covers a wide field of vision over a full semicircle. There is a small overlap in front of the face, and a "blind spot" directly behind. Never approach a horse from behind, because you will startle it.

Seeing straight ahead
A horse makes little use of stereoscopic vision for judging distances—for example, when jumping—so a one-eyed horse can still judge distances. A horse loses sight of a fence as it takes off, so it has to trust in its rider knowing it is safe to jump.

HEARING

The mobile ears, wide range of vision, and flexible neck allow the horse to keep informed of what is happening behind it

Use of the ears
Horses use their sense of hearing a great deal, moving each ear independently to pick up sound waves. Talking to a horse is a good way to let it know that you are there and that you are not a threat.

Preparing to flee
When a horse hears a sound, such as a dog barking, it lifts its head, looks toward the source, and assesses the significance of the noise. It will not turn its whole body because it would then be less able to run away from the danger.

TOUCH

Sensitivity

The horse has an acute sense of touch over its whole body, enabling it to detect the presence of a single fly and whisk it away with its tail with unerring accuracy. So don't be surprised if your horse is startled when you touch it without warning.

Whiskers

The whiskers, and the long hairs around the eyes, are important for sensing nearby objects. You should never cut whiskers when clipping a horse, even if you are preparing the horse for a show.

SMELL

Obtaining information

Smell enables a horse to detect undesirable items in its food. It is also important in social interactions; horses greet friends or identify strangers by touching muzzle to muzzle.

Scent analysis

This action, known as flehmen, may involve "smelling" with the sensitive membranes inside the lips, as well as the nostrils. It is usually seen in sexual activity, so it may detect pheromones, the sex hormones released into the air. Many horses will do this when they come across an unusual smell or feed for the first time.

TASTE

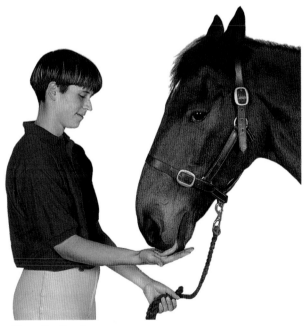

Favorite foods

Horses like salty and sweet things, but not bitter or sour ones. Many horses like peppermints. This may be because they once licked someone's hand, which was salty, received a peppermint as a bonus, and came to associate the taste with nice people. A treat should be an occasional reward for good behavior. If it becomes a habit, the horse may also develop habits such as nipping you in anticipation.

BODY LANGUAGE

The horse is a herd animal and needs to be able to communicate with other members of the herd. Of course, horses do not have philosophical discussions, but they do need to convey basic emotions, such as fear, and to establish a hierarchy of dominance without resorting to violence. Domestic horses treat us as members of their herd, so they use the same body language with us.

CONTENTMENT

Signs of happiness
A contented horse is not worried about any other horses that may be around. It shows off its best features by carrying its head high and holding its tail up, and tends to make its movements more extravagant than usual.

In the field
Because horses like company, they are usually pleased when they see a human being whom they recognize and trust. They will approach you without fear, rather than running away from you.

In the stable
If a horse wants to be left alone to enjoy a rest, it will turn away from other horses. A stabled horse may turn its back to the door to show you that it does not want to talk.

IMPATIENCE

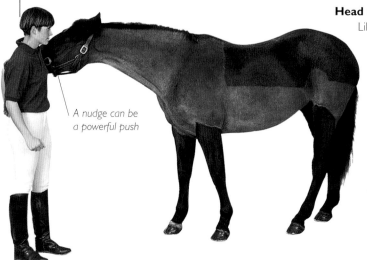

A nudge can be a powerful push

Head movements
Like children, horses may not like being ignored. A horse may demand a human's attention by nudging with its muzzle.

Stamping feet
A horse can get impatient waiting for food or when restricted. It may then stamp or kick the stable door to make a noise.

ANNOYANCE

Ears back

Teeth bared

Biting other horses
When its patience is exhausted, a horse may express anger by biting. The horse's teeth are not designed to cause wounds when it does this, as the teeth of a carnivore might, but the bite says, "I have a position within the herd that allows me to bite you if I want to."

Biting you
A horse may bite you for the same reason as it would bite another horse. Never tolerate this—it would tell the horse that you accept it as the boss. Distract it before it bites; if it does get you, slap its muzzle.

FRIGHT OR FURY?

White of eye visible

Body ready for action

UNHAPPINESS

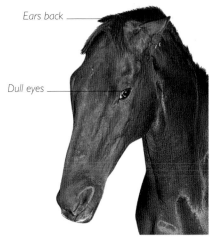

Ears back

Dull eyes

Signs of fright and aggression
There is a big difference between an aggressive and a frightened horse, although both may show the whites of their eyes and bite or kick. A scared horse will stand its ground or run away.

It is very unusual for a horse to be aggressive, but if one is, it will move toward you. A frightened horse is more likely to run away: wait for it to come to you, no matter how long it takes.

Causes of unhappiness
Horses can get depressed during illness or if they are bullied. They will look uninterested and unhappy, and may become aggressive. Riders used to boast about breaking a horse's spirit, but this is just not acceptable today.

THE HORSE AT LEISURE

Even with the finest stable management, horses need to have periods of rest from their work for humans. This may involve letting them out in a field for an hour every afternoon, or turning them out for days or weeks. You should never suddenly change a horse's routine from strenuous and regular work to field rest; you must allow its digestive and movement systems to adapt over at least a week. Most horses thrive when turned out (except for a few Thoroughbred-type horses that cannot adapt, like workaholic people who cannot relax on vacation). Many horses perform at their best when they return after a rest period. Whether this is due to mental relaxation in a more natural state, or because the access to grazing provides good natural nutrition, is not known. We often give "Dr. Green" the credit anyway.

RELAXING

Sunbathing
Turned-out horses lie down much more often than stabled horses, especially in sunny weather. When relaxing in this way, they may look unconscious, but if you make a sudden noise, you will see that they are awake enough to be aware of possible danger.

Playing
Young horses learn their communication skills from play. Like all youngsters, they have mock fights. They also seek a lot of physical contact. This is a point to remember if keeping a solitary horse; because it has no horse friends, its owner must provide all social contact.

ROLLING

Why do horses roll?
Horses roll for pleasure. They also roll when they have colic, or abdominal pain. If you regularly watch a horse both before and after it rolls, you should have very little trouble telling which kind of roll it is. Rolling involves almost all the muscles of the body, and when horses roll for pleasure they seem to enjoy it in the same way as humans would enjoy a good stretch. Horses also roll to rub their back, and often roll in dust for a cleansing bath.

Choosing the place
A horse often uses one particular spot whenever it wants to roll. Like a dog settling on its bed, it may turn around on the spot once or twice.

Settling down
A horse goes down front first. It may be that this leaves its hind legs ready to operate in case it suddenly has to run from danger.

The ears are laid back slightly

Dozing

Horses are able to sleep standing up. They can lock one or both of their stifle joints to keep themselves upright. As a horse goes to sleep, its eyes will half-close and its head will sink down a little. When horses are in a group, one of them usually stays awake grazing while the others doze off in this way.

The lower lip may hang loosely

Two horses greeting each other
Horses communicate by actions as much as by sounds. The two horses here will be in no doubt that the other is a friend.

Resting a hind foot
Many horses rest a hind leg. This is done not to take weight off the foot (most weight is taken on the front feet) but perhaps to relax the stifle-locking mechanism. If a horse often rests a particular leg, take note if it rests a different one; this may indicate pain.

The foot is tilted, with just the toe touching the ground

Rolling around
Usually, a horse rolls until its legs are vertical in the air, then back down on the same side, several times. It may even roll all the way over.

Getting up
A horse gets up from the ground with its front legs first. Its priority is to get its head up high so that it can see if any danger has appeared.

Shaking the dust off
Finally, a horse usually gives itself a good shake, to remove any excess dust that was picked up during rolling.

THE HERD

A herd of wild horses will include animals of both sexes and all ages. In a domestic situation, geldings (castrated male horses) and mares can be mixed in a field, but this is more likely to lead to fights about leadership, so they tend to be segregated. Stallions are usually kept away from both mares and geldings. It is natural for stallions to collect and mate with mares and fight other male horses. Within any group, there is a hierarchy, and each horse is responsible for protecting those lower down the order.

Safety in numbers
Horses prefer to be in a group with other horses, even those they do not know. This impulse is so strong that horses that have lost their riders will gallop with the others on the racecourse or in a group out trail riding, and single horses who are grazing may make determined efforts to escape and join other horses that happen to pass nearby.

Fighting
Most fights between horses are triggered by a need to preserve a particular position in the hierarchy, or a desire to challenge another horse and perhaps gain a higher position. As a result, there is much ritual posturing rather than serious physical damage.

A fight will take on a new intensity when a stallion has collected a harem of mares and is challenged by an outsider. As a general rule, though, horses are not aggressive; where instinct is concerned, they prefer "flight" rather than "fight."

Arguments

Even in a group of only mares or only geldings, there will be horses that establish dominance within sub-groups. A dominant horse will try to bring more members of the herd into their group, so arguments may occur between group leaders.

Caring for young

The herd is an extended family, and many members contribute to the care and education of foals. Young horses naturally gather together, and the nearest adult will usually act as "nanny," even if it is a gelding. This is not as altruistic as it seems— all the adults want to establish dominance over the young ones, not just the dams.

Friendship

Some horses within a group may develop strong attachments to each other. When they are stabled, this can mean that if only one horse is taken out for a ride, then the stay-at-home friend becomes upset. If two good companions are turned out together, they will usually stay fairly close to one another. If one of the friends dies or is sold, the remaining horse may show all the signs of grief.

Rounding up

In a herd, stallions round up their mares. This is to ward off the slightest sexual threat from a rival stallion, rather than to protect the mares from danger. In many domesticated groups, horses of either sex will round up horses that they dominate as part of their efforts to reinforce that dominance.

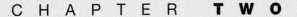

CHAPTER **TWO**

GENERAL CARE

WILD HORSES HAVE CONSIDERABLE TACTILE AND SOCIAL

CONTACT WITH OTHER HORSES, BUT DOMESTICATED

HORSES OFTEN HAVE VERY LITTLE. A DOMESTICATED

HORSE NEEDS CONTACT WITH PEOPLE INSTEAD, AND

THIS IS GIVEN THROUGH ACTIVITIES SUCH AS GROOMING

AND EXERCISING. STABLE MANAGEMENT TASKS MAY BE

BORING FOR YOU, BUT DO NOT TRY TO COMPLETE

THEM AS QUICKLY AS YOU CAN; THEY ARE INTERESTING

DIVERSIONS FOR THE HORSE. STABLED HORSES WITH

NO STIMULI MAY DEVELOP HARMFUL HABITS IN

RESPONSE TO STRESS.

OWNING A HORSE

When you decide to own a horse, it means you are accepting full responsibility for the horse's welfare. To fulfill your obligation, you must understand the horse's needs, both mental and physical. Ignorance of these can lead to your abusing the horse, albeit unintentionally. Owning a horse is a major financial and time commitment. Budget for one-and-a-half times what you think it will cost. You will need to spend money whenever the horse needs veterinary attention, or new clothing or shoes, not just when money is available.

THE HORSE'S NATURAL INSTINCTS

Nourishment

One of the horse's natural instincts is to eat and drink. Food and water provide the horse's body with the things it needs to function. To obtain enough nourishment from its natural food of grass, a horse needs to spend most of the day grazing. In the wild, it will eat the food around it and then move to a new area to find more.

Survival

When a zebra runs from a lion, it is using its natural instinct for survival. The horse has the same "fright and flight" response to danger, even after domestication. So don't be surprised if a horse runs away from something unusual without stopping to decide if it is really dangerous.

Reproduction

Another instinct of the horse is to reproduce. Even when a domestic mare or stallion is not being used for breeding, its reproductive system is still active. Mares come into season for five days every three weeks in the summer, ready to breed. A mare may become temperamental and more difficult to handle when it is in season.

THE HORSE'S BASIC RIGHTS

Companionship
The horse is a herd animal and needs companionship. If you keep a horse on its own, then you must provide the physical contact and mental stimulation that it would normally receive from other horses in a herd.

Food
A domesticated horse depends entirely on its owner for food. If you expect your horse to work, then you may need to give it food other than just grass or hay.

Careful treatment
A horse may take orders even from children because it accepts being dominated by a human, as it might be by a member of a herd. There is no need to make a horse submit to you out of fear.

YOUR COMMITMENT

Hard work
Keeping a horse involves hard work such as mucking out, carrying hay and water, and grooming. A stabled horse needs exercise every day, and a grass-kept horse must be checked twice a day, especially in bad weather.

Expense
The many costs associated with keeping a horse are not optional. Food, blankets, farriery, veterinary visits, and shelter are all necessities.

KEEPING A HORSE HEALTHY

It is better to prevent disease than to have to treat it once it occurs. Horses can be vaccinated against specific diseases, such as tetanus and equine influenza, but the best general disease prevention is good stable management and a sharp eye for deviations from normal health. You must get to know what is normal for your horse. Give it a mini health check once a day; then you will spot a problem if it occurs. Be extra-vigilant if your horse has been mixing with strange horses—for example, at a show—and consider isolating it from other horses when you get home, in case it has picked up an infection.

Signs of health
You should visit a turned-out horse twice a day. Check that its feet are in good order, that it does not have any cuts or injuries, and that any blanket is in place and not rubbing. If possible, bring the horse in during really bad weather.

Disinfecting the stable
Never introduce a new horse to a dirty stable. The stable should first be cleaned thoroughly and then disinfected. Dirt, especially feces, renders many types of disinfectant inactive, so disinfection on its own is not an alternative to cleaning—it is a vital element of it.

Check the color of the eye and mouth membranes

Feel the legs for signs of inflammation

Pick out the feet several times a day

Checking all over
Every day, you should run a hand over literally every part of your horse's body. Look for the classic signs of inflammation: heat, swelling, and pain. Naturally, you should be familiar with the size of any existing lumps and bumps on your horse. The skin should be supple and not show any signs of sweating. Horses often rest one leg more than the others, but look out for any variations in this habit.

Worming

It is essential to worm your horse regularly (see p. 150). The main goal of worming is to prevent worm eggs from passing out in the feces to reinfest the horse at a later date.

A PROFESSIONAL CHECK

Horses should have their teeth checked by a vet or an equine dental technician annually, with some older horses requiring more frequent examinations. Professionals will use a gag to hold the jaw open and may use electrically driven files to remove the sharp points that develop on a horse's teeth during natural wear.

Examining the mouth

Look inside the horse's mouth and make sure that there are no ulcers on the tongue or insides of the cheeks caused by sharp points on the teeth. Watch your horse eat. If it drops appreciable amounts of food out of its mouth, there may be a dental problem (see p. 145).

CHECKING THE RESPIRATION, TEMPERATURE, AND PULSE

Respiration

While at rest, a horse normally takes 8–16 breaths per minute. (A breath is counted as one out–in movement of the ribs.) It may be hard to see and count such slow breathing. Stand behind the horse at a safe distance and watch the ribs rise and fall as it breathes.

Temperature

A healthy horse has a temperature of 101–101.5°F (38.3–38.6°C). At first, ask an expert to help you take the temperature. Grease the thermometer with petroleum jelly, shake it hard, then insert it, bulb first, into the rectum, holding on to it tightly. Read the mercury level after about one minute.

Pulse

The normal pulse rate of a horse is 30–50 beats per minute. It takes practice to feel it. Rest the tip of your fingers on the artery that passes over the edge of the lower jaw, and count the beats. Expect the rate to be three or four times the respiratory rate, even after exercise.

STABLE VICES

Although horses are quick learners, not all the activities they learn to perform are desirable. A group of repetitive, or stereotypic, behaviors can be seen in individual horses the world over. These behavior patterns are known as vices, because the horse does not appear to have any choice as to whether it will continue to perform the activity—if the appropriate stimulus is there (and this may not be obvious to us), the horse will behave accordingly. The horse seems to be addicted. Cribbers, like horses showing other vices, will crib more before mealtimes, before exercise, or when people come into the yard or stable—any time when the stress or excitement levels increase. There have been various theories about what causes horses to develop the repetitive behavioral habits that we call vices. One of these is that the horse performs the activity when stressed because it releases natural morphinelike substances that give pleasure.

CRIBBING

Cribbing
The horse grinds its incisor teeth on a solid object, most commonly the top edge of the lower stable door. This can cause considerable damage to the door and abnormal wear on the incisor teeth. Attempts to estimate the horse's age from the wear on those teeth are unlikely to be successful.

Stabling
Horses stabled for most of the day may be more susceptible to developing repetitive behavioral patterns because they are unable to relax naturally and so become more stressed.

Installing a grille

Weaving describes a horse's standing and moving its head and neck from side to side. Many horses perform this activity with their head over the stable door, and so owners may install a grille to the upper door opening to stop the horse from weaving while still allowing it to look outside the stable. It is possible that physically preventing a horse from performing its vice may be even more stressful to the horse.

A large toy

Providing a large toy for a horse that is kept in a stable for a prolonged period of time may distract the horse from the kind of stress or excitement that would otherwise trigger a vice. Like a child, over time a horse will lose interest in the toy, which consequently needs to be replaced with a different stimulus. In certain cases, this may be providing a more acceptable repetitive activity than the vice.

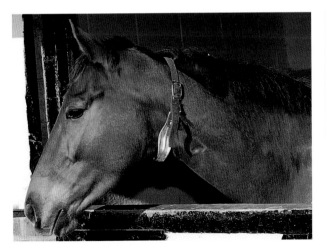

Anti-wind-sucking strap

Wind-sucking is a vice where the horse fixes its upper and lower jaws around a solid object and "swallows" air. Many, but not all, wind-suckers are originally cribbers. It has been thought that wind-suckers are more prone to colic and weight loss because their stomachs fill up with air. Some horses wind-suck even when turned out in a paddock, and may loosen the fence posts by repeatedly using them for this activity.

Newly weaned Thoroughbred foals

For a long time it was thought that horses acquired vices by imitating another horse who already exhibited the behavior. Scientific efforts to prove that the behavior can be spread in this way have been unsuccessful. What we do know is that many vices have their origin in what happens at weaning, and the diet fed to the foal at that time. It has been suggested that feeding antacids to horses that crib or wind-suck may reduce the behavior.

HANDLING A HORSE

How you first approach and handle a horse will affect everything else that follows. If you make a horse nervous, it will be suspicious of even the most routine action. Walk up to it steadily, as if you expect it to stand still and wait for you. If it turns away, stand still and wait until it turns around again and is approachable. Talk to the horse all the time, so that it can hear who you are, and reassure it in a friendly tone of voice, rather than give it orders. Make sure that your movements are smooth and unhurried, so as not to startle the horse. Its natural instinct is to move quickly away from anything that might be dangerous before it stops to think. It will not spend time making allowances for your inexperience or reasoning that you mean it no harm.

APPROACHING A HORSE

1 Approach the horse from the front, at a slight angle from the center of its head so that it can see you clearly. Make sure that the horse hears you and, when you are close enough, hold out a hand so that it can smell you also.

Allow the horse to smell and lick your hand

2 Pat the horse gently on the neck. This physical contact is pleasant for the animal and helps to bond it to you. It also shows the horse that you are not afraid of it.

PUTTING ON A HALTER

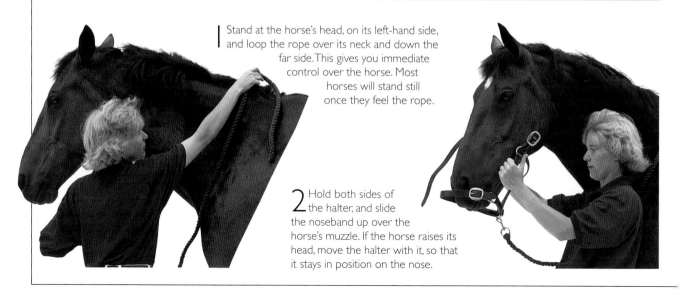

1 Stand at the horse's head, on its left-hand side, and loop the rope over its neck and down the far side. This gives you immediate control over the horse. Most horses will stand still once they feel the rope.

2 Hold both sides of the halter, and slide the noseband up over the horse's muzzle. If the horse raises its head, move the halter with it, so that it stays in position on the nose.

Leave the lead rope over the horse's neck

Use both hands to fasten the buckle

3 Use your right hand on the far side of the neck to flick the strap over the horse's poll. Do this calmly. Some horses may be frightened when they feel the strap on the left side of their neck, especially if it is flapped suddenly.

4 Make sure that the strap is fitting snugly just behind the horse's ears before you actually fasten it to the buckle on the cheekpiece. For safety, do the buckle up properly, with the end of the strap tucked in so that it cannot come undone.

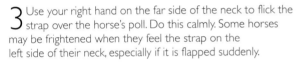

5 Finally, check that the halter fits the horse correctly and adjust the buckles if necessary. Make sure the clip on the lead rope is facing away from the head, or it may pinch the horse's skin.

THE ROPE HALTER

A rope halter is a type of universally adjustable halter. It can be made of webbing or rope. The noseband should lie over the bridge of the horse's nose, with the fastening on the left side of the head. You should always tie the rope with a knot at the side. If you don't, the halter may loosen—in which case it could easily come off over the horse's ears—or it may become too tight.

Correct fit
If the halter is too tight, it will be uncomfortable; if it is too loose, it will not provide safe restraint. The noseband should lie about halfway between the eye and the corner of the mouth, and you should be able to fit at least two fingers under it.

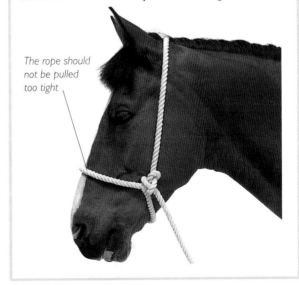

The rope should not be pulled too tight

METHODS OF CONTROL

You will need to restrain your
horse for its own good as well as
for your convenience. For example,
you may need to put on a dressing,
check its teeth, or give it worm
paste. You cannot expect it to
understand when and why you
want it to stand still. A horse's
natural reaction to anything
unexpected or unpleasant is to
move away. Therefore, you must
apply enough restraint to control
the horse without causing it pain.
If physical methods fail, your vet
will be able to sedate the horse
for a short period using drugs.

WHY CONTROL?

Effective control
A domestic horse must learn that it
cannot get its own way by rearing or
kicking. If it achieves its aim once, it will
use the same tactics in other situations.
Use brain rather than brawn to
control it. It is probably bigger
than you and is certainly
heavier. In trials of
strength, your
horse will
win every
time.

TYING UP A HORSE

Tie the rope to a loop of string fixed securely to a ring

Using a halter
The simplest
form of restraint is a
halter and rope. When you
tie a horse up, tie the rope
to a string, which will break
if the horse pulls back in
fright. This will stop it from
panicking even more.

Quick-release knot
You should always use a quick-release
knot when you tie up a horse. If the
horse gets into any difficulties, such
as trapping a leg in a badly positioned
haynet, then it is important that you can
release it quickly. Quick-release knots are
easy to undo, even if the knot has been
tightened by the horse's pulling backward.

1 Thread
the rope
through the
string and
form the
loose end
into a loop.

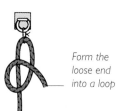

Form the loose end into a loop

2 Make another
loop with the
loose end and
thread this
under and
through the
first loop.

3 Leave the
second loop
hanging, then
tighten the knot
securely by pulling
it, and the rope
attached to the
horse, at the
same time.

Untie the knot by pulling the loose end

OTHER METHODS OF RESTRAINT

Distracting with food
During simple, painless tasks, you may be able to distract your horse with food. A haynet is best because it will keep the horse occupied for a reasonable length of time.

Fitting a lunging cavesson
A lunging cavesson may be useful in controlling a fractious horse. It looks rather like a sturdy halter, but the long lunge rein is attached on top of the horse's nose, not under its jaw. This makes it easier to stop the horse from rearing.

The noseband should be well padded and fit the horse snugly

Lifting a foot
Lifting up a foot may help to restrain your horse if you are doing something to one of the other legs. Horses can stand comfortably on three legs, but be careful—some horses will stand on two legs and kick with the third.

Hold the foot up so that all the leg joints are flexed

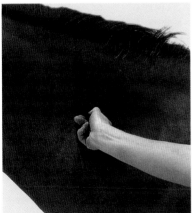

Twisting the skin
Stallions grasp a fold of skin to restrain mares. You can use the same technique by twisting a handful of loose skin on the horse's neck.

Using a humane twitch
As a final resort, a twitch applied to the top lip can make a horse oblivious to unpleasant stimuli. It causes the release of endorphins, or natural painkillers, into the bloodstream. Always use a rigid metal twitch; a rope twitch can be twisted too far and can cause rope burns.

Apply a twitch for only a few minutes

LEADING IN HAND

A well-behaved horse can be led safely, even past traffic, although this is not a natural form of behavior for it. A horse has to learn how to be led every bit as much as how to jump. Most horses learn when they are foals, but you must be prepared for a horse to revert to its natural instinct of flight at any time. It is traditional always to walk on the left side of the horse, because most people are right-handed, and this means your strongest arm is next to the horse. Practice leading on both sides, however, so that the horse gets used to it. If the horse is used to being led only from the near side, it will have to learn as if from scratch when you find you have to lead from the other side.

LEADING IN A HALTER

Walk at the horse's shoulder; if you walk in front and pull, or stare it in the face, the horse will resist

Holding the rope
With one hand, hold the lead rope 12–18 in (30–45 cm) from the halter, and hold the end off the ground with the other hand. You will then have a better chance of holding on if the horse suddenly pulls away from you. Never wrap the rope around your hand. If the horse bolts, you will not be able to release yourself, and you may get seriously hurt.

LEADING IN A BRIDLE

More control
A bridle gives you more control than a halter. When leading a horse in a bridle, bring the reins over the horse's head and hold them in the same way that you would hold a rope. Do not loop the reins around your arm or wrist.

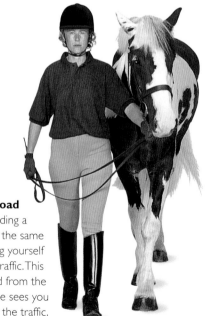

Leading on the road
Always use a bridle when leading a horse on the road. Walk in the same direction as the traffic, putting yourself between the horse and the traffic. This means you may have to lead from the right-hand side. If the horse sees you there, it is less likely to mind the traffic.

TURNING AROUND

1 Being a large, four-legged animal, a horse needs more space to turn than a human being needs. It cannot "about-face" like a soldier. When you turn a horse, steady it first, then turn its head away from you, keeping yourself on the outside of the circle.

The hindquarters should not swing out, because this unbalances the horse

When you turn, you should always be on the outside of the horse

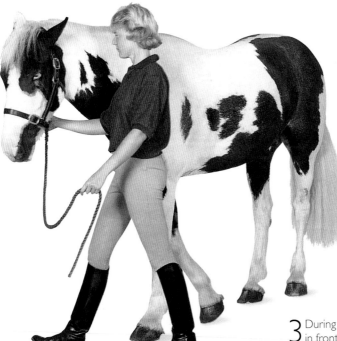

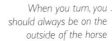

2 As you turn the horse's head away from you, the horse will have to bend its neck, and you will then not have to pull it around.

3 During the turn, you will inevitably move slightly in front of the horse's shoulder. Once the turn is completed and the horse is walking in a straight line, position yourself correctly again.

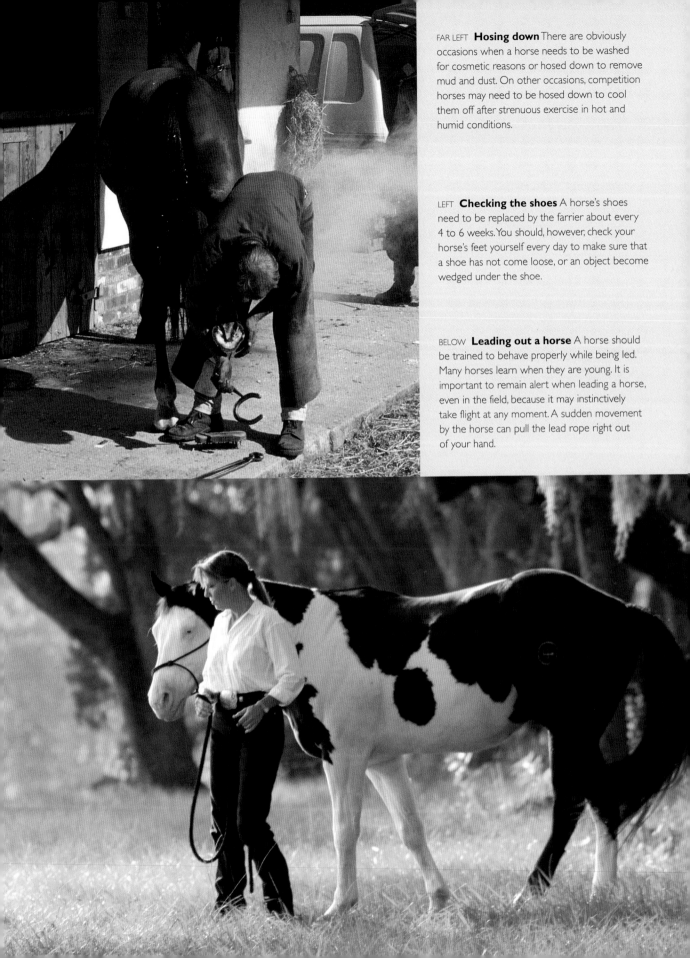

FAR LEFT **Hosing down** There are obviously occasions when a horse needs to be washed for cosmetic reasons or hosed down to remove mud and dust. On other occasions, competition horses may need to be hosed down to cool them off after strenuous exercise in hot and humid conditions.

LEFT **Checking the shoes** A horse's shoes need to be replaced by the farrier about every 4 to 6 weeks. You should, however, check your horse's feet yourself every day to make sure that a shoe has not come loose, or an object become wedged under the shoe.

BELOW **Leading out a horse** A horse should be trained to behave properly while being led. Many horses learn when they are young. It is important to remain alert when leading a horse, even in the field, because it may instinctively take flight at any moment. A sudden movement by the horse can pull the lead rope right out of your hand.

CHECKING A HORSE'S FEET

There is a well-known saying: "No foot, no horse." The vast majority of lameness problems originate in the feet (*see p. 138*), so anything that has a harmful effect on the feet is painful for the horse and reduces its ability to work. You need to check all four feet every day. This includes picking them out, looking for injuries, and checking that any shoes fitted are not loose. The feet must be checked regularly by a farrier and trimmed if necessary, whether or not the shoes are worn out. If a shoe comes off, ask the farrier to come as soon as possible. Never work a horse with only three shoes; it is better to remove the shoe on the other side to keep that pair of feet level.

NEGLECTED FEET

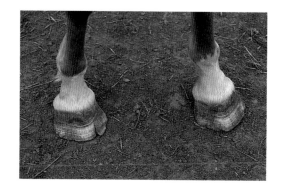

Signs of neglect
On neglected feet, the hoof walls start to crack and break away at the bottom. The walls splay out, becoming concave. Some problems, such as laminitis or a sudden change in diet, result in horizontal ridges in the hoof wall.

LIFTING A FRONT FOOT

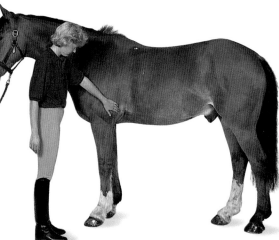

Stand close to the horse's shoulder, facing the tail. Place the hand nearest the horse on the animal's shoulder, and move it down toward the leg. This lets the horse know you are about to pick up its leg, so it will not be startled.

2 Reach around the back of the horse's leg and then run your hand down the inside. Keep a light but firm pressure on the leg.

3 Press backward and upward on the back of the pastern to encourage the horse to lift its foot. If it does not, grip the pastern and pull the foot up and back.

4 When the horse lifts its foot, support the leg by putting your hand around the hoof wall, with your palm against the inside wall. If you need to examine the foot or use a hoof pick, tilt the sole up.

LIFTING A HIND FOOT

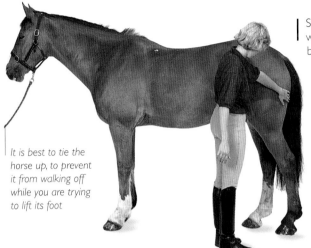

It is best to tie the horse up, to prevent it from walking off while you are trying to lift its foot

1 Stand close to the horse; that way, if it kicks, it will hurt less because the leg will have built up little momentum. Run your nearest hand down the horse's hindquarters.

2 Bring your hand around to the front of the leg just below the stifle. Then run it down the inside of the lower leg, maintaining a light but firm pressure.

3 Take hold of the back of the fetlock. Squeeze it gently, and pull the joint upward and forward. This should encourage the horse to lift its foot up off the ground.

Bend your knees to avoid straining your back

4 Raise the foot so that it is well clear of the ground, but do not hold it up too high or you will unbalance the horse and cause it discomfort. Hold the foot steady by putting your other hand around the toe while you release your grip on the fetlock.

5 Support the leg by taking hold of the toe of the foot from the inside with your original hand. Let the foot rest in your palm. You cannot tilt the foot as much as a front foot.

USING A HOOF PICK

Pick out the feet at least twice a day, and check the foot at the same time for any disorders. Choose a hoof pick that is not too sharp. Clean the grooves beside the frog first, then the sole of the foot. Always work toward the toe to avoid damaging the frog or the horse's leg, should the pick slip. Remove all mud and debris and any flaking horn.

HORSESHOES

Horses were not designed to travel long distances. Wild horses spend most of their time grazing, moving on only to find food or to escape danger. Domestic horses are asked to cover relatively long distances, often on hard roads. Their hooves cannot take the wear and tear, so iron shoes are used to protect them. Horses that are not worked regularly on hard ground may not need shoes. Seek expert advice if you are considering working a barefooted horse.

SHOES AND NAILS

Types of shoes

Ready-made shoes come in different sizes for different-sized horses. Most shoes have a groove in the underside, called fullering, to make them lighter and to give better grip. Non-fullered shoes are called plain-stamped. A horse's shoes should always suit its planned activities.

FULLERED SHOES

Fullering

Nail hole

NAILS

Nails come in sizes to match shoe sizes, and the correct size must always be used

PLAIN-STAMPED SHOE FOR SLOW WORK

"CIRCULAR" FRONT SHOE

"DIAMOND-SHAPED" HIND SHOE

STUDS

Studs are used in predrilled holes in the heel of a shoe to increase grip. A wrench is needed to screw them in tightly. Studs must be removed for work on roads or hard ground, because they tilt the foot and reduce the area in contact with the ground.

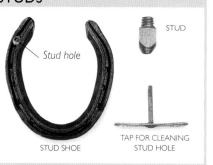

Stud hole

STUD

STUD SHOE

TAP FOR CLEANING STUD HOLE

SIGNS THAT RE-SHOEING IS NECESSARY

Checking shoes

Watch for signs that your horse needs shoeing before its scheduled time. For example, a shoe may come loose, in which case you will be able to move it slightly with your fingers; a nail might come loose or fall out; or the shoe may be worn. Do not wait until shoes have worn out before you call the farrier. The hooves may need trimming before that.

Heel of the shoe pressing on the frog

POORLY FITTED SHOE

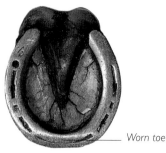

Worn toe

SHOE THAT HAS WORN EARLY OR UNEVENLY

KNOCKING DOWN A CLENCH

If you notice a raised clinch on one of the horse's hooves (see p. 58), you may be able to knock it down and keep the shoe on until the farrier arrives. First stand the horse on a hard surface, then position yourself safely and knock the clinch down with a few firm downward blows of a hammer.

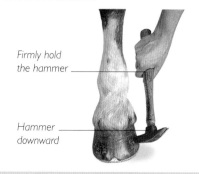

Firmly hold the hammer

Hammer downward

REMOVING A SHOE

In an emergency, when the farrier cannot come right away, it is better to remove a loose shoe than leave it only partly fastened to the foot and risk injuring the horse. To remove a front shoe, hold the foot between your knees to leave both hands free. Straighten the clinches using a hammer and buffer (see p. 60).

Don't hold the foot so high that it is uncomfortable for the horse

2 Grasp a heel of the shoe with pincers so that the jaws are between the shoe and the hoof. Loosen the shoe with a sharp, strong movement toward the toe. Do the same with the other heel.

3 If it is difficult to free the shoe, try removing one or more of the nails first. This is easiest with nail pincers, but you can use ordinary pliers if necessary. Loosen the shoe gradually down both sides, levering carefully toward the toe.

4 When you reach the toe, remove the shoe completely. Lever it off sideways so as not to split the hoof. Be sure not to leave any old nails on the ground, where the horse could step on them and injure itself.

Removing a hind shoe

When you have to remove a hind shoe, hold the leg up over one knee rather than between your knees. Stand with your back to the horse's head, and let the hoof lie on the inside of your knee. Press your side into the angle of the horse's hock to restrict its ability to kick. Remove the shoe in the same way as a front shoe. It is more difficult to hold a hind leg than a front leg, and the procedure does take practice.

THE BAREFOOT TRIM

Increasing numbers of people work horses without shoes. Barefoot trimming does not simply mean not fitting a shoe, though—it is a specific way of trimming the feet. The principal goal of such trimming is that the horse should take little or no weight on the wall of the hoof. This is achieved by trimming so that the heel is short, the toe is shortened from the front, and the frog extends over two-thirds of the length of the sole to take the weight.

SHOEING PROCEDURE

Arrange to have your horse shod regularly. On average, a farrier will need to visit every four to six weeks. Even if the shoes are not worn out, the hoof will have grown and will need trimming. Having your horse shod properly is expensive, but do not leave the shoes on in an effort to save money. Badly fitting shoes are painful for the horse and can cause permanent damage. Shoeing a horse can be carried out either hot or cold. In hot shoeing, the shoes are heated so that the farrier can shape them to fit the feet. In cold shoeing, only small alterations to the shape of the shoe are possible. Never be tempted to shoe a horse yourself, even if you are just replacing a nail. Shoeing is a skilled craft that, for the horse's sake, should be left to farriers.

TRIMMING EQUIPMENT

Some of a farrier's tools are specialized tools, used only for shoeing. A pritchel is used to carry a hot shoe from the forge to the horse. Clinching tongs are used to bend over the trimmed end of the nails, called clenches, to hold the shoe in place. A buffer is used with a hammer to knock up the clenches when removing a shoe. A hoof knife is for paring and trimming the foot and the frog.

PRITCHEL

BUFFER

DOUBLE PRITCHEL

CLINCHING TONGS

PINCERS

NAIL PULLER

HOOF NIPPER

HAMMER

HOOF KNIFE

RASP

HOT SHOEING PROCEDURE

After removing the old shoe, the farrier's first step is to pare away all the loose flakes of horn from the sole. This allows the length of the hoof wall to be assessed in relation to the sole.

2 The appropriate length of wall is then trimmed off using the hoof nippers. The goal is to return the hoof wall to the length it was when the horse was last shod. More horn usually needs to be removed around the toe than around the heel, because this area grows quickest.

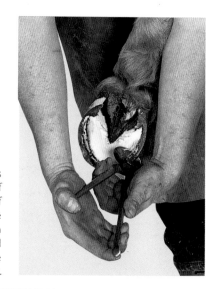

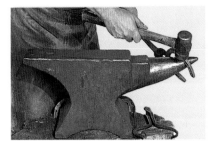

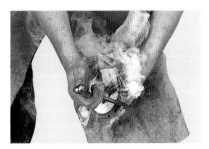

3 The uneven surface left by the small bites of the hoof nippers is filed level with a hoof rasp. It should not be necessary for the farrier to file away significant amounts of the wall at the toe. Too much filing is called "dumping."

4 The shoe is heated until it is red-hot and then shaped by hammering it against an anvil. The shoe will need to be returned to the furnace to reheat it during the shaping process. Hammering iron that is not hot enough weakens the metal.

5 When the shoe is ready, the farrier holds it gently in position against the hoof. This is not to burn a seating for the shoe but to discolor any protruding areas of horn, which would prevent the shoe from fitting properly. These areas are then rasped level.

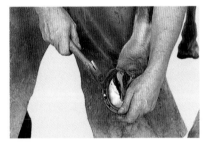

6 When the farrier is satisfied, the shoe is cooled in water and nailed in place. There is no definitive number of nails that must to be used, just the fewest possible to keep the shoe secure—traditionally four on the outside and three on the inside.

7 The ends of the nails are twisted off and bent over with the clinching tongs, to form clinches. The farrier will usually rest the horse's foot on a special tripod. This makes it easier to form the clinches because it frees both hands to use the tongs.

8 The foot is finished off. Sharp edges on the clinches are rasped away, and the hoof wall is rasped lightly where it meets the shoe. This is to reduce the risk of the hoof cracking, not to make the foot fit the shoe. Any clips are tapped gently into place.

SIGNS OF GOOD SHOEING

The final result

Good shoeing produces a symmetrical hoof, with the inside and outside wall the same length. The edge of the shoe should follow the wall of the toe. The heels of the shoe must be long enough so that the whole bottom of the hoof is protected. A shoe can be slightly larger than the hoof— the hoof will spread to fit—but it must never be smaller than the hoof. Ask someone to recommend a good farrier. Proper shoeing takes time. The best farrier will probably not be the quickest or the cheapest.

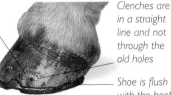

Clenches about one-third of the way up the wall

Toe is not dumped

Clenches are in a straight line and not through the old holes

Shoe is flush with the hoof

Toe clip fits neatly into the hoof

Frog and sole are trimmed neatly but not excessively

Nails are the correct size to fit the shoe

NATURAL BALANCE SHOEING

A natural balance shoe is shaped differently at the toe than a traditional horseshoe and is set back beneath the hoof. The goal is that the point of breakover— where, during movement, the foot rotates as the heels start to lift— should be underneath the foot rather than at the tip of the toe.

Toe is straight rather than rounded

NATURAL BALANCE SHOE

GROOMING EQUIPMENT

A grooming kit is not a random mixture of brushes, but a collection of specific grooming tools. Each one is designed to do its job without hurting the horse's often sensitive skin. If you use the wrong piece of equipment at any stage, you could hurt the horse, and if a brush does not do its job properly, you will be wasting your time. A grooming kit should be kept clean, because any dirt from an implement may be brushed into tiny cuts in the skin and subsequently cause infection.

You could use a household plastic tray for a grooming kit

Individual kits
Each horse should have its own, labeled grooming kit. This prevents the spread of diseases such as ringworm from horse to horse. There are a variety of commercial boxes in which you can keep a grooming kit.

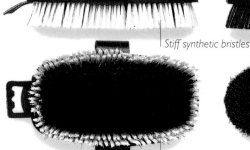

Stiff synthetic bristles

Soft fiber bristles

Metal curry comb
This curry comb should never be used on the horse. It is used only for cleaning the body brush (see p. 65). Keep it free of hair to maintain its effectiveness.

Body brushes
These brushes are used to remove dust and scurf from a stabled horse's coat. They have short, closely spaced bristles. Body brushes vary in stiffness. The finer the horse's coat, the softer the brush should be. You should also use a softer brush on a summer coat than you do on a winter coat, because the coat will not be so thick.

Curry combs
Plastic and rubber curry combs are used for removing dirt, especially dried mud on turned-out horses. They can be used directly on the horse, although care should be taken when using them on horses with a thin coat or sensitive skin.

PLASTIC CURRY COMB

RUBBER CURRY COMB

Cactus cloth
This can be used dry or damp to remove dried mud or sweat. Soak it before you first use it, to soften it.

Dandy brush

This is the first brush to use on a dirty coat. The bristles are long and well spaced. Do not use it on sensitive or clipped areas.

Metal mane comb

This separates the hairs of a tangled mane. Do not pull too hard on the hairs—it can hurt.

Hoof pick

A hoof pick must have a blunt end. If the point is sharp, it could cut the sole of the foot, or puncture the sole if the horse steps on it. A hoof pick is a vital grooming tool. Keep it where you can find it.

Massage pad

This is used on a clean, working horse, to help develop the muscles and stimulate the blood supply to the skin. This massaging is called wisping (see p. 66).

Water brush

This can be used to train a mane and tail (see p. 67). It is also useful for removing difficult stains from a pale-colored coat. Use it slightly damp, not soaking wet.

Sponges

You need two soft, good-quality sponges—one for the eyes, nose, and mouth, and one for the dock area under the tail. Do not use a deteriorating sponge, because bits of sponge may get into the horse's eyes.

Grooming cloth

Usually made of linen, a grooming cloth can be used to give the coat a final polish. It should be washed regularly.

MAKING A MASSAGE PAD (WISP)

Traditionally, wisping, or massaging, is done with a wisp made from straw or hay. To make a wisp, dampen some straw or hay and twist it into a "rope" 6½–8 ft (2–2.5 m) long. Make two loops at one end of the rope, one slightly bigger than the other. Wrap the long end in tight figure-eights around the loops down to the end. Twist the rope through the end of each loop, and tuck the end in securely.

Make the loops the size you want the wisp— it should fit comfortably in your hand

Make the twists as tight and as neat as possible

Tuck the end into the wisp

Hoof oil

Hoof oil can be clear or black. You can brush oil on clean, dry hooves to protect them and to enhance their appearance (see p. 67). Applying hoof oil does not improve the quality of the existing horn.

GROOMING A HORSE

Wild horses survive perfectly well without being groomed, but domestic horses are expected to be free from mud, stains, and dust. Turned-out horses should not be groomed excessively because the grease in their coat helps to keep them warm and dry. Just pick out their feet and remove any mud and stains, especially from those areas where tack will lie. A full grooming of a stabled horse is known as strapping. It removes dirt and massages the muscles and skin, stimulating the release of natural oils into the coat and improving the circulation. Strapping is most effective after exercise, when the horse is warm. Most horses enjoy being groomed, but some are ticklish in places. If possible, groom outside, so that the dust and hairs blow away and are not just redistributed.

GROOMING FOR COMFORT

Mutual grooming
Horses will groom each other with their teeth to form social bonds as well as to provide a welcome scratch. They will also roll in dust, as a form of dry shampooing, and rub against trees, which is the equivalent of being brushed.

QUARTERING

Give your horse a quick groom before you exercise it in the morning in order to make it comfortable and neat. Pick out the feet, sponge the face and dock, brush the coat lightly, and remove major stains with a sponge or water brush. This procedure is called quartering, because a blanketed horse is done a quarter at a time with the blanket folded back or forward.

REMOVING MUD

1 | Pull the hoof pick down each side of the frog from heel to toe to remove manure or mud. You may also need to run the pick around the inside of the shoe.

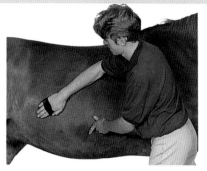

USING A RUBBER CURRY COMB

2 Remove any dried mud from the coat with a rubber curry comb or dandy brush. Use them in a straight line, following the lay of the coat.

USING A DANDY BRUSH

The dandy brush is relatively harsh, so avoid using it on the horse's tender parts such as the belly, on clipped areas, or on a thin coat.

USING THE BODY BRUSH

Flip the mane to the other side

1 After removing mud, use the body brush to clean and massage the skin. Start along the crest of the neck, brushing in the direction of the lie of the coat with short circular strokes. Press hard so that the bristles reach down to the skin.

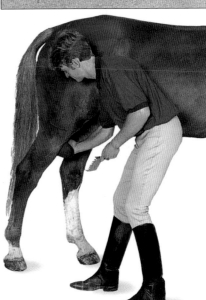

Cleaning a body brush
Keep the body brush clean with a metal curry comb. After every four or five strokes, push the bristles across the curry comb. From time to time, tap a corner of the curry comb on a hard surface, away from the horse, to dislodge dirt.

2 When you have brushed the crest of the neck thoroughly, flip back the mane and work on it a few locks at a time. Use your fingers to remove any tangles, then brush the mane down the neck from the roots downward.

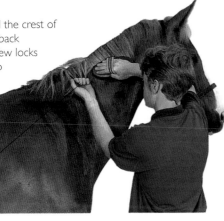

Be careful not to pull the hairs as you untangle them

3 Brush all parts of the body, working toward the tail. When you brush sensitive areas, such as the inside of the legs and the groin, stand close to the horse and to the side so that it cannot kick you.

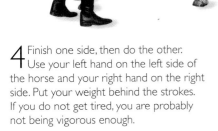

4 Finish one side, then do the other. Use your left hand on the left side of the horse and your right hand on the right side. Put your weight behind the strokes. If you do not get tired, you are probably not being vigorous enough.

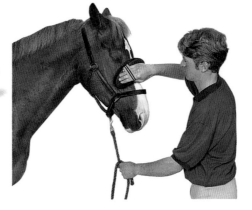

5 Dispense with the curry comb for grooming the face. Untie the horse and hold the rope while you groom with a soft brush. Move the halter or take it off and buckle it around the neck, so that you can groom underneath the straps.

BRUSHING THE TAIL

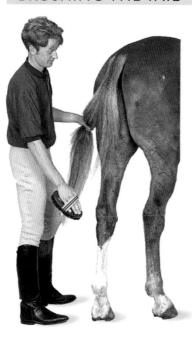

Removing tangles
Untangle any knots with your fingers, then brush the tail with a body brush. Take care not to pull hairs out, and never use a dandy brush or curry comb on the tail. Hold the tail in one hand, and shake a small section free. Brush this with long flowing strokes starting at the bottom. Brush in more hairs bit by bit until you have finished the whole tail.

MASSAGE

Start with five bangs on each area and increase the number gradually

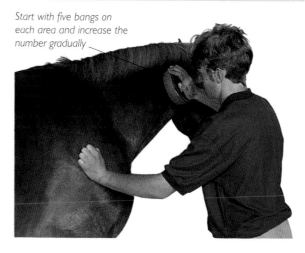

Toning the muscles
Massage only the neck, shoulders, quarters, and thighs to tone the muscles. Bang the pad or wisp down with reasonable force and make a short stroke in the direction of the coat.

SPONGING THE EYES, MUZZLE, AND DOCK

The eyes
The sponge should be damp, but not wet enough to release water into the eye. Do not attempt to open the eye; the idea is to clean the eyelids. Start at the outside corner and sponge inward, so that you do the dirtiest part last.

The muzzle
Sponge around the lips, then sponge the nostrils. You can put the sponge right into a nostril to clean inside it. Then remove any discharge from the outside.

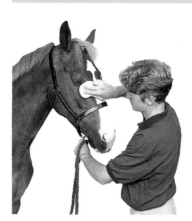

Lift the tail out of the way

The dock
Use a different sponge for the dock area. Gently sponge the underside of the dock and the whole area under the tail.

TRAINING THE MANE

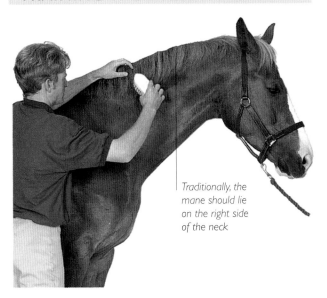

Traditionally, the mane should lie on the right side of the neck

Flattening the hairs
Training the mane encourages the hairs to lie flat and look neat. Wet the water brush and shake it once to remove excess water. Place it on the base of the mane and brush from the roots downward.

TRAINING THE TAIL

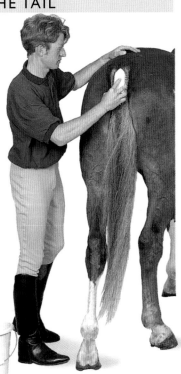

Smoothing the tail
Lay the top of the tail with a water brush in the same way as the mane. Pay particular attention to the short hairs, which would otherwise stick upward. When you have finished the tail, you can bandage it to keep it neat (see p. 198).

USING A GROOMING CLOTH

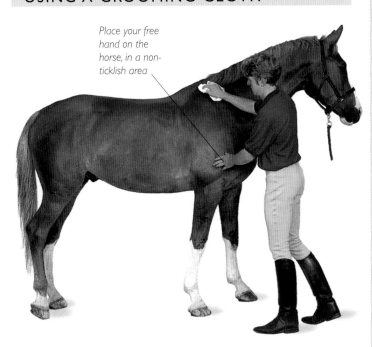

Place your free hand on the horse, in a non-ticklish area

Polishing the coat
Slightly dampen the grooming cloth and fold it into a flat pad. Wipe all over the body in the direction of the hairs to remove any remaining dust.

OILING THE HOOVES

Brush any mud off the hooves before applying oil. In muddy conditions, it may be necessary to wash them. If you do wash the hooves, dry them thoroughly or the oil will not be effective. Never apply oil to a dirty hoof, because this will seal in the dirt. Cover the whole hoof, from the bulbs of the heel up to the coronet, with a thin, even coating of oil. Oil the sole of the hoof, too. This will help to prevent mud, ice, and bedding from getting packed into the foot.

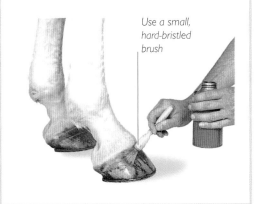

Use a small, hard-bristled brush

PREPARING FOR A SHOW

Your horse will probably know it is a special day before it gets to the show, and may be excited from the moment you arrive at the stable. Its anticipation may be triggered by small changes in routine on previous days, or it may sense your mood. You will have to start early in the morning because there is a great deal of work to be done. There is no point doing this the night before, because the horse may roll, and then you will have to do it again.

WASHING

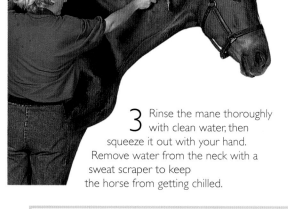

Washing the mane

1 Wet the mane thoroughly, using a sponge and warm, not hot, water. Be careful not to get water in the horse's eyes. Do not forget the forelock; bring it back behind the ears to join the mane. Make sure that the water penetrates down to the skin at the roots of the hairs.

2 Use a mild soap or shampoo to soap the mane. Do not use a detergent. Work the lather well into the base of the hairs, to remove any scurf from the skin. Leave the lather in place for several minutes.

Start at the top of the neck

3 Rinse the mane thoroughly with clean water, then squeeze it out with your hand. Remove water from the neck with a sweat scraper to keep the horse from getting chilled.

Washing the tail
You can wet much of the tail in a bucket, but you will need a sponge to wet the top. Do not forget the underneath, and make sure that you wash right down to the roots of the hairs Use several buckets of water to rinse, because it is vital that all the shampoo is removed.

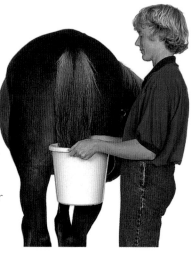

WASHING EQUIPMENT

SHAMPOO

BUCKET

SPONGE

SWEAT SCRAPER

PULLING

Pulling the mane
Thin or shorten a mane by pulling. Take a few hairs from underneath, wind them around a comb, and pull them out with a sharp tug.

Pulling the tail
Tail pulling can be painful for a horse, so if you have to pull a tail, take the underneath hairs and only pull a few in a single session. You will need to start well in advance of the date of a show.

PULLING EQUIPMENT

COMB

BRAIDING

Braiding the tail
1 You cannot just divide the hairs into three groups and braid the tail, because the hairs grow around the dock. Instead, take a small group of hairs from the center and each side of the tail at the top.

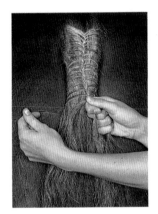

2 Braid down the tail. Bring in successive groups of hairs from each side and join them into the braid as you continue down.

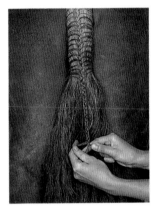

3 Braid one-third of the way down the tail, then continue without adding any new hairs. Loop the end under and secure it with thread.

BRAIDING EQUIPMENT

NEEDLE AND THREAD

SCISSORS

ELASTIC BANDS

Make an uneven number of braids

Braiding the mane
1 Divide the mane into bunches. Braid each one, adding in a 12-in (30-cm) thread, doubled, a third of the way down. Cut the thread, leaving a 3-in (8-cm) end.

Separate the bunches with elastic bands

2 Thread the needle, then wind the thread around the braid and sew the end under. Leave the thread hanging. Follow the same procedure with all the braids before going to the next stage.

Be careful not to prick the horse with the needle

3 Sew through the top of the braid from underneath to fold the braid in half, and in half again. Pull the thread tight, wind it around the braid, then sew through several times to secure it.

CLIPPING AND TRIMMING

Clipping lets a horse lose more heat during work than it can if wearing its winter coat. If you let a horse sweat too much, it will lose condition, and risks getting chilled unless it is dried properly. The clip you use depends on the work your horse does. If it never sweats, then it doesn't need clipping. Few horses like being clipped; all have sensitive areas, such as the belly, and some take time to accept the noise of the clippers. When learning how to clip, ask an expert to show you, and then to supervise you. In any case, you will need a helper to calm the horse. A clipped horse must wear a rug (*see p. 192*) to replace the insulation you have removed.

THE NATURAL COAT

Winter protection

A horse naturally grows a thick winter coat to protect it against the cold. It is a highly effective form of insulation—more so than many people realize. Snow that falls on a horse's back will not melt right away because the coat stops heat from escaping from the body. Turning a horse out wearing a thick blanket discourages coat growth and reduces this natural protection.

TRIMMING EQUIPMENT

ELECTRIC CLIPPERS

Tension adjuster for blades

On–off switch

Hole for lubricating oil

MOVING BLADE

FIXED BLADE

CLEANING BRUSH

Clipping

Clippers can be either AC- or battery-powered. They have two cutting blades, one of which is fixed while the other moves from side to side— just enough to let the hairs enter the channels in the blades. A cleaning brush is good for removing hairs from the clippers after use.

Try to use clippers that are quiet—an advantage of battery-powered models—but as powerful as possible so that they do not become too hot. Battery-powered clippers are particularly useful for sensitive or awkward areas such as around the head. They also avoid the danger of you or the horse tripping over the cord. Make sure you check your clippers for electrical safety before you use them. You may find that a horse resents either the noise or the vibration from the clippers. If this happens, try applying a twitch (see p. 51). This might override the irritation and encourage the horse to stand still. However, some horses may require sedation before they will allow themselves to be clipped.

USING CLIPPERS

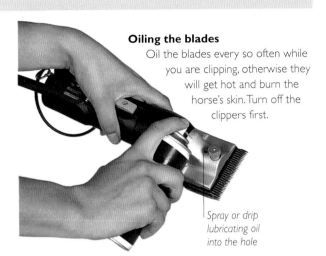

Adjusting the tension
Blades that are too loose rattle and pull the coat instead of cutting properly. If they are too tight, they put a strain on the motor and get very hot. To tighten them, slowly turn the screw. When the noise changes, as the blades stop moving freely, loosen the tension very slightly.

Oiling the blades
Oil the blades every so often while you are clipping, otherwise they will get hot and burn the horse's skin. Turn off the clippers first.

Spray or drip lubricating oil into the hole

TYPES OF CLIPS

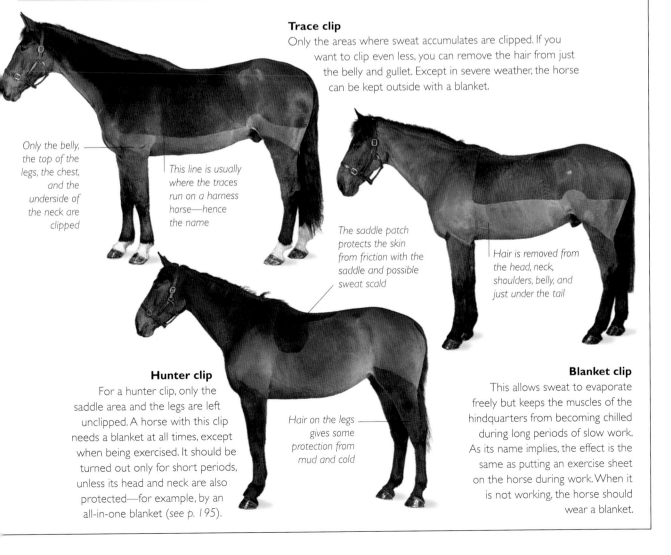

Trace clip
Only the areas where sweat accumulates are clipped. If you want to clip even less, you can remove the hair from just the belly and gullet. Except in severe weather, the horse can be kept outside with a blanket.

Only the belly, the top of the legs, the chest, and the underside of the neck are clipped

This line is usually where the traces run on a harness horse—hence the name

The saddle patch protects the skin from friction with the saddle and possible sweat scald

Hair is removed from the head, neck, shoulders, belly, and just under the tail

Hunter clip
For a hunter clip, only the saddle area and the legs are left unclipped. A horse with this clip needs a blanket at all times, except when being exercised. It should be turned out only for short periods, unless its head and neck are also protected—for example, by an all-in-one blanket (see p. 195).

Hair on the legs gives some protection from mud and cold

Blanket clip
This allows sweat to evaporate freely but keeps the muscles of the hindquarters from becoming chilled during long periods of slow work. As its name implies, the effect is the same as putting an exercise sheet on the horse during work. When it is not working, the horse should wear a blanket.

CLIPPING A HORSE

1 Draw the outline of the clip you want with chalk. (This horse will have a blanket clip.) Don't just start work and hope that the clip will turn out symmetrical with straight edges.

Follow the line of the muscles in the leg to make a nice shape

Bandage the horse's tail to keep it out of the way

Stand between the horse and the electrical cord so there is no danger that the horse will step on it

2 The shoulder is the best place to start; most horses will accept the clippers here. Use smooth strokes against the lay of the hairs. Keep the blade parallel to the skin. If you tilt it down, it will nick the skin, and if you tilt it up, it will not cut well.

Ask someone to hold the horse and help keep it still

Wear rubber-soled shoes or boots for safety when using electric clippers

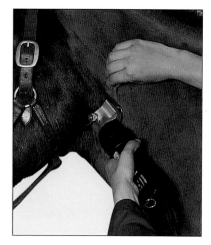

3 In certain places, the skin is very loose or, because of the shape of the body, the area to be clipped is concave. These places can be difficult to clip neatly without nicking the skin. The solution is to stretch the skin with your other hand so that you are still clipping a firm, flat surface.

If a helper is not holding the horse, tie the horse up, preferably with a haynet to keep it occupied

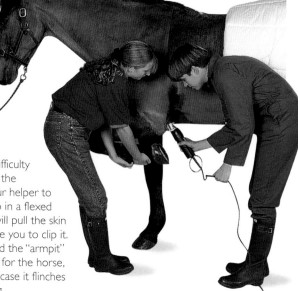

4 A similar difficulty arises with the elbow. Ask your helper to hold the leg up in a flexed position. This will pull the skin tight and enable you to clip it. Clipping around the "armpit" may be ticklish for the horse, so be ready in case it flinches and jerks its leg.

TRIMMING

Ears
Hold the ear with one hand so that the two edges touch each other, then trim the hairs that stick out beyond these edges. Use scissors with rounded ends. Never cut the hairs inside the ears; these protect the inner parts from dirt and infection. Cut upward, away from the horse's face, to avoid stabbing the horse in the eye if it moves its head.

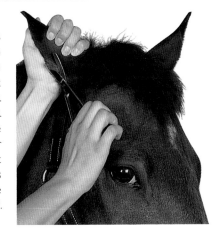

TRIMMING EQUIPMENT
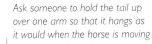

COMB

CURVED, BLUNT-ENDED SCISSORS

Face
Long hairs under the horse's chin and lower jaw should be trimmed with scissors, but not the whiskers. These are part of the horse's touch apparatus. Lift the hairs to be cut with a comb so that no whiskers are included.

Ask someone to hold the tail up over one arm so that it hangs as it would when the horse is moving

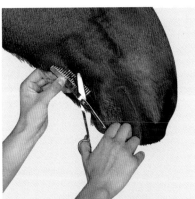

Tail
Neaten the bottom of the tail by cutting across, parallel to the ground. When the horse is carrying its tail properly, the end should be a hand's width below the hocks.

Heels
You may need to trim the feathers (the long hairs on the back of the leg, the fetlock, and the heel) so that the skin can be easily kept clean and dry. This helps to prevent mud fever. Run the comb upward through the hair and cut the ends neatly, but not too close.

TRANSPORTING A HORSE

There are two types of vehicles designed for transporting horses by road. A horse van is really a covered truck. A horse trailer is towed behind a car or pickup truck. Some commercial vans can transport 10 or more horses, while most trailers can carry only two; in either case, check with your state's motor vehicle division to find out if you need a special driver's license to transport horses. Even the best van or trailer may not provide ideal ventilation for all its passengers. Make sure there is plenty of fresh air (but no drafts) flowing through, and never travel for more than six hours without stopping. Avoid transporting any horse with a respiratory problem.

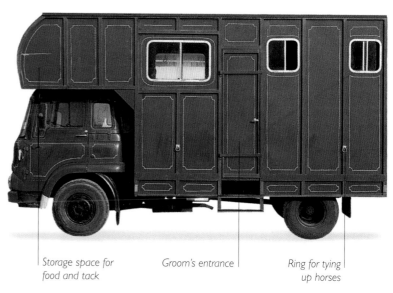

Storage space for food and tack *Groom's entrance* *Ring for tying up horses*

Horse van

There are a number of points to consider when choosing a horse van. The vehicle's overall weight may affect whether a special driver's license is needed. The layout may require horses to travel facing either sideways or front to back; both methods have their supporters. Some boxes load at the rear, but others load at the side. Avoid vehicles that have luxurious living quarters for the people but cramped and poorly equipped facilities for the horses.

Trailer

Before using a trailer, check that it has been properly maintained and its loaded weight is within the car's safety limit. The car's license plate must be shown on the rear of the trailer. Hitch the trailer to the car as shown here. Never travel in a trailer—it is too dangerous.

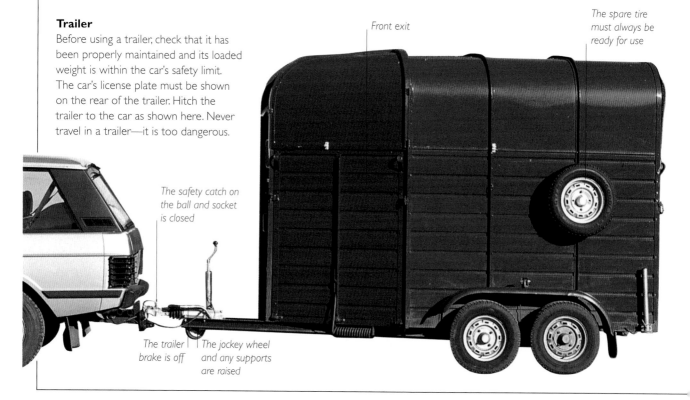

Front exit

The spare tire must always be ready for use

The safety catch on the ball and socket is closed

The trailer brake is off *The jockey wheel and any supports are raised*

Long journeys

You should not try to travel for more than a total of eight hours in any one day, even with stops, and not for more than four to six hours without a decent rest. When you do stop, open all the doors and windows of the trailer or van, and untie the horse's head so that it can cough or put its head down. Do not transport horses at night unless you have a good light inside the trailer for loading and checking during transit.

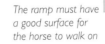

The walls and partition should have some padding on which the horse can lean

There should be a tape, chain, or bar as a rear restraint for each horse

The floor should be easy to clean, with a good grip for the horse's feet

A front ramp is preferable for unloading

Rear supports are necessary to stabilize a trailer during loading and unloading

Rear blinds should be lowered only in very bad weather, because they reduce ventilation

The breast bar must be sturdy and well padded, since horses may lean against it during braking

There must be a means by which you can secure the partition during travel

The ramp must have a good surface for the horse to walk on

On arrival

When you arrive at an event, lower the rear support on the trailer, and put the brake on. Unload the horses, and walk them around in hand for five minutes. This will loosen any muscles that they were using to brace themselves against movement during the journey. Then tie the horses up outside the vehicle, in the shade. Give them access to fresh water, and provide a haynet if appropriate.

CAREFUL DRIVING WITH A TRAILER

Before attaching a trailer to your vehicle, make sure the combined weight of the trailer and horse is below the vehicle manufacturer's recommended maximum towing weight. If you have ever tried to travel standing up on a bus without hanging on to anything, you will realize what it is like for a horse to travel. Always think ahead, braking and accelerating gradually. Take corners slowly. Trailers can easily skid when water or ice reduces road adhesion. You should not tow a trailer unless you have practiced backing up with it, in case this is necessary in an emergency.

LOADING AND UNLOADING

Horses do not naturally enjoy walking into an enclosed space such as a van or trailer. Remain calm and be prepared for the horse to stop suddenly, rear, or go backward. Use as long a lead rope as possible—you must be able to keep hold of the horse even if the unexpected does happen. A helper makes loading easier and safer, but most horses will go into a box or trailer with no problems if they have traveled before with no ill effects and have confidence in you.

WHAT THE HORSE SHOULD WEAR

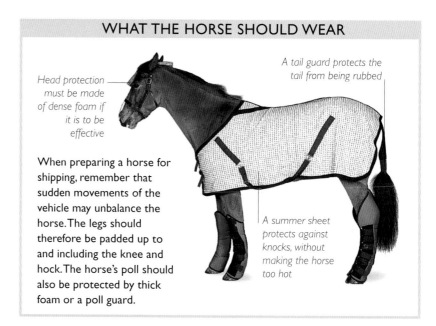

Head protection must be made of dense foam if it is to be effective

A tail guard protects the tail from being rubbed

A summer sheet protects against knocks, without making the horse too hot

When preparing a horse for shipping, remember that sudden movements of the vehicle may unbalance the horse. The legs should therefore be padded up to and including the knee and hock. The horse's poll should also be protected by thick foam or a poll guard.

LOADING

Walk confidently up the ramp

The helper should be behind and to one side of the horse, just within its field of vision

1 Approach the trailer from a distance, so that the horse has momentum when it steps on the ramp. Walk in a straight line up the center of the ramp. If possible, ask someone to walk a little way behind the horse. Once the horse knows that there is someone there, it is less likely to stop. If you have a problem, try attaching a long rope or lunge rein to either side of the trailer and ask two people to cross over behind the horse with the ropes.

2 If a single horse is to travel in a dual-horse trailer, put it on the side closest to the middle of the road, for a smoother ride. Ask your helper to fasten the bar or chain behind the horse and close the ramp once you are inside the trailer. Next, tie the horse up, making sure that the rope is long enough for the horse to stand against the partition; it may want to lean against it during the journey. You can provide the horse with a small haynet to prevent it from becoming bored during the journey.

UNLOADING

I If the trailer gives you the option to unload at the front, always use this exit. First remove any equipment that is stowed in front of the horse. (If you do store something here during a journey, make sure that it cannot slide around.) Untie the head, and then remove the breast bar. In vehicles containing two or more horses, unload the horse closest to the ramp first.

A helper should stand near the ramp on the side away from you, to deter the horse from stepping sideways off the ramp

2 Lead the horse out calmly. Do not let it pull you out. If there is another horse in the trailer, secure the first one, then untie the second, move the partition over to widen the exit, and lead the horse out.

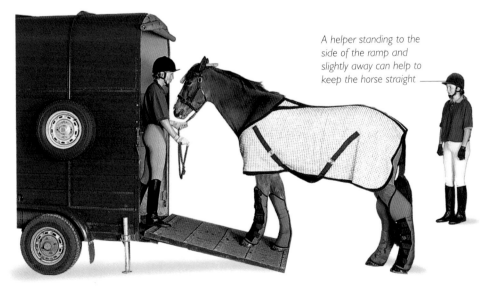

A helper standing to the side of the ramp and slightly away can help to keep the horse straight

Rear unloading

Unloading from the rear can be difficult. Horses do not move backward easily, and the shipping boots restrict movement further. Untie the head when you are on the same side of the breast bar as the horse. Ask a helper to undo the rear bar or chain, and be ready in case the horse pulls backward. Guide the horse out; you cannot expect it to be able to keep itself straight.

THE HORSE AT WORK

The change from rest to full work must be gradual. As a guideline, a horse should spend at least a week just walking, a week walking and trotting increasing distances, and a week introducing the canter. To get a horse fit to compete, spend longer on each stage. A change from work to rest must also be gradual. It is bad for a horse suddenly to do nothing.

WARMING UP

Warming up
Before riding, walk and trot a stabled horse up and down in hand a few times to loosen it up. Ride at the walk and trot for at least 20 minutes before fast work, to increase the blood flow to the horse's muscles. Exertion produces lactic acid, which must be washed away from the muscles as soon as it forms.

AFTER WORK

Cooling off
A horse must be cooled off slowly after hard work. Walk for 10 minutes at the end of a fast hack or other work. Then wash sweat off to make the horse comfortable.

FOOD AND WATER

Horses must get used to drinking during exercise. When ridden for long periods, they can become dehydrated if the fluid they lose is not replaced. After hard exercise, a horse should be given a little water at a time, to which you can add electrolytes. However, do not give a horse a large meal immediately after work; its digestive system will not be able to cope because the blood will still be concentrated in the muscles.

1 Sponge down sweaty areas, especially the saddle area, between the legs, and under the belly. In cold weather, make sure the horse is not in a draft.

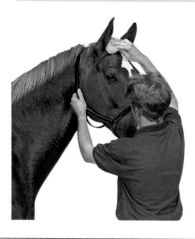

2 Untie the horse, then move back the halter so that you can sponge the dirt and sweat away from areas where the bridle has rested. If the horse is tacked up again without being washed, this dirt will rub the skin.

3 Use a sweat
scraper to remove
excess water. In hot
weather, let the
horse dry slowly;
the evaporation of
the water gives a
cooling effect.

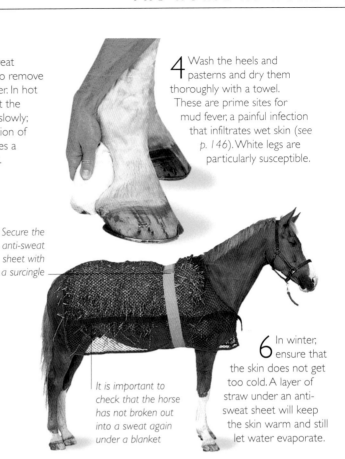

4 Wash the heels and
pasterns and dry them
thoroughly with a towel.
These are prime sites for
mud fever, a painful infection
that infiltrates wet skin (see
p. 146). White legs are
particularly susceptible.

*Secure the
anti-sweat
sheet with
a surcingle*

5 Quietly walk the horse around until all
sweat or water has evaporated from the
coat and the horse is dry. Do not leave the
horse standing in a stable when still wet.

*It is important to
check that the horse
has not broken out
into a sweat again
under a blanket*

6 In winter,
ensure that
the skin does not get
too cold. A layer of
straw under an anti-
sweat sheet will keep
the skin warm and still
let water evaporate.

AT A SHOW

Caring for the horse

Make sure that you warm the horse up adequately
before each class. Between classes, do not just tie
your horse up and abandon it;
check that it is
comfortable
and has clean
water and
possibly a
haynet.

Sponging the mouth

At a show, the horse may wear a bit
for far longer than normal. Moisten
the inside of its mouth with a wet
sponge at least before each class.

Cooling off

When you have finished an
event, tend to your horse.
Walk it around in an anti-
sweat sheet to allow it to
relax and to make sure that
its temperature is stable before
you load it to take home.

PHYSICAL DEMANDS

The activities we ask our horses to perform place a variety of different physical demands on them. Over the years, people noticed that a certain type of horse performed better at a certain activity. They then tended to select horses of that type for that particular activity and to use the successful horses for breeding. The result is that we have selected a range of physical attributes in our horses that we take full advantage of in our equine pursuits. Originally, we grouped these attributes together as good or bad "conformation." We now know that some of the attributes go much deeper than just physical appearance.

Przewalski's horse
Przewalski's horse is thought to be as close as we can get to the original wild horse of Mongolia. It spends 90 percent of its time grazing, but we have taken advantage of its ancestors' "fright and flight" instinct to provide speed in our modern domesticated horse.

YOUR HORSE'S BACK

Ill-fitting tack or slight lameness may result in pain along the muscles of a horse's back. Beware of untrained "experts" who offer to manipulate the problem away. You can get help from certified physiotherapists who specialize in horses—your vet should be able to recommend a local practitioner, and advise whether a saddle fits properly or not.

Endurance riding
Horses used for endurance events are relatively thin and wiry, like human marathon runners. This is because the muscle fibers have to have very good contact with the blood supply that constantly brings oxygen and removes carbon dioxide. The horse has tremendous stamina—its body reserves of fat are sufficient for 400 miles (640 km) of walking and trotting.

Show jumping
The horse is not a natural jumper; some horses would not naturally jump over a very low fence. However, the horse learns quickly, and humans have encouraged jumping ability. Show jumpers tend to be well-muscled horses. Because they need just a few explosive bursts of energy and can then rest, they have thick, powerful muscle fibers that use stored energy rather than relying on close contact with the blood supply.

Taking a cross-country jump

A cross-country course places great demands on a horse because it requires both stamina at speed and bursts of explosive energy for the jumps. No horse in the wild would canter or gallop such a distance without stopping. The variety of obstacles also requires a horse that is prepared to trust its rider even when it does not know what lies on the other side of the obstacle.

Dressage

Dressage is all about precise muscle control. The horse must have as much concentration as its rider. The patterns of nerve impulse and muscle contraction that collectively produce controlled movement are learned subconsciously by repetition. The combination of hours of repetitive work and movements that reveal any lameness is taken seriously in the ring. Horses competing in dressage should be fit, with very fluid movements.

Sprinting

Sprinters are all about power. They have large masses of muscle that can produce maximum effort, but only for a short time. They even have a specially adapted type of muscle fiber that makes maximum use of stored energy. Quarter horses, for example, can run faster than any other horse.

Hacking in the hills

Four-legged animals have difficulty walking down a steep hill. Walking up a hill requires increasing effort with every stride. Slow work up and down hills can be used in fitness training as an alternative to fast work, which may put more strain on the joints and tendons.

Pony pulling a cart/carriage

Pulling heavy loads puts a great strain on the hind legs, which usually take just 40 percent of the horse's weight. Blinkers may stop the fear of the carriage behind, but they restrict the horse's ability to maneuver.

CHAPTER THREE

THE HORSE OUTDOORS

HORSES ARE GRAZING ANIMALS, SO AN OPEN AREA OF GRASS IS THEIR NATURAL ENVIRONMENT. IN THE WILD, THEY HAVE SPACE TO MOVE AROUND AND CHOOSE WHAT THEY EAT AND WHERE THEY SLEEP. A HORSE CANNOT DO THIS WHEN IT IS CONFINED TO A FIELD, SO MAKE SURE THAT THE FIELD YOU PROVIDE IS SAFE AND ATTRACTIVE TO IT. MAINTAINING A SAFE FIELD, SUPPLYING SUITABLE FOOD AND SHELTER, AND HANDLING A HORSE CORRECTLY WHEN YOU TURN IT OUT AND CATCH IT ARE ALL IMPORTANT ASPECTS OF HAVING A HORSE TURNED OUT.

THE FIELD

Horses are very selective grazers. They graze some areas right down to the soil but leave other areas untouched and use them only for defecating. The uneaten area grows long and coarse and becomes infested with weeds. If horses are left on their own to graze a field, the weedy area gets larger and the field becomes both an eyesore and unsuitable for grazing. The secret of maintaining a good horse paddock is to keep it all cut to the height that horses prefer to graze. This cutting can be done by other animals, such as sheep or cattle, or by mechanical means. It is best to divide the available area into two or three separate fields and then use them in rotation. This mimics nature and provides you with the opportunity to maintain the quality of the grazing.

IDEAL CONDITIONS

A tall hedge provides shelter and extra security

The shed is positioned so that a horse cannot get trapped between it and the fence

The access road has a hard, level surface that will remain good in winter

Fresh drinking water is supplied in a trough

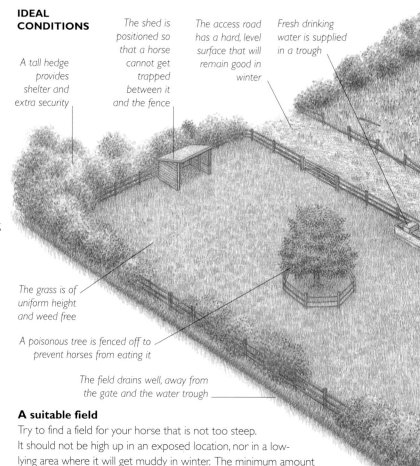

The grass is of uniform height and weed free

A poisonous tree is fenced off to prevent horses from eating it

The field drains well, away from the gate and the water trough

A suitable field
Try to find a field for your horse that is not too steep. It should not be high up in an exposed location, nor in a low-lying area where it will get muddy in winter. The minimum amount of grazing if no supplementary food is available is 1.25 acres (0.5 hectares).

FIELD MAINTENANCE

SEASON	MAINTENANCE PROCEDURES
Spring	Grass growth is at its most rapid at this time and may exceed the horse's ability to eat it, so cutting may be necessary. In early spring, some poisonous plants may sprout before the grass and tempt horses, so watch carefully and remove any potentially dangerous plants.
Summer	Grass growth varies greatly with the rainfall. Irrigation may be necessary to help a paddock recover in dry weather before it is grazed again on rotation. Harrowing breaks open dung and reduces worm larvae levels. It may be possible to take a crop of hay off one of the paddocks.
Fall	The time for boundary maintenance—laying hedges and applying preservative to wooden fences and field shelters. Watch out for acorns and other poisonous fruits and seeds, which may need to be gathered up to prevent horses from eating them.
Winter	Keep an eye on hedges, which may develop holes when the foliage dies. It may be better to feed hay than to have all the grass eaten early in the season. Watch areas that get cut up and muddy. Take steps, such as moving the feeding points, to stop this from happening.

UNSUITABLE CONDITIONS

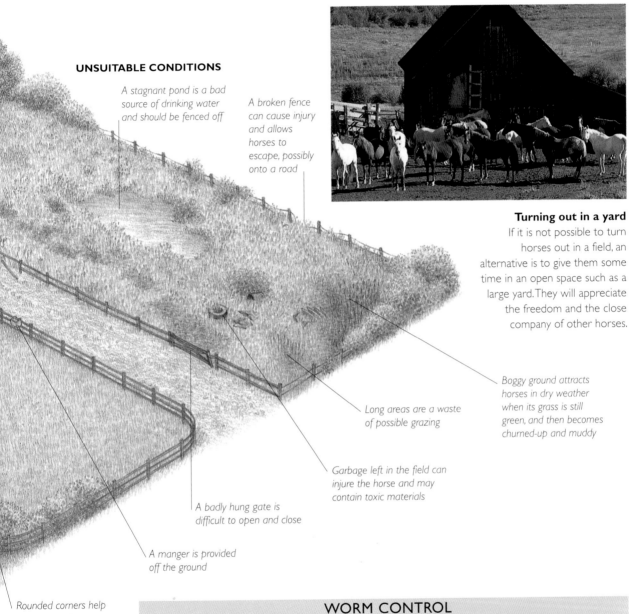

A stagnant pond is a bad source of drinking water and should be fenced off

A broken fence can cause injury and allows horses to escape, possibly onto a road

Turning out in a yard

If it is not possible to turn horses out in a field, an alternative is to give them some time in an open space such as a large yard. They will appreciate the freedom and the close company of other horses.

Boggy ground attracts horses in dry weather when its grass is still green, and then becomes churned-up and muddy

Long areas are a waste of possible grazing

Garbage left in the field can injure the horse and may contain toxic materials

A badly hung gate is difficult to open and close

A manger is provided off the ground

Rounded corners help to prevent a horse from getting trapped in the corner and injured when horses gallop around the field together

WORM CONTROL

Grazing sheep or cattle with a horse reduces the number of infective worms available to the horse. Worms usually affect only one animal species, and the larvae of worms that affect horses die in cattle and sheep. Cutting the grass also helps, because worm larvae move to the top of the grass in order to be taken in by a horse (see p. 150). Harrowing breaks open dung, leaving larvae and eggs to dry up, but it also spreads the larvae slightly.
It is better to remove the droppings, and therefore the worm eggs, every week.

FENCING AND GATES

Effective fencing keeps a horse safe and also prevents it from straying. Many municipalities have laws requiring owners to use adequate means to contain their horses in a field. The type of fence needed depends on the type of horse. For example, a high, single-rail fence that keeps in a 17-hand hunter may also allow a Shetland pony to walk underneath. Similarly, a draft horse could just push through a fence that presents a formidable obstacle to a pony. A thick hedge is the best kind of fencing, but it must not contain any poisonous plants (*see pp. 94–5*). It also provides shelter from the weather. Remember that a fence can be less effective in winter; snowdrifts reduce the effective height, and holes can appear in a deciduous hedge, making it easier to push through.

FENCES

Post and rails
This type of fencing is strong and attractive but can be expensive. Use good-quality, weather-proofed lumber. The top rail should be 4 ft (120 cm) from the ground for a horse, or 3ft 6in (105 cm) for a pony. The lower rail should be 18 in (45 cm) high.

Plain wire fencing
If it is well built, with the wire stretched taut, a plain round-wire fence may be effective. Use five or six strands, with the bottom one at least 1 ft (30 cm) above the ground. There is a danger that the horse may not notice the strands and gallop into the wire. Use markers, such as strips of white cloth, to make the wires visible.

DANGEROUS FENCING

Fencing should not rely on pain for its effect. Barbed wire, for instance, may be acceptable for sheep or cattle, but it is not safe for horses with their fine skin. Every year, many horses sustain a nasty wound from a barbed-wire fence. If a strand breaks, it is very dangerous because it can wrap itself around a horse's leg. A loose strand of any kind of wire is dangerous for the same reason. Wire mesh is unsuitable, too, because if a horse puts its foot through the mesh, it may be unable to pull its leg free without sustaining an injury.

Flexi-fencing
This consists of strong plastic tape stretched between wooden posts. It may not look as nice as post and rails, but it is cheaper and can be just as effective. The white tape is also highly visible to the horse. It is long-lasting because it does not rot.

Electric fencing
This is effective, especially if used with another fence. When a horse touches the wire, it gets a small shock. Do not use it with a thin-skinned horse, and make the wire visible. The wire is not a good barrier if the current is off. Horses learn that they will get a shock only if they can hear the characteristic ticking.

MAINTENANCE
Check fencing and gates regularly and mend them if necessary before a horse escapes or injures itself. Strands of wire can stretch, so they may need tightening. The ends of wooden fence posts, which are buried in the ground, rot faster than the parts above ground, so they need to be checked carefully. Store any spare posts in dry conditions, otherwise they will start to deteriorate even before you install them. Paint wooden fences with nontoxic preservative about every two years.

GATES

Wooden gates
Gates should open into the field so that the horse cannot push its way out. Wooden gates are relatively light. Like fences, they need regular painting with nontoxic preservative. It is worth installing good-quality hinges and fastenings, which make opening and closing the gate much easier.

Metal gates
Heavy-duty metal field gates are strong and long-lasting if properly rust-proofed, but they are expensive. Metal gates can be heavy and difficult to handle; in addition, if a horse does try to get over the gate or gets its leg trapped in the bars, it can be seriously injured because the bars do not break.

WATER AND SHELTER

The absence of either clean water or adequate shelter can seriously affect a horse's health. A lack of water can cause dehydration and death. Exposure to hot sun, flies, and pouring rain can cause skin diseases (*see pp. 146–47*) and be very unpleasant. The water and shelter must cater to every horse in the field. The water must be clean and unpolluted from industry or agriculture. If it is not, it must be fenced off. The shelter must be sited so that no horse can get trapped behind it.

WATER

Natural water source

A clean, running stream is an ideal water source if the banks allow easy access for the horse. The stream must have a gravel bottom. If it is sandy, the horse may take in sand with the water, which can cause colic. A pond may be suitable if it is fed by a spring, or is large enough to remain clear. Stagnant ponds and drainage ditches must not be used.

Trough and piped water supply

Water troughs should be constructed of nonferrous metal that will not rust. Ideally, the trough should be fed by water on a demand valve. Flush and scrub it out occasionally to keep the water clean and fresh. The trough should be sited where the drainage is good so that the surrounding area does not become very muddy, and not under a tree where leaves will fall in it. A horse needs about 5 quarts (5 liters) of water a day for every 220 lb (100 kg) of body weight.

IN WINTER

Check twice a day in winter that the water supply has not frozen. This involves more than breaking the ice. Both the feeder valve of a trough and the supply pipe can freeze. If they do, you must provide the horses with a new source of water.

Bucket and tire

If you use a bucket as a water source, use one without a handle so that the horse cannot get its foot trapped in it. Stand the bucket inside a tire so that it cannot be kicked over. Buckets must be checked and refilled at least twice a day.

SHELTER

Standing together
Horses use each other as shelter from the weather. They often also stand head to tail and use their tails to swish flies away from each other's heads. A horse on its own will usually point its rear end toward the wind, because the large muscle masses of its quarters, with their generous blood supply, stay warm more easily.

Trees and hedges
A tree or hedge can provide shelter in summer and winter. Trees provide shade from the sun, and hedges give shelter from the wind. Horses need to be able to stand downwind from a hedge when the prevailing wind is blowing.

Open shed
A shed is a good type of shelter. If the floor gets muddy, put down some bedding, such as straw. The shed may be used very little. The point of a shelter is that it is there for a horse to use when it decides it needs to. When it does use the shed, you can be sure that shelter was vitally necessary.

The back wall of the shelter should face the prevailing wind

The open front prevents a horse from being cornered or injured inside

Open barn
A large barn in a field has the advantage that a number of horses can shelter together and continue their social interaction under cover. The main goal is to provide shelter from the hot sun in the summer while allowing any cooling breeze to flow through. It will also provide some protection from winter weather. There must be enough room in the barn for all the horses in the field.

LEFT **Fencing** A fence should be easily visible so that a horse does not accidentally gallop into it. Horses may rub themselves against fences, which must be sturdy enough to withstand the force and movement.

RIGHT **Out to grass** Grass is the horse's natural environment, where it can relax and feed. Your horse will also benefit from the vitamins and minerals in the other plants that are ideally part of the herbage.

BELOW **The benefits of blankets** We put blankets on horses for various reasons. A horse with a clipped coat may get protection from cold or rain. In hot weather, a light rug may protect the horse from biting insects.

GOOD AND BAD GRAZING

Just turning a horse loose in a field of green vegetation does not guarantee that it will get enough to eat. First of all, the nutritional value will depend on which plants are present. A field of thistles is of little use as food. Secondly, it will depend on the stage of growth of the plants. Most grasses are at their most nutritious before they go to seed. Finally, it will depend on the height of the grass. Horses prefer to graze shorter rather than longer grass.

GRAZING AREAS

Long and short
Horses prefer areas rich in good grazing plants; these areas are cropped short. Areas with unpalatable plants are left to grow. The uneaten plants produce seeds and multiply, thereby making that area worse.

GOOD PLANTS

Annual bluegrass (*Poa annua*)
Sometimes called meadow grass, this used to be common in water meadows in temperate climates. It provides good ground cover, and is enjoyed by horses.

Fescue (*Festuca*)
Fescue grasses are relatively hardy. They are less palatable to horses than some other types, so may be ignored if horses have alternative species to graze.

Ryegrass (*Lolium*)
Ryegrass grows quickly. Most seed mixes for farm use in temperate climates contain a high percentage of ryegrass. It is not very drought-resistant, but grows well early in the season.

Timothy (*Phleum pratense*)
This is not a terribly hardy grass, but it is very palatable and is much sought-after by horses when it is present. Timothy is also a tasty and nutritious element in hay.

Cocksfoot or orchard grass (*Dactylis glomerata*)
Cocksfoot is able to withstand spells of really dry weather during its growing season. It does not have a high carbohydrate content.

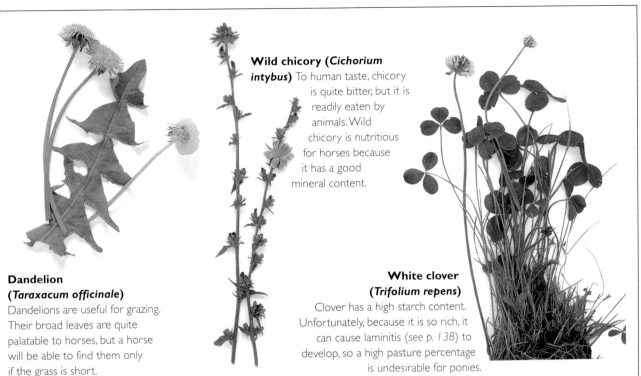

Wild chicory (*Cichorium intybus*) To human taste, chicory is quite bitter, but it is readily eaten by animals. Wild chicory is nutritious for horses because it has a good mineral content.

Dandelion (*Taraxacum officinale*)
Dandelions are useful for grazing. Their broad leaves are quite palatable to horses, but a horse will be able to find them only if the grass is short.

White clover (*Trifolium repens*)
Clover has a high starch content. Unfortunately, because it is so rich, it can cause laminitis (see p. 138) to develop, so a high pasture percentage is undesirable for ponies.

BAD PLANTS

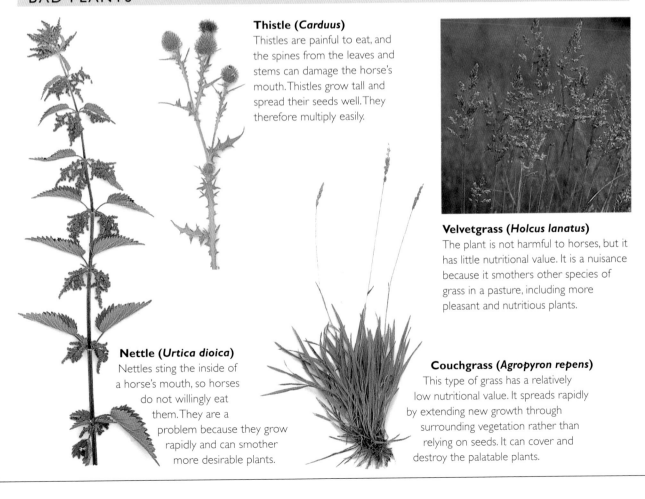

Thistle (*Carduus*)
Thistles are painful to eat, and the spines from the leaves and stems can damage the horse's mouth. Thistles grow tall and spread their seeds well. They therefore multiply easily.

Velvetgrass (*Holcus lanatus*)
The plant is not harmful to horses, but it has little nutritional value. It is a nuisance because it smothers other species of grass in a pasture, including more pleasant and nutritious plants.

Nettle (*Urtica dioica*)
Nettles sting the inside of a horse's mouth, so horses do not willingly eat them. They are a problem because they grow rapidly and can smother more desirable plants.

Couchgrass (*Agropyron repens*)
This type of grass has a relatively low nutritional value. It spreads rapidly by extending new growth through surrounding vegetation rather than relying on seeds. It can cover and destroy the palatable plants.

POISONOUS PLANTS

Most poisonous plants have an unpleasant taste, but if a horse acquires a taste for a plant, it will often go out of its way to find it. Even after several months of stabling, horses may go straight to the plant when turned out again. You must check pastures weekly for any signs of poisonous plants. If the horse gets there before you, there may be little to see, so learn to look carefully. It is best to dig up and burn small numbers of plants. Weedkillers may be used, but you must usually wait a couple of weeks after applying them before the paddock can be grazed again.

Treating pastures
The more there is of a poisonous plant in a field, the harder it is for a horse to avoid eating it. If the plants are growing when grass is limited, it is tempting for a horse to eat them.

Oak (*Quercus*)
Oak leaves and acorns are poisonous, probably because they contain tannic acid. They cause constipation and kidney damage.

GOLDENCHAIN LEAVES

Goldenchain tree (*Laburnum vossii*)
All parts can be deadly, especially the seeds. Affected horses develop nervous malfunctions and go into a coma.

GOLDENCHAIN TREE IN FLOWER

Senecio jacobaea (Ragwort)
Toxic even when dried, ragwort causes acute liver failure in horses. In some countries, owners of land on which it grows are liable to prosecution.

Sorghum (*Sorghum vulgare*)
This can be harmful due to its cyanide and nitrate content. It can cause breathing problems and death. Young plants are not toxic.

Deadly nightshade (*Atropa belladonna*)
The plant contains atropine, which dilates the pupils, so this is a symptom of poisoning. Affected horses may be unable to stand.

The deadly nightshade berry is highly poisonous

The shiny yellow flowers may warn animals not to eat buttercups

Buttercup (*Ranunculus*)
Buttercups are mildly poisonous when they are alive. The plant is not poisonous when it is dried—for example, in hay.

Bracken (*Pteridium*)
This is cumulatively toxic in large amounts and remains so in hay. An affected horse will stand with its back arched and feet apart, growing more and more sleepy.

Locoweed (*Oxytropis splendens*)
The entire plant is toxic. Affected horses become unpredictable and dangerous, and are slowly paralyzed.

Flax (*Linum usitatissimum*)
Both the seeds and the wilted plant are poisonous. Boil the seeds in water to make them safe to feed as a laxative.

Potato (*Solanum tuberosum*)
Don't be tempted to feed waste potatoes to your horse. They may cause choking and, if they are green from exposure to sunlight, colic.

All parts of yew are poisonous, even when dead

St. John's wort (*Hypericum*)
This causes white skin to become sensitive to light and sunburn painfully.

Horsetail (*Equisetum*)
This grows in moist, rich soils. A horse poisoned with horsetail will start to stagger, and after a while will fall over.

Yew (*Taxus baccata*)
This is the most toxic plant. It causes sudden death—a horse may die with leaves still in its mouth.

The leaves have a distinctive, feathery shape

TURNING OUT A HORSE

Putting a horse out in a field not only allows it food and exercise, but also gives it the opportunity for social interaction. It is important that the horse has times when it is its own master, as a contrast to the discipline that you impose. You can learn a lot about a horse's character by watching how it behaves when turned out with others. You can, for example, find out which horses are its friends, which it would like to be exercised with or stabled near, and which ignore or bully it.

GETTING EXCITED

Jumping for joy
Some horses get very excited when they are turned out. Keep an eye on them until they settle down, in case they injure themselves. If you make sure the horse is hungry enough when turned out, it may prefer to put its head down and feed rather than gallop around.

MEETING OTHER HORSES

The horse stretches its head forward, keeping its body as far as possible from the other horse's hooves

Approaching strangers
When a horse greets a strange horse, or one that is not from its close circle of companions, it does so head-on. Both horses want to see each other as clearly as possible and be confident that they cannot be kicked by the other horse.

Greeting friends
When a horse greets a companion, the two animals do not bother to turn and face each other. They will deliberately move close together, often nuzzling each other to provide physical contact, and may touch muzzle to muzzle.

BULLYING

Flattened ears show tension

The unwanted horse is driven away from the herd

Displaying dominance . . .
Every herd, however small, has a hierarchy of dominance. Initially, this social order is established by a mixture of physical threats, biting, and kicking. Later, it is maintained by just body language.

. . . and hostility
Sometimes several horses will pick on a submissive horse and bully it almost constantly without reason. In these circumstances, it is best to remove the victimized horse from that group and try to let it establish itself in another, more friendly group. Bullying of one horse by another may represent a fight for dominance in which the bullied horse never accepts the dominance of the other.

SEASONAL NEEDS

Summer
In warm weather, flies can really irritate a horse, especially when they land on its head. The flies like to suck moisture from around the eyes; a fly fringe can be very useful for preventing this. The horse soon learns to shake the fly fringe by moving its head.

Winter
Clipped horses must wear blankets for warmth when turned out. Rain and wind are the factors that cause chills, not the actual air temperature. Most horses prefer to be out, well blanketed, rather than confined to the stable.

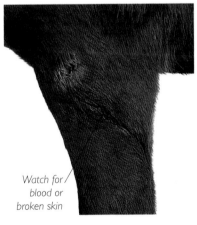

Watch for blood or broken skin

Battle scars
Kicking out at another horse is a natural way for a horse to assert or defend itself. Kick injuries can occur out at pasture, especially if the horses are wearing shoes. During your visits to the field, check each horse visually for any injuries, especially any horse standing away from the others. Make sure that you have a first-aid kit available on your visits.

TAKING A HORSE INTO A FIELD

The process of turning a horse out may be daunting for the inexperienced. The horse is excited because it is looking forward to its freedom, and it doesn't want to wait any longer than it has to. At the same time, if you are nervous or unsure of how to proceed, the horse will know it. Owners often make life difficult for themselves by not maintaining gates. Opening a stiff gate can require all your strength and concentration, leaving neither for controlling the horse. Often, all that is needed is a little oil. It must always be you who turns the horse out, never the horse turning itself out. If you release a horse just in front of an open gate it may gallop through, but horses can go in reverse, too. Never release the horse until both of you are in the field and the gate is shut. It could be disastrous if you don't do the job properly.

DON'T DO THIS!

Managing two horses
Trying to turn out two horses at once is more than twice as difficult as dealing with one. The horses seem to know instinctively how to go in opposite directions at the crucial moment. It is far better to use one person per horse, or to make two journeys.

CORRECT PROCEDURE

1 Position yourself between the horse and the gate, so that you can control the gate and stop it from hitting the horse. Hold the horse firmly and unlock or unfasten the gate. Open it wide enough for both you and the horse to pass through easily at the same time.

2 Lead the horse into the field. Don't let it push in front of you so that you find yourself following the animal into the field. Then, while still holding the horse, turn back and close the gate.

3 Lead the horse a good distance into the field and well away from the entrance. If there are other horses in the field, keep your horse clear of them. Turn around again so that the horse is once more looking toward the gate.

4 Face the horse and take the halter off quietly. Hold the halter and the lead rope carefully, so that you do not frighten the horse. Then pat the horse and step back from it. Do not slap it on the neck or rump, because this may excite it and encourage it to gallop around the field.

5 Once you have turned the horse loose in the field, do not turn your back on it. Instead, walk backward steadily toward the gate, watching the horse all the time. By doing this, you will encourage the horse to stay where it is or even move farther into the field. As a result, it is unlikely to follow you toward the gate. It will then be easier for you to open the gate and let yourself out of the field. At the same time, you will also be watching to see if the horse kicks out in excitement and will have a chance to get out of the way.

DEALING WITH A DIFFICULT HORSE

If you anticipate trouble, take precautions. Wear a hat and gloves, and protect the horse by putting boots on it, so that it does not injure itself. Never let go of the horse until you are fully in control and well into the field. Use a long lunge rein as a lead rope. This allows you to stand farther away from the horse if it rears or bucks, and still hold on to it. Sometimes a horse that is already in the field can cause difficulties when you lead another one in. If this is the case, first go in by yourself, and put some feed on the ground away from the gate before taking your horse in. This will distract the other horse until you can safely release the one you are holding.

CATCHING A HORSE IN A FIELD

Every horse is born wild. Its instinct is to avoid potential danger, including humans. To catch a horse in its field, you first have to overcome its basic wariness. It is frustrating to want to go for a ride yet be unable to catch the horse. It is also vital that you are able to catch a horse when it needs veterinary care. Unfortunately, some horses associate being caught with an unpleasant experience and are difficult to catch. To cure this, catch your horse sometimes just to feed it or talk to it. It will then learn that being caught can lead to something pleasant.

THE BASIC METHOD

Approach at a slight angle to the horse, rather than head-on

1 Slowly approach the horse from the front and slightly to its left. Hold the halter behind your back. Talk to the horse all the time, so that it both sees and hears you. If it first notices you only when you are very close to it, it may be startled and its natural instinct will be to move away from you.

2 A horse is naturally curious, so it will probably look up as you approach. When it looks at you and acknowledges your presence, stand still and keep its attention until it starts to move toward you. Let it see your open hand and perhaps offer it some food. If it moves away, walk around in an arc until you are in the correct position relative to the horse and start the approach again.

Wait for the horse to come to you before showing it the halter

3 Let the horse touch you first, possibly to take food from your hand, rather than move your hand to stroke its head or neck. Do not make a grab for the forelock or mane. Bring the halter into view slowly so as not to startle the horse. If you lay the lead rope over its neck, the horse will probably feel restrained and not move away.

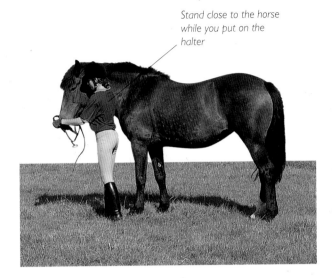

Stand close to the horse while you put on the halter

Once the halter is in place, lead the horse away quietly

4 Hold both sides of the halter and gently raise the noseband until it is in its approximate final position. Keeping your left hand steady, work the headpiece up the far side of the horse's neck in your right hand, and put it over the top of the horse's head. Fasten the buckle, then show the horse that you are pleased with it by patting its neck.

5 Do not relax yet. The horse may still try to pull away suddenly. If it does escape from you, it will be more difficult to catch the second time. Do not wrap the rope around your hand. If you are worried about the horse pulling the rope through your hand, tie a knot at the end of the rope and wear gloves to prevent rope burns to your hands.

CATCHING A DIFFICULT HORSE

Dos and don'ts

Ask someone to help you, then approach the horse from both sides. Avoid making eye contact with the horse or it may feel threatened. Do not frighten the horse by moving suddenly or approaching it from behind. If it runs away, do not chase it, but walk up and start again. Never fasten a rope around its neck; if it escapes, the rope could be dangerous. Do not vent your irritation on the horse when you finally catch it; instead, reward it.

The horse starts to move after its friend as the other horse is led away

1 If your horse is grazing with a companion, the bond between them may be stronger than the horse's desire to avoid being caught. So, if the companion horse is easy to catch, catch it first.

2 Lead the other horse away until your horse follows. If possible, ask a helper to catch it. If not, tie one horse up, then catch the horse you really want.

CHAPTER FOUR

THE STABLED HORSE

LIVING IN A STABLE IS NOT NATURAL FOR A HORSE.
IT DOES NOT HAVE 24-HOUR-A-DAY ACCESS TO ITS
CHOICE OF GRAZING, WHICH IT WOULD HAVE IN THE
WILD, AND IT IS SEPARATED FROM OTHER HORSES, SO
IT IS DENIED SOCIAL INTERACTION. WHEN YOU STABLE
A HORSE, YOU DO IT FOR YOUR OWN CONVENIENCE,
NOT THE HORSE'S, SO YOU MUST TRY TO PROVIDE AS
GOOD AN ENVIRONMENT AS POSSIBLE. CONSIDER THE
PSYCHOLOGICAL AMENITIES THAT YOU PROVIDE AS
WELL AS THE FOOD, WATER, AND BEDDING.

THE STABLEYARD

Over the centuries, various ways have evolved to provide stabling for horses. The most common types of stable used today are box stalls and straight stalls. Box stalls are like individual "rooms" for horses. These may open to the outside, or they may be enclosed in a larger barn. Straight stalls are equipped with solid partitions and, at most, a single bar across the front. A straight stall is relatively narrow, but the horses are usually tied up and so do not turn around.

Straight stalls are useful for keeping large numbers of placid horses, such as draft horses, but they are not suitable if the horses need to be stabled for 24 hours a day.

Site and buildings

The ideal yard has covered areas for horses, feed, tack, and storage and other uses. It is built on two or more sides of a square, with the back of one part facing the prevailing wind so that the yard is sheltered. The site should be level; if it slopes, the lowest point must be free from buildings to ensure good drainage. There must be easy access to paddocks.

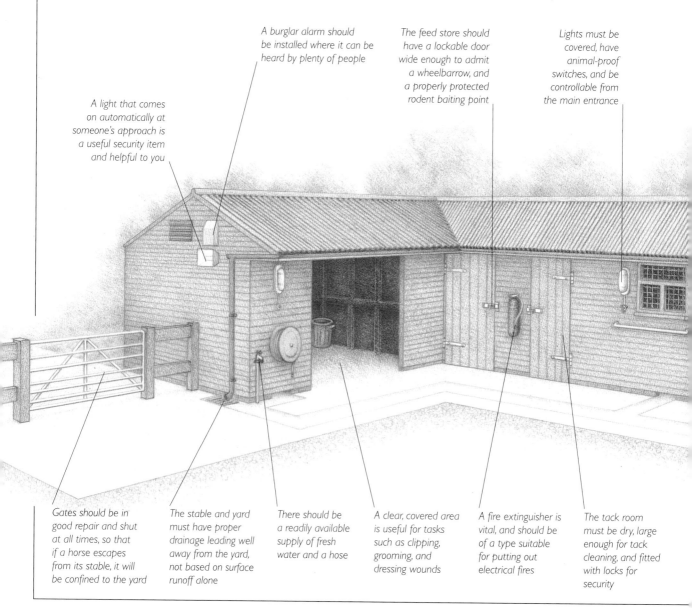

A burglar alarm should be installed where it can be heard by plenty of people

The feed store should have a lockable door wide enough to admit a wheelbarrow, and a properly protected rodent baiting point

Lights must be covered, have animal-proof switches, and be controllable from the main entrance

A light that comes on automatically at someone's approach is a useful security item and helpful to you

Gates should be in good repair and shut at all times, so that if a horse escapes from its stable, it will be confined to the yard

The stable and yard must have proper drainage leading well away from the yard, not based on surface runoff alone

There should be a readily available supply of fresh water and a hose

A clear, covered area is useful for tasks such as clipping, grooming, and dressing wounds

A fire extinguisher is vital, and should be of a type suitable for putting out electrical fires

The tack room must be dry, large enough for tack cleaning, and fitted with locks for security

American barn

In this type of stabling, loose boxes face each other across a central aisle, with the whole area covered. This is a better environment for both horses and their attendants, especially in extremes of hot or cold. Being able to see and communicate with each other provides stimulation for the horses. Disadvantages are the common air space and ventilation problems, which allow respiratory diseases to spread rapidly.

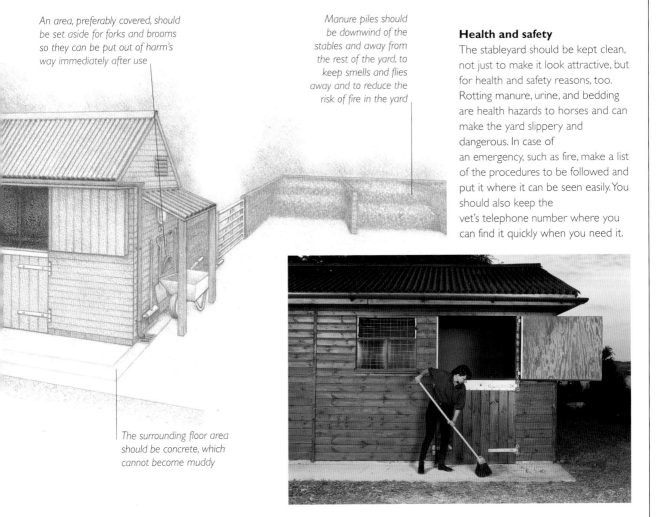

An area, preferably covered, should be set aside for forks and brooms so they can be put out of harm's way immediately after use

Manure piles should be downwind of the stables and away from the rest of the yard, to keep smells and flies away and to reduce the risk of fire in the yard

The surrounding floor area should be concrete, which cannot become muddy

Health and safety

The stableyard should be kept clean, not just to make it look attractive, but for health and safety reasons, too. Rotting manure, urine, and bedding are health hazards to horses and can make the yard slippery and dangerous. In case of an emergency, such as fire, make a list of the procedures to be followed and put it where it can be seen easily. You should also keep the vet's telephone number where you can find it quickly when you need it.

THE STABLE

When a horse is put in a stall, it cannot choose when or where to find shelter, or when and what to eat and drink. You must therefore take full responsibility for all aspects of its daily life. It is unfair to house it in a stable with dangerous fixtures that may cause injury, or in one with such poor ventilation that the horse develops respiratory problems. Even though the horse is in an unnatural environment, try to make it as happy as it would be out in a field. If a horse is stabled full-time, it can become bored, so make sure that it can see what is going on around it.

The size of the stall

The minimum size for a horse stall is usually 12 ft (3.6 m) square and 9 ft (2.7 m) high. The sides should be at least one-and-a-half times the horse's length.

The floor must be hard-wearing, impervious to moisture, and have a nonslip surface, and should slope gently for drainage

Window

Windows are a source of light, as well as part of the ventilation system. In many cases, they do not need any glass, merely window bars. If you do wish to glaze them, consider using plexiglass-type materials rather than glass, which is dangerous if it is broken. Louver openings may be better than a single opening.

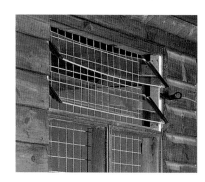

INTERNAL FIXTURES

Tie rings

These should be fixed firmly to the wall—one at the horse's ear height for a haynet, and one lower down for tying up the horse.

Water bucket

If possible, hang this on a wall. If it is on the floor, it can be knocked over or get full of bedding.

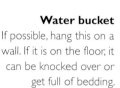

Manger

This should be fixed so that the top is at the horse's natural nose height. The corners should be rounded so that food does not lodge there. Anti-spill bars across the top are useful.

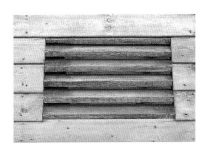

Air vent
There should be an air vent near or in the roof of the stable, to make air flow around the stall and then be pushed out by fresh air coming in through the door. The vent should not be placed where it just causes a draft.

Roofing material must not be too noisy when hit by rain or hail, and must not become too hot in direct sunlight

The doorway should be at least 4 ft (1.2 m) wide and 6 ft 7 in (2 m) high

The horse must be able to move around and lie down in the stall

The bottom door of the stall should be at least 4 ft (1.2 m) high

Overhang and drainage
It is important that the stable roof has efficient guttering, and that captured water runs into a drain or large rain barrel. If it does not, the stableyard can become a muddy mess as horses and people walk through the puddles. There should be an overhang on the roof, to protect the horse and its bedding from the rain, which might otherwise blow in through the open door.

Hook on door
The top stable door should always be left open but never left to swing loose, because it could hit the horse's head. It should be hooked back.

Horse-proof bolt
The bottom stable door must have fastenings at the top and the base. The top bolt needs a safety device, because some horses learn to open bolts.

The safety catch of this horse-proof bolt has to be held up to allow the bolt to be slid open

Kick bolt
The bottom bolt braces the door against any kicking by the horse. A kick bolt is opened with the foot. It enables you to open the door with one hand without bending down, which is useful if you have a heavy bucket or are leading a horse.

IDENTIFICATION

There are two main reasons why we may want to identify a horse. The oldest reason is to denote ownership. Branding horses with a red-hot iron has been carried out for this purpose for hundreds of years, but it does involve significant pain for the horse. We still need to be able to prove ownership of horses that might have been stolen, but today we may also need to give it a specific identity. Competitions are all about comparing one horse with another, and if the results are to be reliable, we need to be sure that the horse involved really is the individual it is claimed to be. Control of disease epidemics may also require the authorities to be able to identify specific horses.

IDENTIFICATION DOCUMENTS

The gold standard of horse identification remains a detailed written description linked to a drawing on which is marked any white areas and hair whorls. An accurate description has the great advantage that it never changes; hair whorls never move and hoof horn color never changes, for example. Increasingly, however, this description is linked with a microchip code. Since 2009, all foals born in the EU must be microchipped. Both the passport and microchip number are recorded in a national database. One reason for this is so the authorities can identify horses that have received drug treatments not allowed for horses that may enter the human food chain. These treatments must be recorded in the passport. In the US, Thoroughbreds are tatooed before their first race and registered with the Jockey Club.

BRANDING

Originally, branding was used to indicate the ownership of a horse and was carried out with a red-hot iron. Now branding is commonly used to identify an individual horse. Branding with a hot iron produces a pattern of hair loss that may be difficult to see, especially when the horse has a thick coat. In freeze-branding, the iron is cooled by immersion in liquid nitrogen and then applied to the skin of the saddle area. This is much less painful than hot branding and produces a permanent mark of white hairs. Unfortunately, parts of the brand sometimes do not take, producing a false mark. It is also possible to alter the freeze brands of stolen horses.

Hoof branding burns the owner's zip code into the horse's hoof. It is a completely painless process but it does need rebranding from time to time as the burned hoof grows down and is eventually worn or trimmed away.

A FREEZE BRAND

HOOF BRANDING

MICROCHIP ID

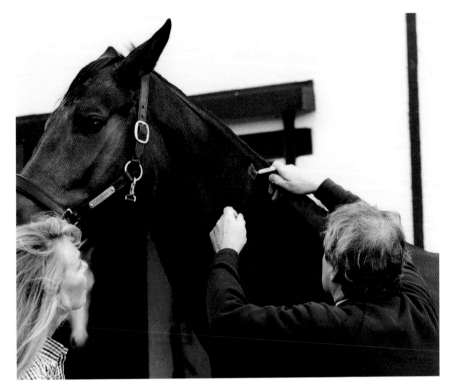

Inserting the microchip
The microchip is inserted down the bore of a hypodermic needle that is no thicker than those used to inject some drugs. There is no universal agreement about where to insert the microchip. The neck is the most common site.

The microchip
The most sophisticated method of identification is by inserting a tiny microchip under the horse's skin. The chip is encoded with an individual number and a central register links the number with a written description.

Scanning
A special scanner detects the chip and decodes its identification number. Microchips can fail electronically and may also migrate through the tissues and not register at the expected site. It is theoretically possible to surgically remove one chip and replace it with another, but the chips are very difficult to locate surgically.

WARNING SIGNS
When you identify a horse as a deterrent against theft, it is important that any potential thief knows what you have done. Microchipping is invisible, and the horse might be stolen before anyone realizes that it is microchipped. A warning sign at the entrance to the stableyard alerts potential thieves that the animals can always be linked back to you.

FAR LEFT **The stable** A stable is an artificial environment for the horse. It is up to us to make it as safe and healthy a place to live as possible. The top stable door should remain open to allow ventilation at all times.

LEFT **Sturdy footwear** Horses are big, heavy animals and do not always worry about where they put their feet. Always wear boots or sturdy shoes when you are around horses—never athletic shoes or other soft shoes.

BELOW **The stableyard** Being able to see its neighbor allows a horse a limited opportunity to socialize, and is an important contributing factor in the overall psychological health of what is by nature a herd animal.

BEDDING MATERIALS

Clean, warm bedding is essential for any stabled horse. Bedding provides comfort and insulation, prevents a horse's feet from being jarred by standing for a long time on a hard surface, and encourages a horse to pass urine and droppings. The most important factor when choosing a material to use as bedding is the comfort of the horse. Other considerations, such as the cost, how clean it keeps the horse, and how easy it is to deal with and dispose of, must be regarded as secondary.

COMFORT

A bed to lie on
Although horses are able to sleep standing up, they like to lie down from time to time. If a horse does not have adequate clean bedding, it will hurt its joints when lying down. This can lead to a capped hock or elbow (see p. 141). Wet bedding feels cold, and can scald the horse's skin.

STRAW

Advantages and disadvantages
Straw, the traditional bedding for horses, is widely available in temperate climates, and fairly cheap. Often, however, it is full of fungal spores, which can trigger respiratory problems (see p. 155). Barley straw is the most widely used. Wheat is good, especially if it has long stems. Oat straw is the least common type, and is quite harsh and prickly.

Oat straw is absorbent

OAT STRAW

Barley straw is yellower than other straw

WHEAT STRAW

Wheat straw drains best

BARLEY STRAW

Dusty bedding
The dust particles seen in a stable containing straw are too big to get into a horse's lungs, but a large amount may be a warning that fungal spores, which cannot be seen with the naked eye, are present. Straw usually contains some fungi, and any plant-based material can become infested if left as deep-litter bedding.

OTHER BEDDING MATERIALS

Shavings

Wood shavings are now readily available as bedding. They are easy to muck out if you have the correct equipment (see p. 114). Clean, dry shavings are a good form of bedding for horses with respiratory problems. The main drawback is that disposal may not be easy, because shavings take time to rot down.

Newspaper

Shredded newspaper, packaged in bales, can be bought fairly cheaply. It is rather like sterile straw when first put down, so can be useful for horses that are allergic to straw. However, once it gets wet with urine, it starts to disintegrate and is rapidly invaded by fungi. Disposal of the waste may be a problem.

Hemp

This is a relatively new bedding for horses, and not as widely available as others. It is made from the core of the stem of a nonnarcotic hemp plant. It rots down more easily than shavings, does not degenerate as much as paper when wet, and absorbs a lot of moisture. It should be dealt with like shavings (see p. 116).

Synthetic flooring sheets need grips to stop them from moving and wrinkling up

Rubber flooring

Porous rubber bedding sheets drain well and so can make a dry floor. On the other hand, they provide little comfort for the horse, and because droppings lie on the surface, they can easily dirty the horse's coat. This type of material can be useful in a trailer or van, where a horse does not lie down and needs a nonslip surface.

Sand

Sand might be considered the natural bed for Arabs and other horses that have a desert origin. It makes a dry bed that molds well to the horse's shape. It is also cool, which is useful in hot climates. It is not organic, so it is not likely to cause respiratory problems. It is important not to give food on the floor; the horse can ingest sand with it, and this may result in colic.

MUCKING OUT

Wet bedding, droppings, and urine fumes are unpleasant for the horse, and must be removed as quickly as possible. A stall should be cleaned out once a day, and if the horse is stabled all the time, droppings must be removed and the bedding leveled out and made comfortable at least three times a day. If the bedding is always damp, it can cause infections, especially of the foot. Thrush, an infection of the frog (*see p. 139*), is a particular danger. Dirty bedding also inevitably leads to a dirty horse, which makes grooming more difficult. The "deep litter" system, in which fresh bedding is added to existing bedding, and the stable is cleared out only every few months, should be avoided. In this situation the bedding will store fumes and fungal spores, and these can affect the horse's health.

TOOLS

Mucking out used to be done with only a fork, a shovel, a broom, and a wheelbarrow. Now there are extra tools to cope with bedding other than straw, and to save time and effort. A shavings fork is essential for beds of wood shavings; it allows clean shavings to fall through the small gaps, while catching droppings and any clumps of wet material. There are also "scoops" you can use to collect droppings and lift them easily into a skip or wheelbarrow.

FORK

SHOVEL

BROOM

SHAVINGS FORK

WHEELBARROW

SCOOP

SMALL RAKE

SKIP

DEALING WITH DIRTY BEDDING AND DROPPINGS

1 First remove any visible droppings with a fork. Search carefully, because some may be covered with bedding. Lift each pile with some bedding underneath the droppings.

2 Tip the droppings into a skip, keeping as much clean bedding as possible. A plastic basket like the one shown here is a good, cheap substitute for a commercial skip.

3 Separate the clean and the dirty or wet bedding. Toss the clean bedding to the sides of the stable, leaving the dirty bedding on the floor.

4 Load all the dirty bedding into a wheelbarrow. Try to avoid pushing dirty bedding into clean areas.

Most horses will usually dirty the bedding in the same place in the stable

5 Toss the clean bedding up into the air and against the wall, forming a pile along the wall. This fluffs it up and allows any further hidden droppings to fall out. Try to pile the bedding against two different walls each day. This ensures that each part of the bank (see p. 116) is broken up every other day.

Toss the bedding to break it up so that it makes a comfortable bed

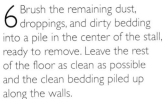

6 Brush the remaining dust, droppings, and dirty bedding into a pile in the center of the stall, ready to remove. Leave the rest of the floor as clean as possible and the clean bedding piled up along the walls.

7 Using the shovel, lift the pile of dirty material into the wheelbarrow.

PUTTING DOWN THE BEDDING

1 Leave the stable to air and dry before you put the bed down. Toss the old bedding on the floor, leaving enough by the walls to form a bank (*see step 2*). Add fresh bedding to replace what you removed. Mix the new bedding in with the old if your horse has a tendency to eat it.

Use the fork to toss the bedding in the air to fluff it up, then spread it on the floor

2 Use the remains of the piles of old, clean bedding to form an even bank of dense bedding all around the stable. This will help to prevent the horse from getting cast on its back if it lies down or rolls close to the wall. Work backward around the stable, using the fork to push the bedding firmly up against the wall, then level the top.

3 When bedding is shaken up, it can look thick, but it will soon be compacted by the horse. To test if the bedding is thick enough, drop a fork into it. If you hear its tines hit the floor, you need more straw.

MUCKING OUT SHAVINGS

1 If you use shavings for the bed, you will find that droppings tend to stay on the surface, so it is not hard to find them. It is easy to collect them with a scoop and small rake.

Tilt the scoop a little to catch the droppings

Use the rake to roll the droppings into the scoop

2 Use a shavings fork to sift the bed for droppings and wet shavings, and to fluff it up. High banks may not be needed; unlike straw, shavings will not move around a lot when the horse is lying down.

MUCKING OUT WITH THE HORSE

Using a barrier across the door
If you cannot turn the horse out while you muck out its stall, fix a wooden bar across the doorway. This will stop the from horse escaping, and will allow you to duck quickly underneath to enter or leave.

Stay clear of the horse while you work

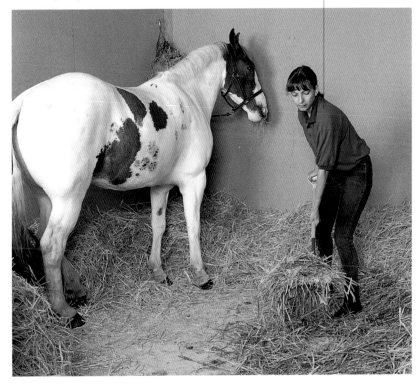

Moving the horse
Use the tools away from the horse so that you do not risk injuring it. Do not work around the horse's feet. Move the horse to one side and then the other while you do each half of the stable.

THE MANURE PILE

Build the heap in an area confined on three sides to keep it neat

Store droppings and soiled bedding neatly, in an area accessible to vehicles for disposal. Make the pile in layers so that it is easy to build and allows the rain to penetrate and aid rotting. Spread a layer of manure over the area and compress it by walking on it. Start a second layer at the back, using a plank on top of the first tier to support the wheelbarrow. At a convenient stage, start a third layer. Complete the layers bit by bit, stepping them down as you go.

CHAPTER FIVE

FOOD AND WATER

A DOMESTICATED HORSE HAS A GREATER RANGE OF

FOOD AVAILABLE TO IT THAN A WILD HORSE HAS, BUT

IT IS IMPORTANT TO REMEMBER THAT IT IS STILL A

GRAZING ANIMAL. WHATEVER ELSE IT EATS, IT SHOULD

HAVE ACCESS TO ROUGHAGE SUCH AS GRASS OR HAY

FOR MOST OF THE DAY. HOW YOU FEED A HORSE

AFFECTS ITS HEALTH, BEHAVIOR, AND PERFORMANCE.

FOLLOW THE BASIC RULES OF FEEDING, BUT DO NOT

STICK RIGIDLY TO FORMULAS. EACH HORSE IS AN

INDIVIDUAL, AND YOU MUST LEARN WHAT IS BEST FOR

EVERY ONE THAT YOU LOOK AFTER.

HOW TO FEED A HORSE

Horses are naturally grazing animals. They cut the grass with their incisor teeth, and chew it with their molar teeth, producing saliva while they chew. The food is mixed with the saliva and swallowed, then it passes into the stomach. The stomach is designed to hold only small amounts of food. This means that a horse doing strenuous exercise may be unable to eat enough grass or hay at one time to replace the energy it has used. By feeding small amounts of "concentrated" feeds (*see p. 126*) this problem can be overcome. Concentrates provide more energy for a given volume of food than grass or hay.

METHODS OF FEEDING

Loose on the ground
Giving food on the ground allows a horse to eat in a natural way, as if it were grazing on grass, but it is wasteful. The food is mixed with soil and spread out so thinly that the horse cannot pick up all the individual pieces. Another disadvantage is that the horse may pick up silt or sand with the food, which can cause colic.

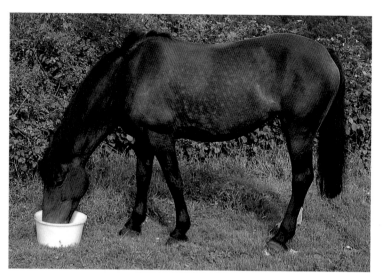

In a bucket on the ground
A bucket keeps food together, making it easier for the horse to eat. Keep one bucket per horse and put it flat on the ground. Use buckets without handles so that a horse cannot get its foot trapped. In a field, put the buckets well apart, so that horses do not try to eat each other's feed. Horses with breathing problems should always be fed with their head down. This lets mucus drain out of the respiratory system and not down into the lungs.

In a manger
Feeding in a manger ensures that the horse cannot spill all the contents, as it could by kicking over a bucket. It also stops a stabled horse from playing with the container if it becomes bored. Another advantage of a manger in a stable is that it gives the horse more floor space.

RULES FOR FEEDING

FEEDING RULE	REASON
Always make any feeding changes gradually.	This allows the digestive system to adjust. It applies to new batches of hay and new brands of a feed, as well as to changes in food type—even grass.
Never increase food in anticipation of a future increase in work.	Feed more concentrates because the horse has lost weight, rather than because you might want to increase its workload in the future. An imbalance between food and work can lead to azoturia or lymphangitis (see p. 153). Reduce feed before reducing a horse's workload, not after.
Feed only good-quality food.	Cleanliness is a reasonable guide to quality for concentrated feeds. If feeds are dull and dusty, their nutritional value will be low. It is not so simple with hay; good, nutritious hay may be a health hazard because of the high number of fungal spores it contains.
Allow the horse access to roughage of some sort for most of the day.	The horse's digestive system is designed to deal with almost continuous amounts of roughage. Its stomach is not designed for large meals.
Always feed by weight rather than volume.	Feeds vary in their volume for a given weight, so a scoop of one feed is not the same weight as a scoop of any other (see p. 126). Each type of feed also varies in its volume for a given weight with every batch you buy.
Do not disturb or work a horse during or immediately after feeding, and do not feed a horse immediately after work.	The blood supply to the horse's muscles is increased during work, so the supply to the digestive system must decrease, causing faulty digestion. Also, if alarmed, a horse may swallow food before chewing it and colic may follow.
Feed concentrates in small amounts at the same times every day.	This evens out the workload of the horse's digestive system, reducing the risk of colic. Feed at regular intervals, not just when it is convenient.
Make clean water always available, but do not let a horse drink too much right after feeding.	Hay and concentrates are drier than grass. They must be mixed with water in the stomach before digestion, but not washed straight through.

CHECKING A HORSE'S WEIGHT

Measure the girth just behind the elbow, where the saddle girth usually sits

How to find out the weight of a horse

Use the horse's weight to assess the effects of your feeding and exercise regimen, not to decide how much to feed. Using a special scale at an animal hospital or vet school is the ideal way to weigh a horse. At home, you can use an ordinary tape measure to find the horse's girth and length (from the point of shoulder to the point of buttock), and calculate its weight using one of the formulas below.

Weight (lb) = girth^2 (in) × length (in) ÷ 300
Weight (kg) = girth^2 (cm) × length (cm) ÷ 12,000

FAR LEFT **Bucket feed** Horses that are turned out in a field may still require supplementary feeding with food in a bucket. Some horses will only allow themselves to be caught if they are first given a bucket of food.

LEFT **Coping with snow** Horses cope with snow very well, although you must watch out for balls of ice that may collect on the soles of their hooves. Supplementary hay will be necessary when the grass is covered with snow.

RIGHT **Drinking water** If your horse has to rely on a river or pond for its drinking water, it is important that this water is clean and has not been contaminated farther upstream.

BELOW **Horses grazing in a field** The size of a field will determine how long a particular number of horses can safely be allowed to graze it. The grass in an overgrazed field will generally take a long time to recover.

NUTRITIONAL NEEDS

Each horse has an individual genetic body structure that determines factors such as its height and shape. It has an individual metabolism that determines how well it digests its food, and how efficiently it absorbs nutrients. Each horse also has its own collection of bacteria within its colon to digest roughage. Therefore, the same amount of food will have a different effect on different horses. Feeding guidelines are provided here, but feed your horse according to its needs, not to a formula. Each horse's needs will vary depending on whether it is stabled or kept in a field, whether it is clipped or not, and what the weather is like. If a horse lacks nutrients, one sign is weight loss. Ask the previous owner how much they fed the horse, to give you an idea how to start.

PARTS OF A BALANCED DIET

PART OF DIET	WHAT IT DOES	WHERE IT IS FOUND
Protein	Proteins are the body's building blocks. Muscle is mostly protein; tendons and ligaments also have a high protein content.	Most horses' needs are met by grass in summer, and hay (as needed) in winter. In pellets, good sources include soybeans.
Carbohydrate	The source of energy, carbohydrates are stored as glycogen in the muscles, ready for instant use during exercise.	Grass or hay gives enough for maintenance but usually not for work. Grains, such as oats, are the major energy source.
Fat	Fats or oils are a valuable energy source because they can be broken down into simple, easily utilized carbohydrates.	Many ready-mixed feeds include vegetable oils. Up to 15% of a horse's energy needs can be efficiently provided by vegetable oil.
Water	Much of the horse's body contains built-in water; it is the main medium for carrying substances around the body.	Spring grass may have a high water content, but most of a horse's needs are met by drinking. Water must be clean and fresh.
Minerals	Bones obviously need minerals, but most of the body tissues have some mineral requirements.	Alfalfa is a rich source. Minerals are taken in with soil during grazing. Salt can be given as a salt lick.

BULK/CONCENTRATE RATIO

Food and work

Even when working hard, a horse should be fed mostly roughage, but grass and hay cannot usually supply all the energy a horse needs for work. The digestive system cannot handle the bulk needed, so extra nutrients are fed as concentrates. However, you must feed according to what your particular horse needs. Some ponies and horses do not need extra concentrates, even when they are working.

Work

Maintenance (no work)
Feed usually no concentrates, just good-quality roughage to maintain normal weight.

Light work
Up to an hour per day of walking with some trotting. Feed up to 15% concentrates.

Medium work
Includes some jumping, cantering, or galloping. Feed up to 30% concentrates.

Hard work
Two hours per day including galloping, or competing. Feed up to 45% concentrates.

Food per day

0%   20%   40%   60%   80%   100%

Roughage

Concentrates

SPECIAL NEEDS

A very thin horse | *An obese horse*

EXTREMES OF CONDITION

Over- or underweight
If a horse is over- or underweight, do not alter its diet suddenly. It is particularly harmful to put a fat pony on a crash diet because its digestive system will not cope. As a guide, you should be able to see where the ribs end but not see the shape of each individual rib.

Feeding in winter
A stabled horse may not need any more food in winter than in summer. A horse living outside will use more energy for warmth in wet, windy weather, so must have extra concentrates. It may also need folic acid supplements to make up for the lower level in grass.

OLD HORSES

In old age, horses may benefit from processed roughage such as chopped straw or complete horse pellets, because lost and long teeth may reduce their ability to deal with hay. They need protein to replace muscle tissue broken down by metabolic aging, rather than carbohydrates for energy. If the horse is still working, frequent, regular feeds will maintain the energy levels.

PLANNING A DIET

Providing energy
When mixing feeds, first decide what work the horse will be doing; that tells you how much energy it must have. You can then combine any feeds that in total will provide the energy, and are concentrated enough for the horse to be able to eat all of it in a day. In equine nutrition, energy in food is usually expressed as megacalories (Mcal) in a pound. (1 Mcal = 1,000,000 calories)

ENERGY VALUE OF FEEDS

- Oats: 1.5 Mcal/lb
- Corn: 1.7 Mcal/lb
- Barley: 1.6 Mcal/lb
- Beet pulp: 1.3 Mcal/lb
- Bran: 1.2 Mcal/lb
- Premixed food: see package labeling for information

ENERGY NEEDS FOR VARIOUS TYPES OF WORK

EXERCISE	1,100-lb (500-kg) riding horse	660-lb (300-kg) family pony
EXTRA 1 HOUR WALKING	1.2 Mcal of energy needed on top of maintenance needs. *Feed: 14 oz (0.4 kg) beet pulp; or 10½ oz (0.3 kg) corn; or 5¼ oz (0.15 kg) corn and 7 oz (0.2 kg) beet pulp.*	0.7 Mcal of energy needed on top of maintenance needs. *Feed: 8¾ oz (0.25 kg) beet pulp; or 9½ oz (0.27 kg) bran; or 3½ oz (0.1 kg) oats and 4¼ oz (0.12 kg) beet pulp.*
EXTRA 30 MINUTES TROTTING	2.4 Mcal of energy needed on top of usual needs. *Feed: 26½ oz (0.75 kg) oats; or 35¼ oz (0.5 kg) beet pulp and 8¾ oz (0.25 kg) corn; or 17½ oz (0.52 kg) oats, and 9½ oz (0.27 kg) bran.*	1.4 Mcal of energy needed on top of usual needs. *Feed: 15¾ oz (0.45 kg) oats; or 35¼ oz (0.5 kg) beet pulp; or 7¾ oz (0.22 kg) oats, and 9½ oz (0.27 kg) bran.*
EXTRA 10 MINUTES GALLOPING	2 Mcal of energy needed on top of other needs. *Feed: 18½ oz (0.5 kg) corn; or 21 oz (0.6 kg) oats; or 7 oz (0.2 kg) oats, 8¾ oz (0.25 kg) beet pulp, and 8½ oz (0.24 kg) bran.*	1.2 Mcal of energy needed on top of other needs. *Feed: 11½ oz (0.33 kg) barley; or 11 oz (0.31 kg) corn; or 4½ oz (0.13 kg) barley and 8½ oz (0.24 kg) beet pulp.*

CONCENTRATED FEEDS

There is a large variety of concentrated feedstuffs available. These include commercial mixes, which can be loose or processed into pellets, and several grains. Commercial mixes provide a balance of nutrients, which your own mixture is unlikely to do. All concentrates are unnatural to the horse, but they provide energy and variety. You must not guess how much feed to give your horse. Do not go "by the scoop," because different feeds weigh different amounts. Many also vary in their volume per unit weight from batch to batch. Each of the feeds shown here is the same weight: 1 lb 5 oz (595 g).

DIFFERENT FEEDS

Bran
Use bran as a bulk food, not as a source of nutrition. It is not good for growing horses because it has too much phosphorus and not enough calcium.

Pellets
There are different pellets to suit different horses, such as "horse and pony" and "racehorse." Buy the right kind for your horse.

Flaked corn
A valuable feed, corn is often processed further by food companies to make it "nonheating" (not liable to make the horse excitable). The nutritional concentration is lowered so that it provides less energy.

Coarse mix
This looks more appetizing than pellets, but a more valid reason to feed it is that it takes longer to eat, which is better for the horse's digestion. It comes in different grades.

Linseed
Uncooked linseed is poisonous. It must be boiled for many hours until the seeds have split. It is a laxative, and it may also help to produce a shiny coat.

Barley
This is often underrated, but it has a high energy content. Take care when feeding it, because even a small change in the amount fed can have significant nutritional consequences.

Alfalfa pellets
Even in this dried form, alfalfa contains good concentrations of the vitamins and minerals found in grass. It is especially valuable for its calcium and fibre content. It has been called "pelleted sunshine."

Oats
The popularity of oats is mostly due to the fact that careless changes to the quantity fed make little nutritional difference because it has a low energy content. It is not a natural food for horses.

Beet pulp
Beet pulp is a valuable feed because it is rich in energy and protein. Pulp is dried beet and must be soaked before feeding.

Beet cubes
Like beet pulp, cubes expand rapidly on contact with moisture, such as saliva, and can cause choking and colic if not soaked first. Never confuse them with ordinary cubes.

1 lb 5 oz (595 g) sugar beet pulp weighs 5 lb 13 oz (2.6 kg) after soaking

Soaked beet
Soak the sugar beet for about 12 hours in sufficient cold water so that at the end of that time, there is still some water that has not been absorbed.

SUPPLEMENTS

Roots and fruit
Carrots and apples probably top the list of healthy treats for horses. Carrots may be fed in large quantities, but do not have great nutritional value. Cut them lengthwise. Square or round pieces can get stuck in the throat and cause choking.

Cod-liver oil
This is a rich source of vitamins. It can be mixed with food to help condition the coat.

Molasses
A palatable supplement, this is a useful binding agent to add to dry or dusty food. It can also be mixed with medicines and put directly into the horse's mouth.

Corn oil
Oils are a rich source of energy. They can be added to the diet of competition horses, which might be unable to eat enough food to supply their energy needs.

STORING FOOD

Keep feeds in a metal or plastic bin to protect them from insects and rodents—and from your horse. Horses need good-quality food, so never buy more than two to three weeks' supply at a time because it will deteriorate, especially in hot, humid weather. Empty a bin completely before you add more food, or you will end up mixing stale food with the new.

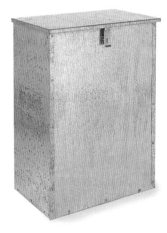

Salt
A salt lick is the best way to supply salt. The horse can have a lick whenever it feels that it needs some.

SOURCES OF ROUGHAGE

The fibrous, bulky part of a horse's diet is called roughage. This may be fed fresh, as grass, or it may be preserved, like hay and silage. The horse's digestive system, unlike that of humans, can obtain nutrients from the plant fiber because it has a very long colon, which has evolved over millions of years for this task. Cellulose, the main component of roughage, is digested in the colon by bacteria that exist in harmony with the horse. The bacteria provide soluble carbohydrates, fatty acids, and amino acids for the horse, in exchange for the chewed-up cellulose on which they live. If a horse does not eat enough bulky food to keep the colon fairly full, colic may result.

Natural food

Grass is the most natural form of roughage for a horse. The horse has no option but to bite off each mouthful, so it is forced to eat slowly. Grass changes its character and nutritional value through the seasons. It is most nutritious in early summer, just before flowering. In spring, it has a high water content, while in winter some grass is as dry as hay.

HAY

Good hay

Hay is dried grass. Meadow hay, shown here, is made from permanent pasture and contains a variety of grasses and herbs; seed hay is made from specially grown grass. Good hay is crisp, smells sweet, and is greenish- brown in color.

DANGERS OF BAD HAY

It is very important to feed horses good-quality hay. Some hay may have little nutritional value; some may contain a high concentration of fungal spores that can trigger respiratory ailments. Be sure not to feed hay containing poisonous plants. They can cause death, even when dried.

Poor-quality hay

Bad hay will contain more stalk than leaf. It may be yellowish-brown in color rather than green because the pigment has been bleached out. If the hay has been made or stored badly, white mold may even be visible.

This poor-quality hay is brown; it also looks dull, in contrast to the springy, glossy appearance of good hay

OTHER FIBROUS FOODS

Vacuum-packed grass
This preserved grass is damp and softer than hay. Horses usually enjoy it, and it has about twice the nutritional value of hay. The grass is vacuum-packed just after harvest, and a cold fermentation then takes place in the bag.

Alfalfa
A good mineral source, alfalfa is fed as hay, or chopped and dried. Its leaves are larger than those of other grasses; this helps to make it more nutritious than the best meadow hay. It is very rich, so feed less of it than you would hay.

Silage
A moist, acid-smelling feed, silage is grass that has been compacted and put through a hot fermentation process to preserve it. If it is made in polythene-wrapped bales, it must be stored carefully; badly stored bales have been blamed for equine botulism.

Chaff
To make chaff, straw is chopped into tiny pieces. Chaff can be readily digested by bacteria in the colon, so it should not cause impactions of the bowel as long straw may do. It may be mixed in with concentrated feeds; it has little extra nutritional value, but adds necessary bulk.

DRIED GRASS

Modern techniques allow grass to be cut at the growth stage, which ensures it has maximum nutritional value. The grass is dried quickly and compressed into a bale equivalent to several normal bales of hay. Always introduce a horse to a new batch of roughage gradually. This allows the intestinal bacteria that digest the fiber to adjust to the new batch, reducing the risk of colic.

Chaff and molasses
These two feedstuffs can be mixed to make a feed that is very palatable to most horses. The molasses also binds the chaff together, slightly increases the nutritional value, and makes it less dusty. The feed can be bought premixed, which saves time but may be expensive; it could be cheaper to buy the chaff and molasses and mix them yourself.

FEEDING HAY

The most natural feeding position for a horse is from the ground. You can feed hay loose on the ground, but much of it will be trampled on and soiled, and therefore wasted. The easiest way to feed hay is in a haynet or hayrack. Divide the horse's daily ration into four roughly equal amounts. Give them at regular intervals, with one first thing in the morning and one last thing at night. When you receive a new batch of hay, keep it separate. Start to feed it gradually over several days, mixing the new hay in with the old. The horse's digestive system can then adapt gradually to the new hay.

Weighing a haynet

Weigh the net on a spring balance to ensure a constant level of feeding. A haynet filled with flakes of hay straight from the bale will contain much more than one filled with loose hay.

FILLING AND WEIGHING A HAYNET

Filling a haynet
Nets made from synthetic twine are best because they do not rot and so last longer. Loosen the drawstring to open the net, then push the hay inside. If you want to make it easier for the horse to pull the hay out, shake it a little to loosen it.

Use your foot to help keep the net open

Estimating weight
A hay bale will break easily into equal flakes, so you can estimate how much you are using. It is useful to weigh one bale from a new batch, because hay varies in weight from batch to batch.

PREVENTING RESPIRATORY PROBLEMS

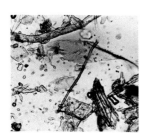

GOOD HAY

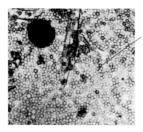

BAD HAY

Fungal spore

Soaking hay

Some of the dust and spores in hay can be washed away by soaking it. Spores also stick to wet hay and are less easily breathed in by the horse. Immerse the hay in running water for about two hours—any longer and you may wash out the nutrients. Warm water is more effective than cold.

Fungal spores
Hay contains microscopic fungal spores. It is these, rather than the visible dust particles, that trigger respiratory problems. These greatly enlarged photographs of hay show how bad-quality hay can have a large number of these harmful spores.

TYING A HAYNET

1 Pull the opening of the haynet shut, then thread the loop of cord through a ring on a wall, a tree, or another suitable place. Whether it is being hung up in the stable or outdoors, a haynet must be hung well clear of the ground. The ring should be just above the horse's eyes.

Thread the cord through one of the mesh links

2 Pull the net up, then thread the cord through the bottom. This helps to compact the net when you tie it up. It also keeps it off the ground when it has been emptied. The net will hang down lower when it is empty, and a horse could get a foot caught in it.

3 Pull the cord tight, bringing the bottom of the net up as high as you can. Tie the cord tightly at the top, using a quick-release knot (see p. 50). Make sure that the loop is not too small.

Tuck the remaining cord inside the net so that it is not left hanging

Turn the knot to the back

4 Finally, turn the haynet around so that the knot is hidden from the horse.

The right height
When you have finished, the haynet should be level with the horse's eyes when it is standing naturally. If the net is lower, the horse may trap its foot in it. If it is higher, dust and seeds will fall in the horse's eyes as it eats.

Hayracks
A fixed hayrack may cost much more to install than a ring for a haynet, but it is easier to fill than a net, and the hay never ends up on the ground. The drawback is that you cannot adjust the height of a hayrack for different horses.

HORSE PROBLEMS & FOALING

EVERYONE RESPONSIBLE FOR CARING FOR A HORSE

SHOULD KNOW HOW TO LOOK AFTER IT IN SICKNESS

AS WELL AS IN HEALTH. IT IS A GOOD IDEA TO LEARN

TO RECOGNIZE SOME OF THE MORE OBVIOUS

SYMPTOMS OF DISEASES AND DISORDERS, SO THAT

YOU KNOW HOW TO TREAT THEM AND KNOW WHEN

TO CALL FOR HELP. IT IS ALSO USEFUL TO BE FAMILIAR

WITH THE PROCESS OF FOALING AND THE CRITICAL

PERIOD IMMEDIATELY FOLLOWING THE BIRTH. IF YOU

ARE EVER IN ANY DOUBT, CALL THE VET. IT IS BETTER

TO BE SAFE THAN SORRY.

POSSIBLE DISORDERS

Many common ailments are linked to domestication. It is not that people knowingly cause disorders but that, when things do go wrong, their management practices can make a problem worse. Ailments may arise due to the work that a horse is asked to do—no wild horse repeatedly performs movements, as is necessary in dressage. Some diseases occur when a horse is stabled—chronic obstructive pulmonary disease (COPD) is triggered by moldy hay or straw. Others can spread through travel. In the wild, equine influenza is usually transmitted only within a herd, but it can spread quickly, even from country to country, when horses mix at competitions.

Warning signs
Inflammation is a symptom of most horse ailments, so you must always be on the lookout for the classic signs—heat, pain, and swelling. Any sudden change from normal behavior should also set alarm bells ringing. You should rely on noticing that a sign of good health (see p. 30) is absent, rather than trying to learn the symptoms of each disease.

INTERNAL PARASITES
(see pp. 150–51)
- *Strongylus* (bloodworm)
- *Cyathostomes* (small redworm)
- *Ascaris* (large roundworm)
- *Anoplocephala* (tapeworm)
- *Dictyocaulus* (lungworm)
- *Oxyuris* (pinworm)
- *Gasterophilus* (bots)

JOINT DISORDERS
(see pp. 140–41)
- Puffy joint
- Ringbone and sidebone
- Windgall
- Thoroughpin
- Spavin
- Curb
- Capped hock or elbow
- Patellar fixation
- Sesamoiditis
- Osteochondrosis (OCD)

SKIN DISORDERS
(see pp. 148-47)
- Mud fever
- Cracked heels
- Rain scald
- Saddle sore and girth gall
- *Trichophyton* (ringworm)
- *Hypoderma* (cattle grubs)
- Sweet itch
- *Haematopinus* and *Damalinia* (lice)
- Mange

FOOT DISORDERS
(see pp. 138–39)
- Bruised sole
- Corn
- Laminitis
- Seedy toe
- Navicular disease
- Pedal ostitis
- Abscess in the foot
- Sand crack
- Thrush

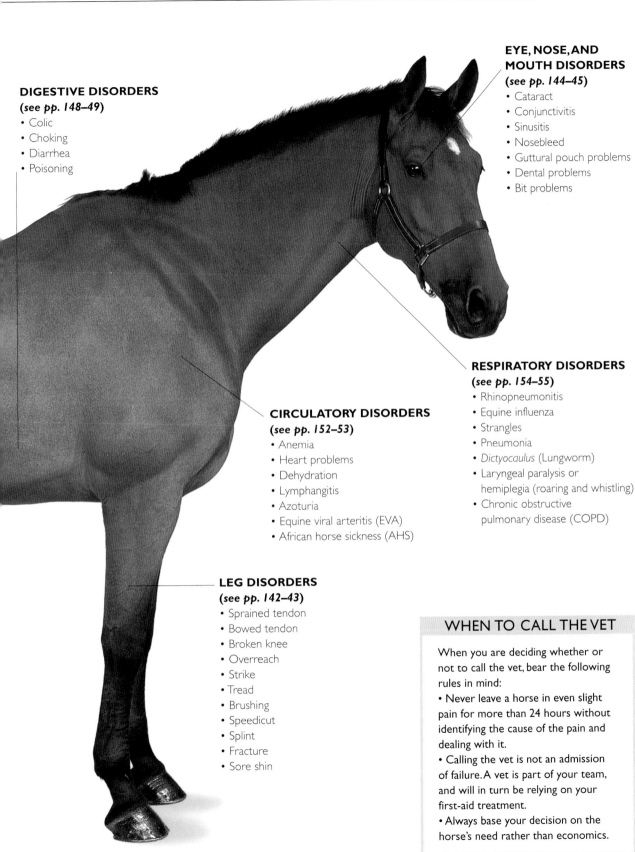

DIGESTIVE DISORDERS
(see pp. 148–49)
- Colic
- Choking
- Diarrhea
- Poisoning

**EYE, NOSE, AND
MOUTH DISORDERS
(see pp. 144–45)**
- Cataract
- Conjunctivitis
- Sinusitis
- Nosebleed
- Guttural pouch problems
- Dental problems
- Bit problems

**RESPIRATORY DISORDERS
(see pp. 154–55)**
- Rhinopneumonitis
- Equine influenza
- Strangles
- Pneumonia
- *Dictyocaulus* (Lungworm)
- Laryngeal paralysis or hemiplegia (roaring and whistling)
- Chronic obstructive pulmonary disease (COPD)

**CIRCULATORY DISORDERS
(see pp. 152–53)**
- Anemia
- Heart problems
- Dehydration
- Lymphangitis
- Azoturia
- Equine viral arteritis (EVA)
- African horse sickness (AHS)

**LEG DISORDERS
(see pp. 142–43)**
- Sprained tendon
- Bowed tendon
- Broken knee
- Overreach
- Strike
- Tread
- Brushing
- Speedicut
- Splint
- Fracture
- Sore shin

WHEN TO CALL THE VET

When you are deciding whether or not to call the vet, bear the following rules in mind:
- Never leave a horse in even slight pain for more than 24 hours without identifying the cause of the pain and dealing with it.
- Calling the vet is not an admission of failure. A vet is part of your team, and will in turn be relying on your first-aid treatment.
- Always base your decision on the horse's need rather than economics.

DIAGNOSING LAMENESS

When a horse is lame, it does not take its weight evenly on each leg as it moves. Lameness may be simple to cure—for example, by removing a stone from the foot. It may be the result of an injury such as standing on a nail. It may be due to wear and tear on the leg joints. The cause may or may not be painful, but you should never work a lame horse except on the instructions of your vet. If the horse is badly lame, call the vet immediately. If the lameness is only slight, stable the horse for 24–36 hours for rest; if it is still lame, call the vet.

SIGNS OF LAMENESS

Holding a front foot off the ground is a warning sign; the foot is probably painful

Unusual behavior
You may spot problems by seeing how the horse stands. If it is lame, it may ease its weight off one leg, or shift uncomfortably when it is resting. Or it may rest a different leg than usual.

FINDING THE CAUSE OF LAMENESS

The use of hoof testers determines whether pressure on the hoof is painful

Veterinary examination
The vet may pinpoint the pain, and the cause of lameness, by using a nerve block—a local anesthetic injected over a nerve, removing pain from the area temporarily. The sole of the foot may need paring, and the shoe may have to be removed.

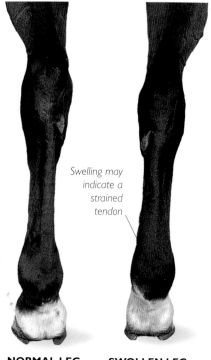

Swelling may indicate a strained tendon

A "big" leg
Never ignore a swelling, even if the horse is not lame. A swollen leg indicates a problem. Use a cold treatment (see p. 161) on the leg until you have a definite diagnosis.

NORMAL LEG   **SWOLLEN LEG**

IDENTIFYING THE LAME LEG

Trotting for the vet

Lameness is most easily seen when a horse is trotted in hand, because only at the trot do horses put an equal amount of weight on each leg. The horse must be trotted on a hard, level surface, so that you can hear whether it is sound or lame. In a sound horse, the noise of all hooves will be identical; with a lame horse, there will be a slightly louder and earlier noise when the corresponding good leg hits the ground. You will be asked to trot the horse up and down in a straight line while the vet watches the front of the horse and then its hindquarters.

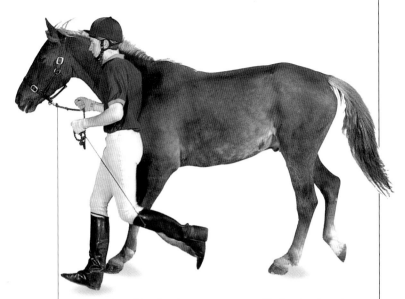

Leave 12–18 in (30–45 cm) of loose rein to allow free movement of the head

The head nods as the horse puts weight on its good leg

SOUND HORSE

LAME HORSE

Good leg

Lame leg

Lameness in a foreleg

When a sound horse trots, its head is held roughly level all the time. When a horse that is lame on a foreleg trots, the head will nod each time the good foreleg lands on the ground, because that leg is taking extra weight. Occasionally, a horse will look slightly lame on a foreleg when the actual physical problem lies in the diagonal hind leg.

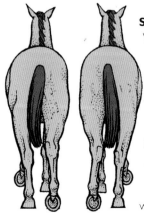

Sound hind legs

When a sound horse is trotted away from the viewer, its hips can be seen to stay level as its hindquarters move. As with sound forelegs, both feet in the pair will be lifted equally high off the ground, and will take an equal amount of weight when they land. The feet will hit the ground squarely.

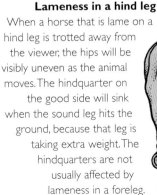

Lameness in a hind leg

When a horse that is lame on a hind leg is trotted away from the viewer, the hips will be visibly uneven as the animal moves. The hindquarter on the good side will sink when the sound leg hits the ground, because that leg is taking extra weight. The hindquarters are not usually affected by lameness in a foreleg.

Lame leg

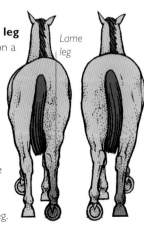

FOOT DISORDERS

Foot problems account for 90 percent of all lameness. It is probably fair to say that most are due, at least in part, to a lack of care by the owner, such as leaving shoes on too long, not picking out the feet regularly, and overfeeding. Foot problems often affect more than one foot at a time, because all the feet undergo the same stresses or neglect. If a horse has a corn in one foot, it may well have a slight corn in one or more of its other feet. There is no point in treating the foot that appears to be lame, only for the horse to go lame on another foot shortly afterward. It is better to check all the feet and learn the extent of the problem at the start, then treat it as a whole.

Paring the foot
In order to inspect the sole of the foot carefully, the vet will remove any flaking or discolored horn with a hoof knife.

FOOT DISORDERS

SYMPTOMS	CAUSE	TREATMENT	PREVENTION
Bruised sole The horn around the white line may be discolored. The horse is sensitive to pressure over the sole, and the lameness is worse on stony ground.	Stepping on a hard object, or repeated pounding on hard ground.	Rest the horse until the inflammation has subsided. It is a good idea to fit a protective pad that covers the sole.	Use a pad to protect the soles of horses with thin soles or flat feet.
Corn—*bruising of the seat of corn, usually on a front foot* Intermittent lameness, which usually worsens with exercise, especially on hard or uneven ground. When the seat of the corn is pared, an area of discolored horn is visible, often pink due to the presence of blood.	Poorly fitting shoes, or shoes being left on for too long before being replaced.	The farrier will remove discolored horn and fit a special shoe that reduces percussion (repeated striking) on the area, because its ground surface is cut away over the corn.	Have your horse shod regularly by a good farrier.
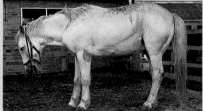 HORSE WITH LAMINITIS SINKING BACK ON ITS HEELS **Laminitis**—*inflammation of the sensitive laminae, usually in more than one foot* The horse tries to take weight off its toes, and sinks back on its heels. In acute cases, it is unwilling to walk. The hooves will be warm.	Overeating, or a toxic process, causes the release into the blood of chemicals that constrict small blood vessels such as those around the sensitive laminae of the feet. In some cases, the laminae die, allowing the pedal bone to rotate and push through the sole of the foot.	Consult your vet and remove the underlying cause. Give the horse a complete rest; only in mild cases should you walk it out. Painkillers will help, and mild sedatives will lower blood pressure, and thus the pain. The feet should be trimmed to ensure a balanced foot (see p. 21), and special shoeing may be necessary.	Be very careful with diet and looking after the feet, especially with ponies, which are particularly susceptible.

FOOT DISORDERS

SYMPTOMS	CAUSE	TREATMENT	PREVENTION
Seedy toe—*infection in the foot* The foot is painful when tapped on the area. Black pus, which may be dry and crumbly rather than liquid, travels up the foot at the toe through the white line.	A combination of poor-quality horn and a long toe, which pulls open the white line and allows the infection to enter.	All the infected horn must be removed.	Pick the feet out thoroughly to remove mud and manure, which can be the source of the infection.
Navicular disease—*condition involving the navicular bone, the overlying deep flexor tendon, and the surrounding tissues in the heel, usually of both front feet* Intermittent lameness in the early stages. The horse may wobble or stumble when it trots. It can be diagnosed by an X-ray or an MRI scan. SHADOWS IN AN X-RAY OF A DISEASED NAVICULAR BONE	Probably wear and tear on the structures around the navicular bone, possibly caused by poor shoeing. This can be made worse by poor circulation.	Remedial shoeing is essential. Circulation can be helped by drugs that dilate the blood vessels. In some cases, surgery may be necessary. AN EGG-BAR SHOE SUPPORTING THE HEEL	Good shoeing can remove a possible cause of wear and tear.
Pedal ostitis—*condition involving the navicular bone* Similar to navicular disease.	Really a stage in the development of navicular disease, rather than a separate entity.	See navicular disease.	See navicular disease.
Abscess in the foot Dramatic lameness—the horse will not even put its foot to the ground.	Puncture of the sole of the foot, which allows infection into the sensitive tissues. The pus that forms has no means of escape, and the resulting pressure causes the pain.	The vet makes a hole in the foot large enough to allow the pus to drain out freely. Antibiotics may be needed. The foot is usually poulticed to encourage drainage.	Check the feet regularly.
Sand crack—*crack in the wall of the hoof* A small, usually vertical crack, which will grow bigger if left. If it reaches the coronet it will prevent normal, uncracked horn from being made. The horse may be lame if the crack extends down to the sensitive tissues. SAND CRACK THAT HAS REACHED THE CORONET	Poor-quality horn that has not been sufficiently protected from stress by the shoe. Very dry conditions can make the horn liable to cracking.	The spread of the crack must be stopped as soon as possible. A horizontal groove above and at least as deep as the crack, or vertical grooves on either side of the crack, may stop it. In severe cases, it may be necessary to cut away some horn and stabilize the crack with an acrylic artificial horn material.	Feed biotin and methionine supplements to ensure good-quality horn.
Thrush—*infection of the frog* The horn of the frog is black and smelly, and appears moist. The horse will be lame only in severe cases.	Leaving the horse to stand in a dirty, ill-drained stable or muddy conditions.	All infected horn must be removed, and it may help to apply an antibiotic spray or a diluted formalin solution to the remaining part of the frog.	Muck out the stable properly, so that the horse stands on clean material. Pick out the feet regularly.

JOINT DISORDERS

There are three important components of a horse's joint: the cartilage, bone, and joint fluid, which acts as both a lubricant for the movement of a joint and the "food source" for the cartilage. There are certain similarities between all the conditions that affect joints.

These problems used to be referred to as arthritis, but now they are referred to as DJD (degenerative joint disease). As a result of DJD, new bone can be formed and other areas of bone become less dense. These changes can be seen on an X-ray. Damage to articular cartilage

exposes raw bone underneath and is painful but cannot be detected on an X-ray; it requires direct viewing of the joint via arthroscopy. Inflammation often results in an increased amount of poor-quality joint fluid, and treatment may involve drugs to replace or improve this fluid.

JOINT DISORDERS

SYMPTOMS	CAUSE	TREATMENT	PREVENTION
Puffy joint Swollen joint, but the horse is not lame and there is no pain.	A slight increase in the amount of joint fluid in response to long-term wear and tear.	No treatment is necessary in most cases. The swelling may decrease with rest.	Regular exercise, not extremes of inactivity and strenuous activity.
Ringbone and sidebone—*joint disease, usually in older horses* The horse is lame. X-rays show large amounts of new bone around the pastern. These may be big enough to feel. Ringbone is an enlargement of the pastern bones on or above the coronet; sidebone is a growth on the cartilage in the heel area.	Wear and tear from repeated concussion (vibration) of the pastern, e.g., during road work.	Usually there is no effective treatment, but painkillers may stop the lameness. If the new bone does not involve a joint (nonarticular ringbone), it may settle down in time.	None.
Wind puff—*production of extra joint fluid* Soft swelling at the back of the leg just above the fetlock, often worse after rest. The horse is not lame. A WIND PUFF	Wear and tear on the fetlock joint.	None necessary.	None possible, although good conformation— with shoulders and pasterns that are not too upright— helps to avoid the problem.
Thoroughpin—*production of extra joint fluid* Soft swelling above the point of the hock between the bone and the tendon. A THOROUGHPIN	Strain on the hock.	None necessary.	None, although good hock conformation helps to avoid the problem.

JOINT DISORDERS

SYMPTOMS	CAUSE	TREATMENT	PREVENTION
Spavin—*bone enlargement* The horse is lame on one or occasionally both hind legs. Sometimes a hard, bony swelling can be seen low down on the inside of the hock.	A form of DJD involving the small bones of the hock joint.	Controlled exercise, with painkillers, if necessary, may result in the painless fusion of bones. Surgical shoeing may help reduce lameness.	None, although good conformation helps to avoid the problem.
Curb—*thickening of the ligament* A firm swelling on the back of the leg at the bottom of the hock. The horse may or may not be lame as a result.	Excessive flexion of the hock joint, spraining the ligament linking some of the bones.	Rest the horse.	Good hocks are less at risk. Avoid working young horses in heavy going.
Capped hock or elbow—*swelling on the joint* Cold, painless swelling on the point of the hock or elbow. (Recent injuries are hot and soft.) A CAPPED HOCK The horse is not usually lame.	May be caused by a blow, but often is the result of too little bedding, so that the horse injures the joint while lying down.	None necessary.	Use sufficient bedding. Fit hock boots (see p. 197). Put shipping boots on for transport.
Patellar fixation or retention—*locking of the stifle* The hind leg is fixed rigidly behind the horse and the horse cannot bend it. This can occur during exercise or after another injury to the stifle joint. A RIGID HIND LEG	The mechanism that enables the horse to lock its stifle and doze on its feet becomes activated by a shortening of one of the ligaments involved. This can be associated with the horse being in poor condition.	If the horse relaxes, it may be possible to relax the locking system by gently massaging the stifle joint. Surgery may be necessary to cut the shortened ligament and allow free movement again.	None.
Sesamoiditis—*condition affecting the sesamoid bone* Pain and swelling at the back of the fetlock joint.	Often the result of general wear and tear, but can occur due to a strain of the ligaments attached to the sesamoid bones.	Rest and treatment with anti-inflammatory drugs.	Avoid letting the foot develop a long-toe/short-heel conformation.
Osteochondrosis (OCD)—*bone disease of young horses* The horse goes lame suddenly, often while standing in the stable overnight. It can affect a number of different joints, such as the stifle, hock, and fetlock. The capsule of the joint is swollen because of an increased amount of joint fluid.	The lameness is caused by the flaking away of a piece of cartilage from the joint, due to a weakness that developed during the first 6–12 months of life. The lameness does not occur until stress is put on the cartilage when the horse starts hard exercise.	The only treatment is surgery to remove any cartilage and bone fragments from the joint.	None.

LEG DISORDERS

Enormous physical strains are placed on both the bones and the tendons of the horse's legs during exercise. For example, at certain stages of the gallop, the whole weight and momentum of the horse is taken by just one leg, so it is hardly surprising that problems arise. Leg injuries take a long time to heal, because it is not possible to prevent a horse from putting any weight on a leg for more than a very short time, so the affected leg can never be rested completely.

Laser treatment
The vet may use laser therapy to treat an injury. This treatment uses light energy to stimulate the horse's natural anti-inflammatory system.

LEG DISORDERS

SYMPTOMS	CAUSE	TREATMENT	PREVENTION
Sprained tendon—*usually the long flexor tendon at the back of the cannon bone* The tendon is thickened, and the tendon sheath that surrounds it becomes puffy and warm to the touch. The horse may be in great pain and does not want to put any weight on the leg. A horse with a severe sprain is said to be "broken down." 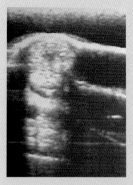 *Area of ruptured tendon fibers is indicated by a black "hole," which will return to normal density as healing occurs* ULTRASOUND SCAN OF A SPRAINED TENDON	Fast exercise, and sometimes a bandage being put on too tightly around the tendon.	Immediate cold treatment on the tendon. Arrange transport for the horse if the injury occurs away from home. Put support bandages on both the affected leg and the good leg, and give the horse complete stable rest in the early stages after the injury. Walk the horse out for 10–15 minutes twice a day, when the swelling has subsided (this may take 10–14 days). After a severe sprain, it may be 6–12 months before the horse can be ridden again. Ultrasound or laser or therapy may help to reduce the inflammation, and anti-inflammatory drugs should be given.	Do not work a horse hard if it is unfit or tired. Never ignore any warning puffiness of the tendon. Feet with a long toe and short heels put extra strain on the tendons.
Bowed tendon—*permanently swollen tendon* A solid, firm swelling down the back of the flexor tendon. The horse is not lame.	This is the possible end result of a sprained tendon.	None. It is too late to treat the tendon. A bowed tendon is always weaker than a normal tendon, so care needs to be taken during exercise.	See sprained tendon.
Broken knee—*injury to the knee* This refers to an open wound on the front of the knee, rather than to a fracture.	The horse stumbling and falling down on hard ground.	Clean and dress the wound. If a lot of skin has been lost, healing will be slow and a scar may form.	Ride carefully on hard ground. Use knee boots (see p. 197).

LEG DISORDERS

SYMPTOMS	CAUSE	TREATMENT	PREVENTION
Overreach—*self-inflicted damage* A horizontal cut or bruise on the heel or the back of the pastern of a foreleg. In very severe cases, the tendon may be cut.	A hind foot hitting a foreleg during exercise, possibly due to faulty action or conformation, or to poorly fitting shoes.	Clean and dress minor wounds. It may be possible to stitch a serious wound if it is fresh. Do not exercise the horse until the wound is healed. Prevent infection which will slow healing.	Trace and remove the cause if you can. Use bell boots (see p. 196) during exercise.
Strike—*self-inflicted damage* Similar to an overreach but higher up the leg, and it can cut the tendon.	See overreach.	See overreach.	As for overreach but use galloping boots (see p. 196).
Step—*self-inflicted damage* Wound in the coronet area.	The horse stepping on itself or being stepped on by another horse.	See overreach.	Protect the leg during shipping (see p. 197).
Brushing—*self-inflicted damage* Wound on the inside of the fetlock joint or the inside of the coronet.	A blow from the foot opposite the injured one.	See overreach.	As for overreach but use brushing boots (see p. 196).
Speedicut—*self-inflicted damage* A wound on the inside of the knee or hock.	A blow from the toe of the opposite leg.	Seek veterinary advice. Do not ride without first seeking advice, because the horse could be unsafe.	Seek veterinary advice.
Splint—*new bone formed on the wall of the cannon bone* The horse may be lame with no obvious cause, but usually there is a hard swelling on the side of the cannon bone, which may be sore in the initial stages. A SPLINT	Stress of repeated concussion (vibration) of the leg bones during exercise. The new bone growth forms to strengthen the wall of the cannon bone.	Cold treatments and anti-inflammatory drugs will help to reduce the inflammation and localized shock-wave therapy may be beneficial. Most splints settle down with time and rest and cause no further problems, although the hard swelling will remain.	None.
Fracture—*broken bone* Extreme pain. The horse will usually be unable to use the affected leg. A FRACTURED LEG	Considerable force, but the stresses on a horse's legs during galloping can be so great that fractures occur with no obvious cause.	With modern technology it may be possible to repair a fracture of the hock, knee, and below. If the fracture is of a major bone higher than this, or if the bone has broken through the skin, the horse usually has to be euthanized.	None.
Sore shin—*a condition of the cannon bone that affects young horses* The horse is lame, and the front of one or both forecannons is painful to pressure. There may be heat and swelling.	Repeated pressure of work, which can overtax immature cannon bones.	Cold treatment and anti-inflammatory drugs combined with rest. Localized shock-wave therapy may be beneficial.	Do not overwork a young horse.

EYE, NOSE, & MOUTH DISORDERS

A horse in the wild would be severely handicapped by disorders affecting its senses. Domestic horses are not so vulnerable, because humans are able to compensate for impaired senses. For example, if we provide food for a horse, it does not need to be able to distinguish between good and bad food or to seek it out. It is interesting that the muscles of the horse's eyelids are much more powerful than those of most other animals. They are able to close their eyes very quickly to protect them from injury—for example, from branches as they gallop through trees. Unfortunately, this can make it very difficult to hold a horse's eye open to put in ointment or eye drops.

Inspecting an eye
The vet may need to look right into the horse's eye using an ophthalmoscope. This shines a light beam into the eye and contains a magnifying glass.

EYE, NOSE, AND MOUTH DISORDERS

SYMPTOMS	CAUSE	TREATMENT	PREVENTION
Cataract—*degeneration of the lens of the eye* The first indication may be that the horse fails to see people or danger approaching from one side. In certain lights, the eye may appear cloudy or white. A CATARACT SHOWING HOW IT PREVENTS LIGHT FROM PASSING THROUGH THE LENS, REFLECTING IT INSTEAD	Most cataracts occur as horses get older. Some are hereditary and affect foals.	The lens can be removed surgically from the eye. This will return the horse's sight, although the horse might lose some of its ability to distinguish fine detail. No other treatment will help.	None.
Conjunctivitis—*inflammation of the conjunctival membranes* The membranes around the eye are red and swollen. There is usually a discharge from the eye; this may at first be watery, but later becomes more puslike. AN INFLAMED MEMBRANE—IT CAN RAPIDLY BECOME INFECTED	An irritant, such as a tiny piece of straw or some shampoo, getting into the eye. Infections can also cause conjunctivitis.	Remove anything in the eye. As long as the cornea has not been damaged, steroid eye ointments may be used to take away inflammation. Antibiotics will kill any infections.	None.

EYE, NOSE, AND MOUTH DISORDERS

SYMPTOMS	CAUSE	TREATMENT	PREVENTION
Sinusitis—*infection in the sinuses* The horse has a discharge from one nostril where pus is draining from the sinus into the nasal cavity. The sinus will sound solid when tapped with a finger, instead of hollow as it should. THIS NASAL DISCHARGE SHOWS THAT IT IS THE LEFT SIDE OF THE HORSE'S SKULL THAT IS AFFECTED	A tooth root abscess is the most common cause, because the roots of the molar teeth extend into the sinuses.	The pus that has accumulated in the sinus must all be drained out. Often, this is best done by removing the tooth whose root enters the sinus, to allow good drainage.	Regular dental checks help to avoid tooth root abscesses.
Nosebleed Blood, which in many cases comes from somewhere else in the respiratory system, drains from the horse's nose. BLOOD DRAINING FROM THE LEFT NOSTRIL	During strenuous exercise horses may bleed into their lungs, and the blood may become visible at the nose. A tumor in the nose can cause significant amounts of blood at the nostrils.	If blood loss has not been too great, clotting will occur if the horse is kept still, possibly by sedating it. The underlying cause then has to be dealt with.	Plenty of fresh air, and not too much strenuous exercise may reduce hemorrhage in the lungs.
Guttural pouch problems—*problems with the large sac, or pouch, that opens off the passageway leading from the inner ear to the back of the throat* Swelling behind the skin immediately below the ear, down the back of the jaw. There may be blood or pus in the sac, which will drain out via the nostrils.	Infections may have become established inside the pouch. The major arteries to the brain, which pass through the pouch, can become blocked.	Surgery may be necessary to prevent a possibly fatal hemorrhage.	None.
Dental problems The horse's performance may be reduced, and it may resent the pressure of the bit. It may drop unchewed food out of its mouth while eating, or it may stop eating altogether.	An abscess will cause a toothache. Sharp edges formed on the outside of the upper molars and the inside of the lower molars can cause ulcerations on the cheeks and tongue.	Any sharp edges must be rasped away. It may be necessary for the vet to remove a tooth. The small wolf teeth found in front of the molars may need to be removed if they cause bit problems.	Have your horse's teeth checked at least once a year.
Bit problems The horse may be unwilling to turn in one direction, or may toss its head in resentment when asked to do so. There may be bruising or ulceration of the gums immediately in front of the molar teeth.	A few horses have a very sensitive mouth, but nearly all problems are caused by a poorly fitting bridle.	Stop riding the horse for a while, then check the fit of the bridle. If possible, use a less severe bit.	Check the bit of a horse's bridle carefully every time you ride.

SKIN DISORDERS

The onset of a skin problem can be difficult to spot, so it is often overlooked for too long. White-haired skin is more susceptible than pigmented skin to many skin problems. Some horses have a very thick coat, especially during winter. This can both hide diseases and provide good conditions for infections to multiply, so check a horse's coat carefully when you are grooming it. Use a grooming kit for one horse only. This prevents the spread of disease from one horse to another, and its importance cannot be stressed enough.

The same applies to rugs and other clothes. Make sure, also, that the blades of clippers are sterile. It is a good idea to clip the hair around any skin problems. This not only lets you see what is happening but also makes the treatment much more effective.

SKIN DISORDERS

SYMPTOMS	CAUSE	TREATMENT	PREVENTION
Mud fever Scabs on the skin, which are very sensitive. They are usually on the legs, especially on the pastern and fetlock, but can extend up to the belly. Sometimes the legs become swollen. SCABS ON A LEG (TREATED)	The infection *Dermatophilus congolensis* enters the skin because the skin is either softened by wet conditions or cracked by dry, dusty conditions. The scabs protect the bacteria underneath.	Remove the scabs to expose the infection to the air. Usually, the whole area must be clipped, because hair stabilizes the scabs. Antiseptic shampoo may soften the scabs, and antibiotic cream will kill the infection. Antibiotic injections may be necessary.	Keep the pastern and fetlock areas clean and dry. If you have to wash mud off, dry the area thoroughly. When the infection has cleared, apply petroleum jelly to protect the skin in the wet.
Cracked heels—*a form of mud fever* Horizontal oozing wounds on the back of the pasterns. Scabs may develop. Horses with white socks are particularly susceptible.	Infection enters the skin. See mud fever.	See mud fever.	See mud fever.
Rain scald—*an infection similar to mud fever* Tufts of hair held together by small scabs all over the body. These often appear after rain or damp conditions. SCAB (TREATED)	Infection with *Dermatophilus*, which spreads rapidly over the wet skin.	As for mud fever, although clipping may not be possible.	Provide the horse with shelter from the rain.
Saddle sore and girth gall—*area of rubbed skin* Raised, inflamed area of skin in the saddle and girth area. It may become raw.	Poorly fitting tack, or a foreign body trapped under the saddle, or girth rubbing the skin.	Remove the cause and do not ride the horse again until the skin has healed.	Ensure that the saddle and girth are clean and fit properly. A gel pad under the saddle (see p. 177) will distribute pressure.

SKIN DISORDERS

SYMPTOMS	CAUSE	TREATMENT	PREVENTION
Trichophyton (Ringworm)—*a fungal infection* Typically round areas of hair loss or slight crusting anywhere on the body. The skin and hair may just look tatty rather than showing such areas. RINGWORM CRUSTING AROUND AN EYE	A fungus weakens the base of the hairs, which break off. The infection can be passed on by grooming kit and tack, or from the stable or wood surfaces. It is often carried by cattle.	Special antibiotics will kill the fungus but it takes time for the hair to regrow. The horse usually becomes immune to infection in time. Because ringworm can infect people, always take strict hygiene precautions during and after handling infected horses.	The fungal spores live for many months. Treat affected surfaces with an antibiotic before using them. Keep the horse away from infected cattle.
Hypoderma (Cattle grubs)—*the larvae of heel flies* A raised area on the horse's back near its backbone, occurring during the winter. In the spring, a hole may appear in the center.	The heel fly lays its eggs on the horse's legs. The larvae burrow into the skin and make their way to the horse's back, where they develop and form swellings. In the spring, adult flies may emerge, although some stay there for a considerable time.	Ivermectin will kill the warble larvae, but it may be necessary to remove the hard lump surgically.	None.
Sweet itch—*an allergy to midges* Lost hair and raw and oozing skin at the base of the mane and tail during the summer. SHORT, BROKEN HAIRS, WHICH ARE THE RESULT OF SWEET ITCH	The horse rubs its mane and tail because of an allergy to the saliva of the small midges that bite the affected areas.	There is no cure for the allergy. Benzyl benzoate lotion will soothe the rubbed areas and kill midges. Calamine lotion is also soothing.	Stable the horse during the evening and morning, when the midges are active. Use fly-repellent washes on the horse's skin and in the stable.
Haematopinus and Damalinia (Lice)—*parasitic insects* Large areas of bald skin in winter. HAIR LOSS DUE ENTIRELY TO RUBBING A LOUSE—WELL-DESIGNED FOR BITING AND SUCKING	The horse rubs itself to relieve the irritation of active lice that bite or suck the skin.	Repeated doses of ivermectin will kill lice. Modern louse powders are based on permethrin rather than more toxic chemicals.	A horse should be treated if it comes into contact with lice, whether it is showing symptoms or not.
Mange—*inflammation caused by tiny mites* (Psoroptes *and* Chorioptes) The affected areas, usually the lower legs, are intensely irritated. The horse stamps its feet and tries to rub them.	The mites bite. There are several families of mange mites. *Chorioptes* and *Psoroptes* are the most common.	When available, benzene hexachloride (BHC) shampoos are effective. Otherwise permethrin or ivermectin can be used.	See lice.

DIGESTIVE DISORDERS

There are several inherent weaknesses in the horse's digestive system (*see p. 29*). This means that the horse is prone to digestive disorders, the main one being colic. There are three types of colic: impaction, spasmodic colic, and physical displacement. Impaction is when there is no movement of material along a portion of the horse's bowel. The horse may still pass droppings initially, as it empties out the bowel contents below the impaction. The pain is low-level, constant discomfort, so the horse may lie on its side, unwilling to move. Impactions often follow a change of diet, when a new type of fiber has not been digested. Sometimes impactions are associated with tapeworm infestations. In spasmodic colic, as its name implies, the pain comes and goes. The pain is usually associated with excess bowel activity. It may follow a disturbance of some sort that upsets the horse temporarily. A physical displacement is often referred to as a twisted gut.

A section of the digestive tract becomes completely displaced, with the result that pressure from the organs interferes with the blood supply to the affected area. Straightforward twisting around of a section of the bowel is relatively uncommon. The pain can be severe, and the horse becomes very shocked. Surgery may be the only form of successful treatment. Rolling may be a symptom of a physical displacement, but it does not cause a displacement in the first place.

DIGESTIVE DISORDERS

SYMPTOMS	CAUSE	TREATMENT	PREVENTION
Colic – *abdominal pain* It is important that you know how to recognize colic in the early stages. The horse usually stops eating and may start to look around at its belly. Areas of patchy swelling appear over its body. It may then start either stamping at the ground with its front feet or kicking at its belly with its hind feet. As the pain becomes more intense, the horse will lie down. In acute pain, it will roll over repeatedly, oblivious to anything or anybody. Its pulse may quicken and increase to 60 or 80 beats per minute.	Many different causes, affecting different parts of the horse's digestive tract, will result in the same colic symptoms.	Call the vet at once. Stable the horse, if possible with a thick bed in case it starts to roll. Encourage it to eat a warm bran mash. Do not walk the horse endlessly around and around; this will not affect the course of the colic, but will tire the horse and may mean that it rolls in an unsuitable place. Do not try to drench (give liquid medicine to) the horse. In its pain, it may not swallow, and the liquid may go into its lungs.	Feed your horse regular amounts of food at regular intervals. Follow a suitable feeding regimen (see p. 124) and make any diet change gradually, over 7–10 days. Follow a comprehensive worming program (see p. 150). Have your horse's teeth checked regularly.

A HORSE PAWING THE GROUND – A SYMPTOM OF COLIC

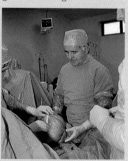

OPERATING TO RELIEVE COLIC

DIGESTIVE DISORDERS

SYMPTOMS	CAUSE	TREATMENT	PREVENTION
Choking—*food stuck in the gullet* The horse is very distressed. Copious amounts of frothy saliva come down its nostrils and drool out of its mouth. The horse cannot eat or drink, and a swelling may be visible on the left side of its neck.  SALIVA COMING FROM THE NOSTRILS AND MOUTH, CAUSED BY CHOKING	Large pieces of apple or root vegetable such as carrot are common things to get stuck. Unsoaked beet cubes can also get stuck, because they swell up quickly on contact with water. The saliva produced cannot drain down past the obstruction, and so it overflows.	Gentle massage of any swelling may encourage the obstruction to pass on. The vet may need to use a stomach tube to remove the saliva, which otherwise might trickle down the horse's windpipe.	Take care to prepare food properly (see p. 127).
Diarrhea Loose droppings, varying from cow-pat consistency to brown water. The horse will start to dehydrate if the diarrhea continues for more than an hour or two. If it persists for several days, the horse will lose body proteins faster than it can take them in, and so will start to lose weight.  A HORSE THAT HAS LOST WEIGHT DUE TO DIARRHEA	There are many causes. Bacteria such as salmonella, heavy worm infestations, and lush spring grass can all cause diarrhea. Diseases that damage the intestinal wall may stop the horse absorbing water from the bowel and result in diarrhea. Stress or excitement may also lead to this problem.	The cause should be diagnosed and treated accordingly. Special electrolyte (salt) mixtures will stop the horse from dehydrating. Codeine can be useful in stopping the diarrhea.	Worm the horse regularly and avoid subjecting it to severe stress.
Poisoning Many poisons start by causing mild constipation, which is then followed by diarrhea. In cases of severe poisoning, the horse can become extremely distressed.	The horse may have eaten a poisonous plant (see p. 94) or ingested one of many toxic chemicals with its grass. These range from lead in a discarded battery to a seed dressing applied to corn.	Give the horse a bran mash or liquid paraffin to speed up the passage of the poison through the system. The symptoms have to be treated, rather than the poison, as there are few specific antidotes.	Check your field regularly and remove all poisonous plants and dumped garbage. Keep chemicals away from the stableyard.

INTERNAL PARASITES

The basic relationship between parasitic worms and horses is that the adult worm lives in the horse's bowel, surrounded by the food that passes through the horse's digestive tract. Often, the worm attaches itself to the bowel wall to prevent itself from being carried through the horse with food and water. It is not in the parasite's interests to kill the horse because, if it does, the worms in that horse will die, too. In the wild, where horses roam over a wide area, they rarely develop a worm burden that is severe enough to be fatal. When they are restricted to grazing a small area continuously, as are domestic horses in a field, the number of worms that they take in can be enormous and possibly lethal.

DEVELOPMENT OF THE WORM

Worms on pasture

A pasture with worm eggs and larvae is like a time bomb, which will explode when horses graze there. There are no chemicals that can kill worm eggs. Drying out and extremes of temperature will kill them in time, but this can take two or three years. When the eggs hatch, the larvae climb to the top of grass stalks. Cutting the grass will remove these larvae; dividing the grazing up and using each area in turn will allow time for the larvae to die in between grazing periods. The larvae develop in the horse and cause more damage than adult worms. You must therefore worm the horse regularly, not just when you know you have a problem (right).

Life-cycle of the worm

The larvae molt several times inside the horse, shedding their skin and getting bigger and bigger until the adult worms develop

The larvae are eaten with the grass by a horse

The adult worms release eggs, which eventually pass out with the horse's droppings

The droppings break down, and the worm larvae hatch and climb up the grass stalks

WORMING PROGRAMS

There are four anthelmintics, or worming drugs, that are active against a reasonably wide range of parasitic worms from which horses suffer. These are moxidectin, ivermectin, pyrantel, and the benzimidazoles (a family of drugs whose chemical names all end in "-dazole"). Don't try to control all the different types of worm with just one wormer— it's just not possible; you must target-worm for the exceptions, and then have one drug for routine use throughout the year. Change the type of wormer every one or two years, but not each time you dose, since this will make it easier for the worms to become resistant to the drugs. Some level of resistance to most wormers now occurs so new worming regimes aim at leaving a certain amount of worm larvae in the horses's intestinal wall to stimulate natural immunity rather than killing all the worms. The worm burden of a horse should be assessed by checking the number of worm eggs in the feces—your vet can arrange this— and only those horses with more than 200–400 eggs per gram of feces should be wormed.

HOW WORMS AFFECT THE HORSE

Does your horse have worms?
You will not be able to tell if your horse has worms by just looking at it. Most worms cause a loss of condition, but there are other factors that make a horse become thin. A large number of adult worms or larvae is usually needed to cause weight loss, anemia, or general poor condition. Worms can be associated with colic (see p. 148). If a horse suffers from repeated attacks of colic, or develops colic where no other cause can be diagnosed, it needs to be wormed. Different tests are required to identify which type of worm is present. The identification and quantity of *Strongylus*, *Ascaris*, *Trichonema*, and *Oxyuris* worms can usually be determined by collecting some of the horse's dung and testing it for the presence of eggs.

THE MAIN WORMS THAT AFFECT HORSES

WORM	TARGET CONTROL
Strongylus vulgaris (Bloodworm) The larvae spend several months in the blood vessels that supply the bowel. They obstruct the blood flow, and so can be dangerous. They emerge in the bowel and can then cause diarrhea. Because they are larvae and not adult worms, their presence will not be detected by a worm egg count.	Use ivermectin or moxidectin, which kill the larvae in the blood vessels as well as the adults.
Cyathostomes (Small redworm) Larvae can lie dormant in cysts in the intestinal wall over winter, before a large number suddenly emerge, causing severe weight loss and possibly diarrhea.	A five-day course of of fenbendazole or the use of moxidectin may kill dormant larvae. Routine worming will only kill the adult worms.
Ascaris (Large roundworm) These pass through the lungs during development, causing coughing and a nasal discharge in young horses. Horses over a year old seem to develop an immunity to them.	Treat young horses from 6 weeks old with either ivermectin, pyrantel, or a benzimidazole wormer.
Anoplocephala (Tapeworm) These flatworms live in the area around the junction between the small intestine and the cecum. They can cause impactions to form at this junction, which can lead to colic. They need an intermediate host—a mite found on grass—to complete their life cycle.	A double dose of pyrantel in the early autumn every 1–2 years.
Dictyocaulus (Lungworm) As their name suggests, these worms live in the lungs, and cause the horse to cough. The immature larvae are carried up the trachea (windpipe) and then swallowed. The full life cycle occurs in donkeys. In horses, it usually stops when the larvae reach the lungs.	Use ivermectin, especially where horses and donkeys are grazed together.
Oxyuris (Pinworm) The adult worms live just inside the rectum. Larvae develop in eggs, then drop to the ground.	Routine worming with most modern wormers will control the worms.
Gasterophilus (Bot) Strictly speaking, these are not worms. The bot fly lays eggs on the horse's skin, which are licked up and pass to the stomach where the larvae develop. The adult fly emerges only after the larvae have been passed in the droppings.	Give ivermectin in winter.

CIRCULATORY DISORDERS

The state of a horse's blood gives a good indication of the animal's health. When a blood sample is taken, the vet examines the red and white blood cells and the blood fluid, or plasma. The number of red cells, and the amount of hemoglobin they contain, indicate whether or not a horse has anemia. White blood cells are affected by infections: bacterial infections cause an increased number of a cell called a neutrophil; parasitic infections increase the numbers of a cell called an eosinophil. Plasma contains substances that have escaped from cells in the internal organs. Background low levels of the substances are present all the time, but if an organ is diseased, the plasma levels will be affected. For example, liver disease will result in a raised level of a substance called gamma glutamyltransferase. Modern technology allows vets to measure about 20 of these different characteristics of blood in their own offices.

Taking blood
The vet may take a blood sample to analyze the red and white cells. The sample must be taken from a horse completely at rest.

CIRCULATORY DISORDERS

SYMPTOMS	CAUSE	TREATMENT	PREVENTION
Anemia—*reduced number of red blood cells in the blood or decreased hemoglobin in the cells* The horse is dull and lethargic. The pink membranes around the eyes and mouth become paler. Anemia will have become severe before symptoms are noted.	A deficiency of folic acid can lead to a decrease in the manufacture of red blood cells. Anemia is caused by chronic internal bleeding or severe bloodsucking by worms. Contrary to popular opinion, it is hardly ever due to an iron or vitamin B12 deficiency.	A folic acid supplement will always be worthwhile. Any other cause should be treated accordingly. Recovery will take some time, because it takes at least a month for the body to replace red blood cells.	Worm the horse regularly. Give access to fresh grass, which provides folic acid.
Heart problems In severe cases, the horse may have edema (filling) of the legs or underneath the belly. The existence of heart murmurs or abnormal heart beats does not mean that the horse will suddenly collapse.	There is no one cause. An electrocardiograph may indicate why the horse's heart rhythms have been affected and ultrasound scans may show physical or blood-flow abnormalities.	There is little precise treatment.	None.

CIRCULATORY DISORDERS

SYMPTOMS	CAUSE	TREATMENT	PREVENTION
Dehydration—*lack of water in the body* The horse is weak and lethargic. It might collapse or appear dazed. If you pull up a fold of skin on the neck and then let it go, it will remain in place rather than go back to normal instantly.	The horse not drinking, or losing too much water—for instance, through diarrhea. Dehydration may also be due to loss of electrolytes (salts) when the horse sweats.	An immediate supply of electrolyte supplement. In severe cases, an intravenous transfusion may be necessary.	Give the horse access to fresh water at all times. Make sure that it drinks during long rides.
Lymphangitis—*damage to the lymphatics (tubes that drain the tissue fluid away)* One or both hind legs are swollen due to the presence of tissue fluid. If the leg becomes greatly swollen, fluid may start to ooze through the skin. SWOLLEN HIND LEG DUE TO LYMPHANGITIS	Imbalance between food and exercise. Lymphangitis was once called Monday morning disease because it occurred in cart-horses after their rest day. (Sometimes, azoturia [*below*] is also called Monday morning disease for the same reason.)	Hot fomentations on the groin area may help circulation. A diuretic drug may remove some of the fluid.	Reduce food on rest days.
Azoturia—*damage to the muscles by high levels of lactic acid* The horse is suddenly very stiff and unwilling to move. It may pass dark red urine. The muscles of the back and hindquarters may be hard and swollen.	Too much food on a rest day, causing a high level of lactic acid to be formed by the muscles during the next period of exercise. The acid cannot be removed effectively by the circulation, and damages the muscles.	Do not exercise the horse any further. Seek veterinary help. Keep the muscles warm with blankets to help the circulation.	Do not overfeed the horse for the work it is doing (see p. 121), as this leads to more lactic acid being formed.
Equine viral arteritis (EVA)—*infectious disease that damages the tiny arteries* Flulike symptoms.	A virus.	No specific treatment.	Vaccination is possible.
African horse sickness (AHS) Large raised areas of swelling on the body. It is usually fatal, because the swellings press on the airways, preventing the horse from breathing.	A virus carried by a midge. It only occurs in countries warm enough to allow the midge to survive through the winter.	No treatment. Affected horses are usually euthanized to prevent them from infecting other horses.	Vaccination is possible.

RESPIRATORY DISORDERS

One of the main symptoms of a respiratory problem is a cough. Coughing is a protective mechanism to keep the airways free of mucus. The vet should concentrate on removing the cause rather than suppressing the cough itself. All horses cough occasionally, but you should note if the horse coughs more than three or four times consecutively.

A cough will spread infection by propelling tiny droplets of water and bacteria into the air. Not all coughs are infectious, though, so a coughing horse does not necessarily pose a threat to other horses.

Listening to the lungs
The vet listens with a stethoscope to the sounds made by air entering and leaving the lungs. Abnormalities in the lungs can be detected this way.

RESPIRATORY DISORDERS

SYMPTOMS	CAUSE	TREATMENT	PREVENTION
Herpes virus infection A nasal discharge and a cough. Occasionally, when more serious, the herpes virus can cause abortion or paralysis.	A virus.	Drugs to keep the airways open and free from mucus.	Vaccination may be possible.
Equine influenza—*flu* The horse has a cough, runny eyes, and a runny nose. It may have a high temperature. Chronic lung or heart problems may follow after the flu has been overcome. In foals, equine influenza can be fatal. A RUNNY NOSE	One of two main families of virus.	There is no specific treatment. Drugs to keep the airways open and to kill secondary infections are usually given.	Vaccination.
Strangles— *a contagious throat infection* Large abscesses under the jaw and around the throat. The horse has a high temperature. In time, the abscesses burst, releasing foul-smelling pus. If they burst internally, the horse will have a pus-filled nasal discharge. A SWOLLEN GLAND DUE TO AN ABSCESS	A bacterial infection.	Antibiotics, given after the abscesses have burst, will kill the infection.	A vaccine is available in some countries. Before mixing with other horses, it is advisable to test horses that have had the disease in the past, and those that have been in contact with other affected horses, to check whether or not they are carriers.

RESPIRATORY DISORDERS

SYMPTOMS	CAUSE	TREATMENT	PREVENTION
Pneumonia—*infection in the lungs* The horse has difficulty in breathing and may have an increased respiratory rate *(see p. 45)*. There may be a cough.	A virus or bacteria that damages the lung tissues. Foals can suffer from a particularly serious form of pneumonia.	Bacterial pneumonias may respond to antibiotics; viral pneumonias never will. There are drugs available that help to remove mucus from the lungs and open the airways.	Make sure that the stable is well ventilated *(see p. 107)*.
Dictyocaulus *(Lungworm) (see p. 151)* A persistent cough that starts while the horse is at grass during the summer.	*See p. 151.*	*See p. 151.*	*See p. 151.*
Laryngeal paralysis or hemiplegia *(roaring and whistling)—paralysis of a vocal cord* Most of the time the horse shows no sign of illness at all. Only during very strenuous exercise may a roaring sound be heard as the horse breathes in. The horse's athletic performance is reduced.	The horse is usually born with the condition. One vocal cord, usually the left, is paralyzed either completely or partially. It cannot be pulled out of the way to allow more air to get into the trachea. *Cartilage* *Paralyzed vocal cord* *Trachea* *Epiglottis* ABNORMAL LARYNX	If performance is affected then surgery will be required to pull the vocal cord out of the way permanently. *Corrected vocal cord* LARYNX AFTER SURGERY	None.
Chronic obstructive pulmonary disease (COPD)—*a restriction of small airways in the lungs* The horse has to make a conscious effort to empty its lungs completely. It may have a cough and a nasal discharge. Athletic performance will be reduced. A "heave" line from the stifle along the belly may be visible, where increased muscle effort has been needed to push air out of the lungs.	An allergy to fungal spores on hay and straw. Occasionally, other particles, such as pollen, can trigger the condition.	Turn the horse out, or make sure it does not come into contact with hay or straw. There are drugs that open up the constricted airways, and nebulizers for drugs that protect the lungs of affected horses. BREATHING VIA A NEBULIZER	Use alternative spore-free bedding *(see p. 113)* and feed vacuum-packed grass rather than hay *(see p. 129)*.

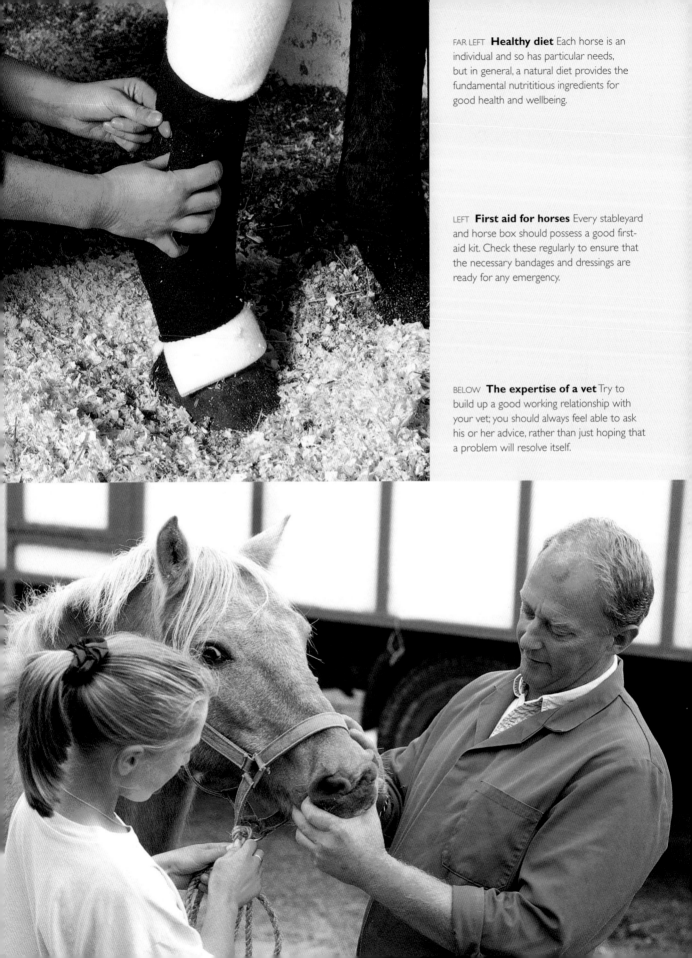

FAR LEFT **Healthy diet** Each horse is an individual and so has particular needs, but in general, a natural diet provides the fundamental nutrititious ingredients for good health and wellbeing.

LEFT **First aid for horses** Every stableyard and horse box should possess a good first-aid kit. Check these regularly to ensure that the necessary bandages and dressings are ready for any emergency.

BELOW **The expertise of a vet** Try to build up a good working relationship with your vet; you should always feel able to ask his or her advice, rather than just hoping that a problem will resolve itself.

WHEN TO CALL THE VET

Use your common sense when assessing whether to call the vet. You should know your horse's habits, past problems, and normal lumps. If you are not sure whether your horse has a serious problem or not, call the vet to discuss it. Never leave a horse with an unexplained condition for more than 24 hours.

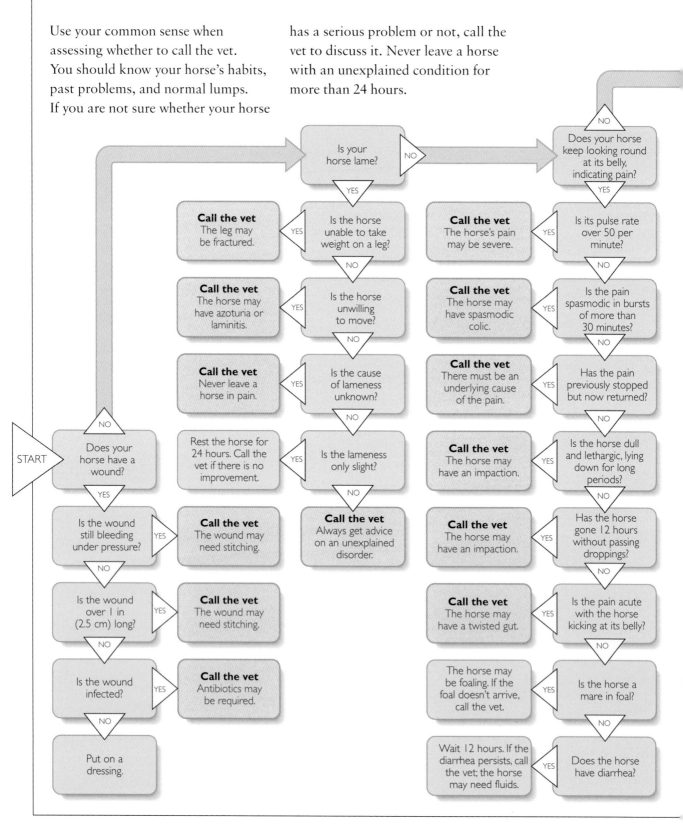

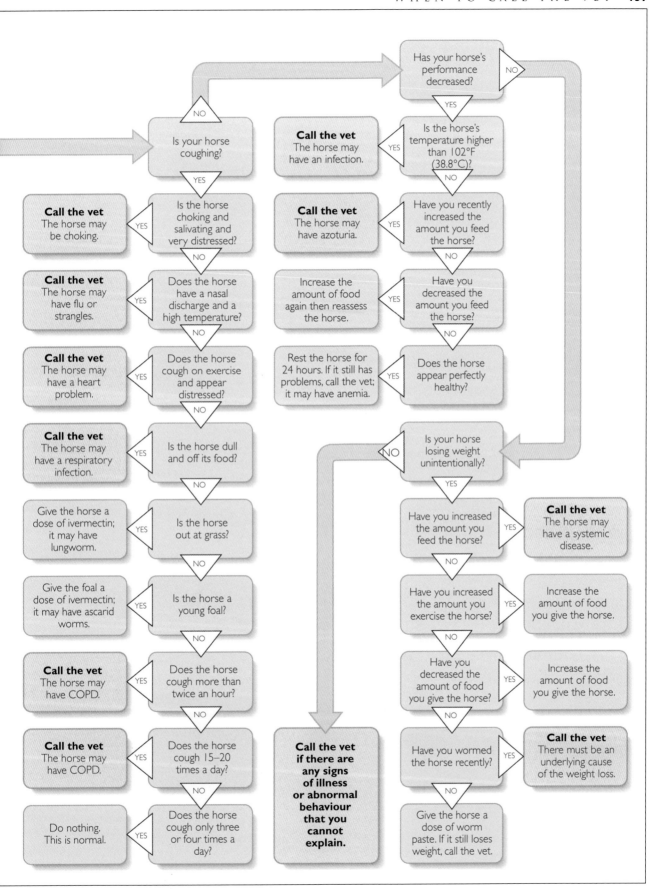

Has your horse's performance decreased?

NO

Is your horse coughing?

YES

Call the vet
The horse may have an infection.

YES

Is the horse's temperature higher than 102°F (38.8°C)?

NO

Call the vet
The horse may be choking.

YES

Is the horse choking and salivating and very distressed?

NO

Call the vet
The horse may have azoturia.

YES

Have you recently increased the amount you feed the horse?

NO

Call the vet
The horse may have flu or strangles.

YES

Does the horse have a nasal discharge and a high temperature?

NO

Increase the amount of food again then reassess the horse.

YES

Have you decreased the amount you feed the horse?

NO

Call the vet
The horse may have a heart problem.

YES

Does the horse cough on exercise and appear distressed?

NO

Rest the horse for 24 hours. If it still has problems, call the vet; it may have anemia.

YES

Does the horse appear perfectly healthy?

Call the vet
The horse may have a respiratory infection.

YES

Is the horse dull and off its food?

NO

NO

Is your horse losing weight unintentionally?

YES

Give the horse a dose of ivermectin; it may have lungworm.

YES

Is the horse out at grass?

NO

Have you increased the amount you feed the horse?

YES

Call the vet
The horse may have a systemic disease.

NO

Give the foal a dose of ivermectin; it may have ascarid worms.

YES

Is the horse a young foal?

NO

Have you increased the amount you exercise the horse?

YES

Increase the amount of food you give the horse.

NO

Call the vet
The horse may have COPD.

YES

Does the horse cough more than twice an hour?

NO

Have you decreased the amount of food you give the horse?

YES

Increase the amount of food you give the horse.

NO

Call the vet
The horse may have COPD.

YES

Does the horse cough 15–20 times a day?

NO

Call the vet if there are any signs of illness or abnormal behaviour that you cannot explain.

Have you wormed the horse recently?

YES

Call the vet
There must be an underlying cause of the weight loss.

NO

Do nothing. This is normal.

YES

Does the horse cough only three or four times a day?

Give the horse a dose of worm paste. If it still loses weight, call the vet.

FIRST-AID EQUIPMENT

You never know where or when an injury may be sustained, so you do not know where or when you will need a first-aid kit. Certainly you must have one at the stables. When you travel to shows you need one in the van or trailer, and if you go out on long trail rides, you should also take a very simple kit with you. The stable kit, and any more basic first-aid items, should be kept in a dry, clean place such as the tack room, where everyone can find it easily. Remember to keep this equipment well out of the way of small children. All first-aid kits should be checked regularly and, if necessary, restocked, so that dressings and other items are always there when needed.

Saddle bag
When you go out riding, take a small first-aid kit in a saddle bag. You can buy a ready-made kit, or make up your own to include enough to deal with a wound: a cleaning agent, a nonstick dressing, padding, and a bandage. You will not have room for more.

ANTISEPTICS

Liquids
The best antiseptic is chlorhexidine. A concentrated liquid antiseptic must be diluted with clean water before use. This is fine for a stable kit, but in a saddle kit it must be ready for use.

Aerosol sprays
An antiseptic in a spray is easier than liquid to apply directly to small wounds to prevent infection. The noise may startle a horse, but the spray only needs to be applied lightly.

BANDAGES

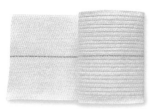

Ventilated elastic adhesive bandage
Usually, you should not use these directly on the skin, but in a few cases this is the only way to hold a dressing. A warm bandage sticks better than a cold one.

Crepe bandage
This has "give" in it, making it cling to the leg, but with use it will lose this. It is secured by splitting the end and tying it around the leg, or with a safety pin and a stable bandage on top.

Zip-up lycra bandage
Bandaging a knee or hock takes practice. There are specially designed zip-up lycra bandages that are easier to put on. They are shaped for particular joints, and come in different sizes.

Padded bandage
These bandages have no tensile strength but provide padding that conforms reasonably well to the shape of the leg. At least three to six layers need to be applied.

Self-adhesive bandage
Cohesive bandages stick only to themselves, and mold to the shape of the leg. They will not stretch or contract if swelling increases or goes down, so they may have to be re-applied if this happens.

DRESSING ITEMS

Scissors

Every first-aid kit needs a pair of good scissors for jobs like cutting dressings to shape and trimming hair. Scissors should have sharp blades with rounded ends. Blunt scissors must be replaced.

Sheet cotton

This material consists of cotton between layers of gauze. It does not shed fibers like plain cotton does. It can be wrapped around a leg, but does not shape to the leg without being trimmed.

All-purpose dressing

Soak prepared dry poultice dressings in warm water before use. Never leave a poultice on for more than 48 hours, or the skin at the wound edges will die. The plastic layer goes on the outside.

Gauze

Impregnated gauze dressings are convenient for stopping bandages and other coverings from sticking to wounds. The dressings contain either petroleum jelly or, more usefully, an antibiotic gel.

Perforated plastic film

Plastic film also does not stick to wounds. The perforations in the plastic film allow fluid from the wound to pass through it, and the fluid is then absorbed by a lint pad on the outside of the dressing.

Hydrophilic polyurethane

This type of dressing provides padding as well as ensuring good conditions for healing. The special foam draws fluid away from the wound, and can absorb up to 10 times its own weight.

COLD TREATMENTS

Freeze pack

Specially designed freeze packs can be bought and kept in a freezer until they are needed. The "bubbles" of liquid in this pack provide flexibility, and allow it to mold to the contours of the horse's leg even when the pack has just come out of the freezer.

Cold pack

A gel that never quite freezes solid is contained inside this type of pack. The pack is kept in the freezer until needed and then stays cold for a considerable length of time. It is rather heavy, so special straps are provided to hold the pack in place.

Hosing boot

The boot allows a continuous flow of cold water to be applied to a horse's cannon. It is directly attached to a flexible hose, and strapped to a horse's leg like an ordinary tendon boot (see p. 196). After use, it must be dried thoroughly before storage.

FIRST AID

First aid is not an alternative to calling the vet. It is what you do first when you find a wound or other problem. Whether you need to call a vet may depend on the results of your efforts. There are situations when you should always seek veterinary help (*see p. 158*). The basis of first aid is calmness. Don't let yourself panic or rush things. If you do, the dressings will slip or the bandages will unroll, and you will get frustrated. Although you know that you are trying to help the horse, the horse does not; an injured horse is entitled to be scared and uncooperative. Try to pass on some of your confidence to the horse.

USING A SPRAY

A small wound on the neck is suitable for a light application of antibiotic spray

Antibiotic spray
Hold the can upright 12–20 in (30–48 cm) from the skin and spray briefly. Some horses dislike the noise, so spray in the air first, to assess the horse's reaction. It will probably get used to it. Cotton balls in the ears may help if there is a problem.

CLEANING A WOUND

When and how to do it
Don't clean a wound unless you are sure you will do more good than harm. Wash your hands first, and make sure that the water and swabs are clean. It is better to use a sterile, dry swab than risk introducing infection with nonsterile water. Never use dirty water from a bucket. Don't keep washing a wound just because it bleeds—washing will disturb the necessary formation of clots. Finally, don't be mesmerized by a little blood and fail to spot a more serious problem.

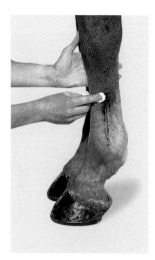

1 Start cleaning at the center of a wound, no matter what size it is. Use clean cotton balls with a either a weak saline or an antiseptic solution.

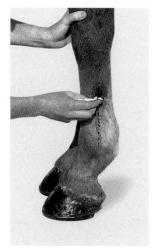

2 Work outward, so that you do not bring dirt into the wound from the surrounding skin. Do not push dirt under any skin flaps.

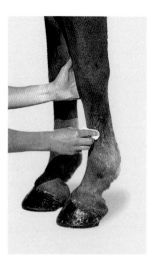

3 Finally, clean the skin surrounding the wound. Never go back to the wound with the same swab, even if the wound is still bleeding.

DRESSING A WOUND ON A LEG

Use of dressings
The main reason for dressing a wound is to use pressure to stop bleeding. In some cases, this is more important than washing the wound. Take care to apply even pressure. If tight pressure is needed, it must be released every 30 minutes to allow the blood flow to the rest of the area. Most wounds hurt much less when dressed.

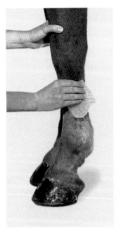

1 Apply a nonstick dressing first. This will not disturb the blood clot when you change it.

2 Wrap padding around the leg. Don't worry if the wound is bleeding—it can take up to 30 minutes to stop.

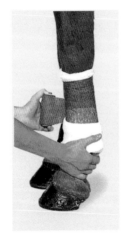

3 Bandage over the padding. Start at the top, to secure the dressing, and then move down to the wound area.

4 Use all the bandage, leaving an edge of padding at top and bottom. Take time to do it well.

APPLYING A FOMENTATION

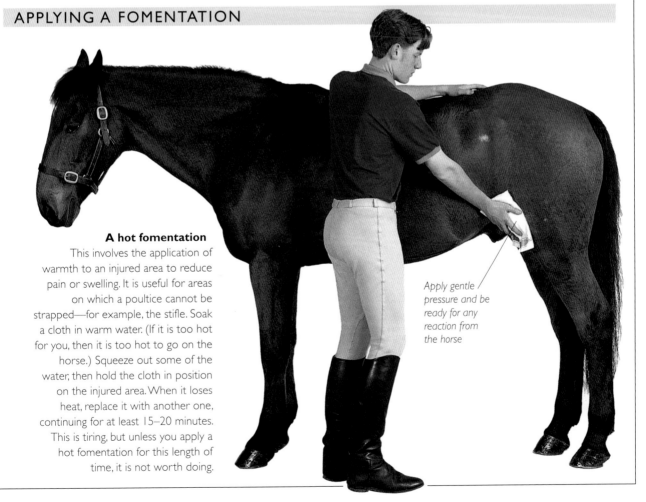

A hot fomentation
This involves the application of warmth to an injured area to reduce pain or swelling. It is useful for areas on which a poultice cannot be strapped—for example, the stifle. Soak a cloth in warm water. (If it is too hot for you, then it is too hot to go on the horse.) Squeeze out some of the water, then hold the cloth in position on the injured area. When it loses heat, replace it with another one, continuing for at least 15–20 minutes. This is tiring, but unless you apply a hot fomentation for this length of time, it is not worth doing.

Apply gentle pressure and be ready for any reaction from the horse

BANDAGING A KNEE

Applying a figure-eight bandage

A horse's knees are vulnerable to injury, but prompt first aid can speed up healing tremendously. A figure-eight bandage is necessary to hold a dressing in place on the moving joint.

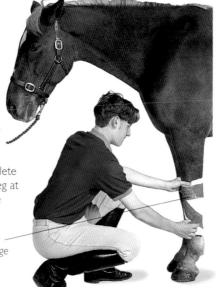

1 Dress the wound, then wrap padding around the leg. Anchor this padding at the top with two or three turns of bandage. Bring the bandage diagonally down across the knee, and make a complete turn around the leg at the bottom of the padding.

Hold the padding in place as you bandage

ZIP-UP BANDAGE

A commercial zip-up bandage is particularly useful if a dressing needs to be changed often, because it is easy to put on and take off. Wrap the bandage around the knee, and secure it in position with the Velcro fastenings. Then close the zipper, being careful not to catch any hairs or dressing in the teeth.

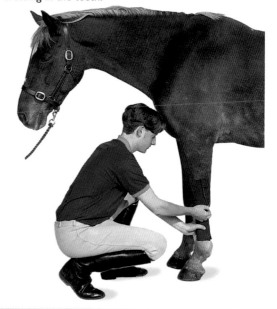

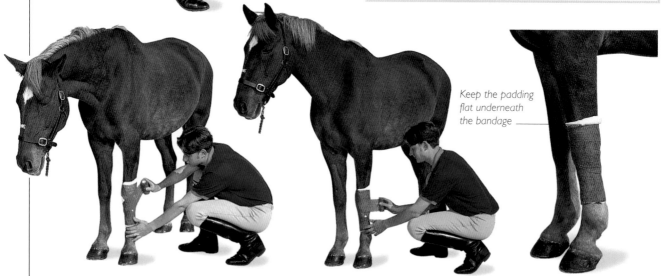

Keep the padding flat underneath the bandage

2 Take the bandage diagonally up across the knee again to produce a cross of bandage on the front of the knee. This applies pressure to a wound on the knee and will not be disturbed when the horse moves its leg.

3 Bandage around the leg at the top and then work downward in the normal way. Overlap at least half of the previous layer of bandage with each new turn until you reach the bottom of the padding. If the bandage is long enough, make a second figure-eight before finishing off.

4 The finished bandage looks just like an ordinary one because the figure-eight is covered. When you bandage, make sure that you keep the same tension throughout and that each layer lies flat.

BANDAGING A HOCK

Covering the hock joint

The hock is awkward to bandage in the ordinary way, because the layers of bandage tend to part above and below the point of the hock when the horse moves its leg. Use a figure-eight bandage instead.

Never kneel on the ground when dealing with a horse's leg; always crouch

1 Make a figure-eight, crossing the bandage over the point of the hock. The first rounds must be tight enough to secure the dressing, but not too tight on the achilles tendon, which runs up the back of the leg above the hock.

2 Finish off the bandage securely. This is especially important with a hock bandage because, if it starts to unravel, the horse will kick out and may reopen the wound.

ROBERT JONES BANDAGE

Life-saving strength

A Robert Jones bandage may save your horse's life. When properly applied, it will immobilize a leg so that even broken bones cannot move. The horse can then be transported for surgery. If a horse will not take any weight on a leg, and you do not know why, apply this bandage immediately so that the problem cannot get any worse.

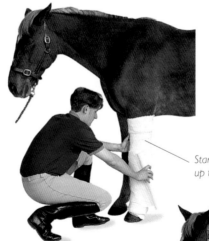

1 You will need at least four wide rolls of sheet cotton and two or three self-adhesive bandages. Wrap the whole leg in two layers of sheet cotton, then bandage tightly around them. This stabilizes the whole bandage, and ensures that it fits securely around the joints. Apply two more layers of sheet cotton.

Start the bandage as high up the leg as you can

Use more than one bandage to cover the leg properly

2 Next, tightly wrap the whole leg again with a cohesive bandage, which will not come loose. The sheet cotton must be tightly compressed.

3 The finished bandage must extend from the top of the leg down to the hoof to be effective. The horse should be unable to move its leg in a Robert Jones bandage.

ICE PACKS

Applying an ice pack

The application of cold to an inflamed area reduces swelling, heat, and pain. If a horse's leg becomes swollen and you do not know the cause, apply cold to the affected area as your first aid.

1 First, protect the leg with a layer of gauze (half a thickness of sheet cotton is fine), so that the ice pack is not in direct contact with the skin. Place the pack directly over and around the swollen area.

PEA PACK

A bag of frozen peas make a good ice pack in an emergency. As the peas thaw, however, the bandage will become loose.

Use a thin layer of padding between the peas and the leg

2 Apply a layer of sheet cotton as insulation to keep the cold in, then bandage the pack in place. The pack may be heavy, so the bandage will need to be quite tight to prevent the pack from moving around on the leg.

COLD HOSING

Simple hosing

Cold-water hosing can be as effective as ice in cooling the leg, but takes more time. Stand the horse near a drain.

Hosing boot

A hosing boot holds water fed in from a hose. Fix it to a flexible hose, so it does not restrict movement of the leg too much.

HOT TUBBING

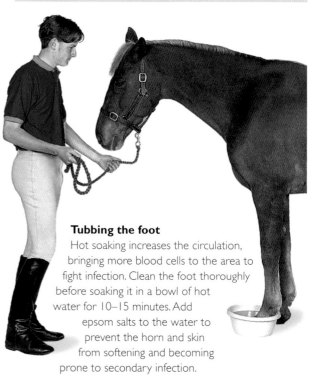

Tubbing the foot

Hot soaking increases the circulation, bringing more blood cells to the area to fight infection. Clean the foot thoroughly before soaking it in a bowl of hot water for 10–15 minutes. Add epsom salts to the water to prevent the horn and skin from softening and becoming prone to secondary infection.

APPLYING A POULTICE

Poulticing a foot

A hot poultice provides warmth to the infected area. Chemicals in a ready-made poultice draw fluid and pus out of the wound. Kaolin clay is also effective, but it is messy.

In an emergency, use a hot bran mash. A poultice must be changed at least every 12 hours because it loses heat and gets contaminated with pus.

1 Cut the poultice dressing to the approximate size of the foot, allowing an overlap all around.

Use safety scissors if you are cutting near a horse

2 Soak the dressing in warm water— not boiling, which would scald you and the horse. Allow it to drain.

3 Place the dressing over the foot. Fold the edges over the hoof to secure it. It is vital that the poultice does not come off.

4 Use a self-adhesive bandage to keep the dressing in place. Start by wrapping the bandage around the wall of the foot, with about a third of the width projecting below the foot. Make two or three turns around to make sure the bandage is firm.

The projecting part of the bandage will curl over the sole

5 Bring the roll of bandage across the sole, and make a further turn around the wall of the foot to secure this length.

Do not let the poultice move while you are bandaging

6 Cross over the sole in the other direction, to produce an "X" of bandage over the sole. Anchor it with another turn around the wall of the foot.

Keep the horse's foot off the ground until you have finished bandaging

Anchor the bandage with a turn around the foot each time you go across the sole

7 Make as many crosses over the foot as the length of bandage will allow. Smooth down all the edges to stick them firmly to the layers underneath. You have now made a bandage boot.

NURSING A HORSE

When a hospital says that a patient is "comfortable," it does not mean that the person is free from pain, but that everything has been done to make life as pleasant as possible in the circumstances. This is what nursing is all about. When a horse needs nursing, keep it in a large, well-lit, draft-free stall. There should be an electrical socket and a source of hot water nearby. A sick horse needs constant attention to keep it warm, clean, and, if its condition permits, well fed. You must be on hand to respond to its needs and any change in its condition.

Nebulizer
Nebulizers can be an effective way to deliver drugs to the lungs as a treatment for respiratory and other conditions. They produce a fine mist of liquid droplets that are small enough to be carried right down into the lungs. There, the drug is absorbed through the very thin blood-vessel walls into the circulating blood.

Giving medicines
These can be mixed with a small amount of the horse's normal feed. If it refuses this, try adding a strong flavor such as molasses, or hiding the drug in a hollowed-out apple or carrot.

Many medicines now come as granules rather than powder

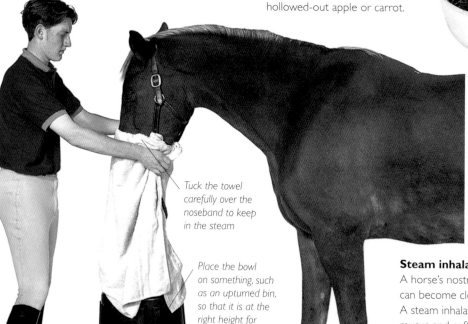

Tuck the towel carefully over the noseband to keep in the steam

Place the bowl on something, such as an upturned bin, so that it is at the right height for the horse

Steam inhalation
A horse's nostrils and airways can become clogged with mucus. A steam inhalation will loosen the mucus and soften any crusting, which might be uncomfortable. Put a few drops of a vapor inhalant into a bowl of hot water. Wrap a towel around the bowl and loosely around the horse's muzzle, so that the horse can breathe only the air containing the medicated steam.

A buildup of straw under the belly restricts movement

Feeling the ears
You can tell whether a horse is feeling cold by feeling its ears gently. Some horses also enjoy being touched in this way. If the horse is cold, put on a blanket. (The ears will not tell you if the horse has a high temperature.)

Providing adequate bedding
Give a sick horse plenty of bedding to lie on, but do not make it too thick, especially if it is straw. If a horse stands miserably shifting its feet, it may build up a pile of straw between its legs that makes further movement difficult. If this starts to happen, move the horse and redistribute the straw.

Keep a blanket over the horse's back to prevent it from getting chilled

Normal routine
Horses like routine, and when they are sick this is all the more important. Give meals and do other tasks at the normal times. Grooming is vital, even for very sick horses; it really freshens them up. If possible, keep the horse within sight of its usual companions and have it nursed by familiar people.

Disinfection
If a horse has an infectious disease, dip its grooming kit in diluted disinfectant after every use, to prevent the spread of infection.

FOALING: THE BIRTH

When the mare's long pregnancy comes to an end, we want the foaling itself to go without a hitch. Because foaling occurs so quickly in mares, you can literally see a pregnant mare with no signs of foaling one minute, go away for half an hour, and return to find a mare and healthy foal. This rapid foaling process leaves you very little time to correct any problems that may occur. It is therefore important to be able to recognize what is happening and to know whether your mare and foal need help or not.

You should always make your preparations well before the foaling date. Keep your vet's telephone number at hand and alert any experienced friends who are going to help you.

Pregnant mother

It is difficult to predict when a mare will give birth. A normal pregnancy may last as little as 310 days or as long as 365 days, although the average is 340 days. When the first stage of labor starts, the mare feels abdominal pain from the contractions and so may roll, lie down, and look at her belly as if she has colic. Beware, though, because mares often have false alarms.

DELIVERY

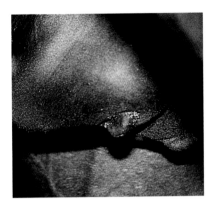

Mare with waxed-up teats
The only visible clue that the birth is imminent is the appearance of drops of honey- or waxlike secretion on the mare's teats. Although not infallible, this usually appears 2–3 days before foaling.

Mare with membranes showing
At the second stage of labor, the mare strains very forcibly. The first thing to appear are the membranes containing the fluid in which the foal has been suspended inside the uterus.

The foal appears
Once the membranes burst, one front leg appears, quickly followed by the other. If it doesn't, or if just a foot appears and after a few minutes of straining, no progress is made, summon help at once.

Mare with both front legs and head of foal showing
By the time the front half of the foal has emerged, its hips will be passing through the mare's pelvic canal. Sometimes the foal can become stuck at this point, with potentially serious consequences. Do not be afraid to give a helping hand by pulling on both legs simultaneously. If the foal still seems stuck, summon help immediately.

The final stages
Even before the foal is fully born, you may see movement of the legs or head. Time is now critical. Call your vet if neither you nor the mare can deliver the foal completely within 2 to 3 minutes. When the birth is over, don't move the foal or tie off the umbilical cord that connects its blood circulation to its mother.

CARE AFTER THE BIRTH

Resist the temptation to help lift the foal up unless the foal still has not stood after an hour; you could hinder the foal-and- mother bond from developing naturally. When possible, check that the entire placenta has been expelled. Even small portions left inside the mare can result in serious or even fatal illness. It should be Y-shaped, with rounded ends to each arm. If in doubt, get an expert to check it for you.

A foal can trot and even gallop alongside its mother within 24 hours of its birth. Make sure the mare does not stay on the move all the time, because the foal can get exhausted and too weak to nurse properly. You should always be concerned if a foal stops suckling, ceases to follow its mother around, repeatedly stands with its tail raised, or seems sleepy.

Don't be concerned if a foal has diarrhea for a couple of days when it is between 3 and 10 days old. The diarrhea will usually clear up without treatment, although if you are in any doubt, consult your vet.

BREECH BIRTH

Most foals are born head end first, but it is not a problem if the birth is breech or backwards. It just means you have to be alert for the hips to become stuck in the pelvis a little earlier in the proceedings.

FOALING: EARLY DAYS

There is no sight more appealing than that of a newborn foal struggling to its feet and taking its first drink. Being born safely is only the start of a foal's potential problems. The first few days may affect its whole life. Foals that do not receive enough of their mother's first milk, or colostrum, will remain significantly more susceptible to infections for many months. The first few hours after the birth are also important for the mother. She is particularly vulnerable to infection or damage to her uterus at this time. Get a vet to check her within 24 hours of foaling.

FIRST STEPS

Foal in the process of standing
The first few hours of a foal's life are very important. The first skill it must learn is how to stand on its own four feet. Miraculously, it will probably be able to do this within an hour of its birth. Do not worry that it falls over many times in the process; it will not hurt itself when this happens.

Foal suckling
The next skill to be learned is how to suckle. It is quite normal for a foal to try suckling between the front legs instead of the back legs—in fact, everywhere but the udder. Most foals suckle within 2 hours. You can help to point the foal in the right direction, but, frustratingly, you cannot make it suckle. Some mares take a little time to stand still enough for the foal to suckle, especially with their first foal. The foal must have the mare's first milk within 24 hours.

CHAPTER SEVEN

TACK AND CLOTHING

HORSE TACK AND CLOTHING TEND TO BE EXPENSIVE,

WHICH IS ONE REASON WHY YOU SHOULD CARE FOR

THEM. ANOTHER IMPORTANT REASON TO KEEP THEM

CLEAN AND IN GOOD CONDITION IS TO PROTECT THE

HORSE: DIRT CAUSES SKIN PROBLEMS. POORLY FITTING

TACK, BLANKETS, AND BOOTS ARE UNCOMFORTABLE

FOR THE HORSE AND MAY CAUSE AN ACCIDENT IF

THEY MOVE OR COME OFF SUDDENLY. IT MAY BE

TIME-CONSUMING TO PUT ON TACK AND CLOTHING

CAREFULLY AND CORRECTLY, BUT YOUR HORSE

WILL BE MORE COMFORTABLE AND RESPOND

MORE WILLINGLY IF YOU DO.

SADDLES AND GIRTHS

A saddle stops a horse's spine from digging into the rider and spreads the rider's weight across the horse's back. It is built around a frame called a tree, which you should protect by storing the saddle on a rack. If the tree breaks, the saddle is useless and hurts the horse. Buy the best saddle you can afford. The best ones are made of leather. Part-fabric or synthetic saddles are cheaper but do not last as long. Faulty stitching, lack of keepers to hold the end of a strap in place, partially severed straps, and rusty buckles all pose potential dangers to the rider.

THE SADDLE

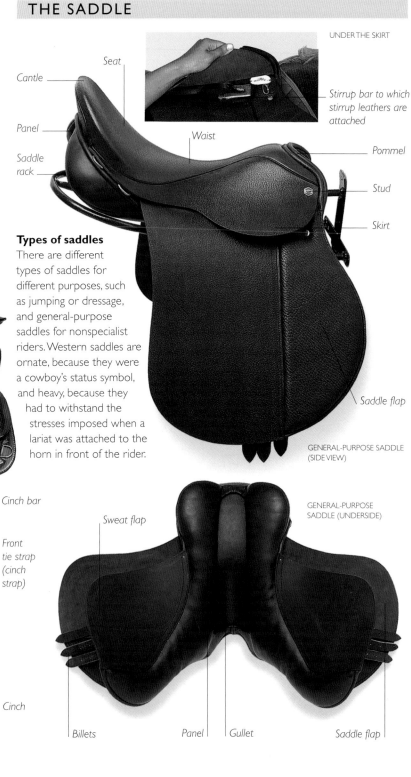

UNDER THE SKIRT

Seat

Cantle

Panel

Saddle rack

Waist

Stirrup bar to which stirrup leathers are attached

Pommel

Stud

Skirt

Saddle flap

GENERAL-PURPOSE SADDLE (SIDE VIEW)

Types of saddles
There are different types of saddles for different purposes, such as jumping or dressage, and general-purpose saddles for nonspecialist riders. Western saddles are ornate, because they were a cowboy's status symbol, and heavy, because they had to withstand the stresses imposed when a lariat was attached to the horn in front of the rider.

Cantle

Seat

Horn

Flank girth billet

Fender

Cinch bar

Front tie strap (cinch strap)

Cinch

Stirrup

WESTERN SADDLE

Sweat flap

Billets

Panel

Gullet

Saddle flap

GENERAL-PURPOSE SADDLE (UNDERSIDE)

SADDLE PADS

Rectangular pad
A saddle pad keeps the underside of the saddle clean and absorbs sweat, which would otherwise allow the saddle to slip around and rub the horse. It can be made from a variety of materials, but some synthetic materials do not absorb moisture well.

Fitted pad
This type of saddle pad is used to protect the horse's back as well as to absorb sweat. It is usually cut in the shape of a saddle. Do not use one as permanent padding for a poorly fitting or badly stuffed saddle—such a saddle should be replaced or restuffed.

Gel pad
A pad made of thermoplastic elastomer gel ensures an even contact between the horse and saddle, and is good for a horse with a sore back. The gel distributes pressure so that it is applied evenly all over.

GIRTHS

Leather girth
Leather is strong and does not stretch much, but it collects sweat and dirt. This makes the girth hard and uncomfortable for the horse if not kept clean. This balding girth is one of several types. It is designed to be narrow behind the horse's elbow without losing strength.

Three separate pieces can move over each other, making the girth more comfortable for the horse

Two buckles spread the tension evenly and provide a backup if one breaks

Roller buckles enable smooth adjustment

The PVC girth is shaped and padded to ensure that it does not pinch the horse's skin behind its elbows

Padded girth
A textured girth is more breathable and grips better than leather, so it is less likely to rub and cause soars. It can be cleaned easily with a sponge.

BRIDLES AND BITS

The bridle enables the rider to control the horse's head. There are two basic kinds of bridle: the snaffle bridle with a single rein, and the double bridle, with two bits—a bridoon, which is a type of snaffle, and a curb bit—with a rein each. Most bridles are made of leather. You should aim to ride your horse in the simplest bridle and bit possible. A double bridle should be used only to give you more precise control over a willing and well-trained horse, not as a means of controlling an unwilling one.

THE BRIDLE

The parts of a snaffle bridle

This simple bridle consists of one set of reins, a browband, a noseband, a crownpiece and throatlatch, two cheekpieces, and a bit. The separate pieces can be taken apart for cleaning, for attaching a different type of noseband or bit, or for substituting a piece that fits better.

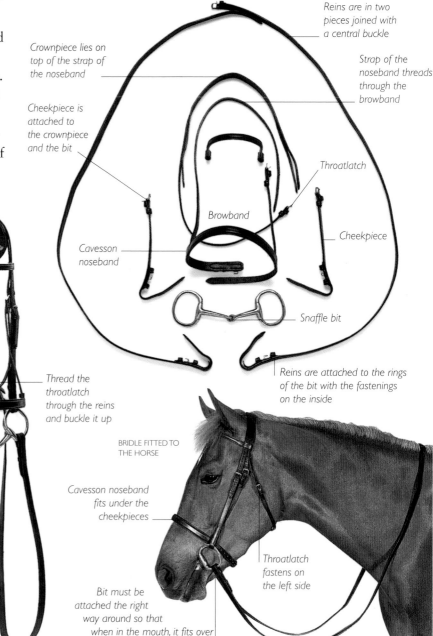

Storing

When off the horse, the bridle should be hung from the crownpiece. It is best to use a broad, circular or semicircular support so that the leather is not bent too sharply. Do not store the bridle, or any tack, in a damp place, because the leather will get moldy and deteriorate.

Reins are in two pieces joined with a central buckle

Strap of the noseband threads through the browband

Crownpiece lies on top of the strap of the noseband

Cheekpiece is attached to the crownpiece and the bit

Throatlatch

Browband

Cheekpiece

Cavesson noseband

Snaffle bit

Reins are attached to the rings of the bit with the fastenings on the inside

Thread the throatlatch through the reins and buckle it up

BRIDLE FITTED TO THE HORSE

Wrap the noseband around the cheekpieces and secure by the keepers

Cavesson noseband fits under the cheekpieces

Throatlatch fastens on the left side

Hang the reins symmetrically

Bit must be attached the right way around so that when in the mouth, it fits over the tongue and does not pinch

Drop noseband
This is used only with a snaffle bit. It stops a horse from getting its tongue over the bit and from opening its mouth wide. It must sit above the nostrils so that it does not restrict breathing.

Cheekpiece must be in front of the line of the lips

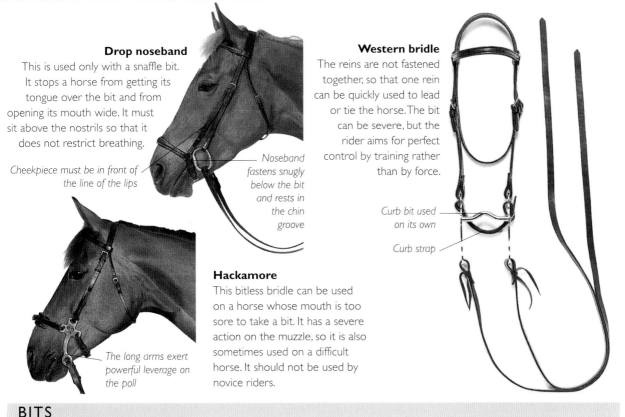

Noseband fastens snugly below the bit and rests in the chin groove

Western bridle
The reins are not fastened together, so that one rein can be quickly used to lead or tie the horse. The bit can be severe, but the rider aims for perfect control by training rather than by force.

Curb bit used on its own

Curb strap

The long arms exert powerful leverage on the poll

Hackamore
This bitless bridle can be used on a horse whose mouth is too sore to take a bit. It has a severe action on the muzzle, so it is also sometimes used on a difficult horse. It should not be used by novice riders.

BITS

Action of the bit
The bit fits over the tongue and rests on the bars of the mouth. Many bits have been designed, appropriate to different situations. Use the simplest bit you can. Usually, the thicker and smoother the mouthpiece, the softer it is.

Vulcanite mouthpiece feels softer than steel

Mullen-mouth snaffle
The straight bar can be made of steel, vinyl, vulcanite, or rubber. The horse can soften its effect by pressing upward with its tongue.

Port, or tongue groove

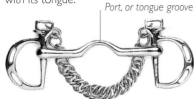

Kimblewick
The "ported" mouthpiece of this single-rein pelham puts pressure on the roof, but allows more room for the tongue.

Smooth side-joint reduces pinching

French-link eggbutt snaffle
French-link bits have a flat plate that lies across the tongue, eliminating any pinching action. One of the softest bits, this snaffle has a curved mouthpiece, so it sits comfortably in the horse's mouth.

Curb chain

Mullen-mouth pelham
A strong bit, the mullen-mouth pelham is used instead of two bits in a double bridle. It is used with a curb chain, which applies pressure to the groove under a horse's chin.

Single-jointed steel mouthpiece

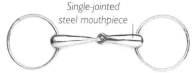

Loose-ring snaffle
Like the eggbutt snaffle, the loose-ring snaffle is a simple bit. The rings can move freely through the mouthpiece, but there is a danger that they may trap and pinch the corners of the mouth.

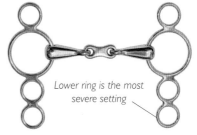

Lower ring is the most severe setting

Elevator bit (French-link gag)
Gag bits exert pressure on the horse's mouth and its poll. Double reins should be attached to the main snaffle ring and either of the lower rings. The more rings the gag has, the more severe its action.

FITTING TACK

It is in the interests of both horse and rider that the tack fits properly. If it does not, it will be painful for the horse, which may cause it to resist the aids given by the rider. A saddle should be specific to a horse. You may need to have one made to measure for some horses, to ensure that it fits perfectly. Loose-fitting tack may fail to pass a given signal to the horse, or may come off, causing a serious accident. If you doubt the equipment you are using, consult an expert at your local tack shop.

THE SADDLE

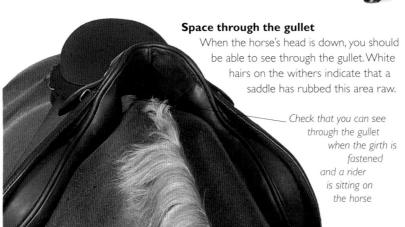

The saddle should not be so long that it puts weight on the horse's loins

Position
The saddle should lie straight on the horse's back, resting on the ribs, not the spine. The sides of the horse's chest are nearly parallel at this point, and this helps to keep the saddle in place.

The saddle must be fitted without a saddle pad

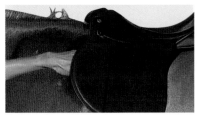

Space through the gullet
When the horse's head is down, you should be able to see through the gullet. White hairs on the withers indicate that a saddle has rubbed this area raw.

Check that you can see through the gullet when the girth is fastened and a rider is sitting on the horse

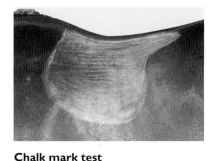

Chalk mark test
Dust the saddle's underside with chalk and place it on the horse. When you remove it, a chalk mark will show if the saddle has been touching the horse where it should not.

Correct width
A saddle must be the same width as the horse's shoulders. If it is too narrow, it will pinch the spine and restrict movement. If it is too wide, it will be low on the withers.

Height of the pommel
The pommel lies over the withers. It must be high enough to allow the horse to lift its head up without causing the withers to press against the pommel.

Snug fit
A well-fitting saddle sits securely even before the girth is fastened. If it moves around too much while you are riding, it will rub the horse's back.

THE BRIDLE

Tightness of the noseband
A cavesson noseband is done up loosely, with room for two fingers between it and the nose. A drop noseband should be tighter, because it is meant to keep the bit in place and stop the horse from opening its mouth too wide.

Level of the noseband
The noseband should lie about midway between the mouth and the projecting cheekbones. You should be able to fit two fingers below the cheekbone. The sidepieces of the noseband must not touch the horse's eyes.

The throatlatch helps to keep the bridle in place

Throatlatch
The throatlatch must be long enough to allow four fingers between it and the horse when it is fastened. If it is tighter, it can interfere with the horse's breathing.

The browband lies under the forelock

Browband
You should be able to fit two fingers under the browband. It must not pull the crownpiece and cheekpieces, but should allow them to lie in a straight line.

The noseband sits on the bridge of the nose

Front view
Look carefully at the bridle on the horse's head from the front. Make sure that it is straight and positioned symmetrically on both sides.

Fitting the bit correctly
A badly fitting bit will be uncomfortable for the horse and can injure the mouth. All bits should lie in the corners of the mouth without wrinkling the lips too much. The horse should look as if it is smiling. If the bit is too high, it will rub the corners of the mouth; if it is too low, it may hit the teeth. The mouthpiece of the bit should protrude approximately ¼ in (5 mm) on each side when you hold the joint straight in the mouth. If it is too wide, it will move from side to side and rub; but if it is too narrow, it will pinch the lips.

CORRECT FIT

TOO HIGH

TOO LOW

TOO WIDE

TOO NARROW

PUTTING ON A SADDLE

You should not tack up a horse until you are ready to ride. Brush off any stable or sweat marks, and any dry mud, especially where the girth and saddle will be. Put the saddle on first. Some horses tend to expand their chests when the saddle is first put on but later relax, leaving the girth loose. By the time you have put on the bridle, your horse will have relaxed, and you can then tighten the girth before you mount. Do not leave a horse standing with its saddle on when you are done riding. If it wants to roll, it will do so even with the saddle in place. This may not only damage the saddle but also hurt the horse's back.

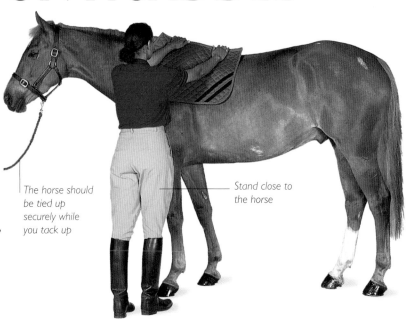

The horse should be tied up securely while you tack up

Stand close to the horse

1 Approach the horse slowly, talking to it all the time. Smooth down the hair on the back, then lay the saddle pad over the withers and saddle area. Put the pad farther forward than the final position of the saddle, to allow you to move it and the saddle back together later, along the lay of the coat.

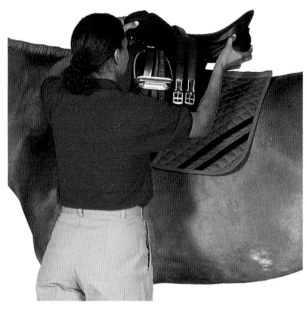

2 Check that the stirrups are run up, and that the girth is fastened on one side and folded over the saddle. Place the saddle on the pad, lowering it vertically so that you do not move the pad. Do not pull the saddle or pad forward, because this will rub the horse's hair the wrong way.

3 Hold the saddle pad well up in the arch and gullet of the saddle, then move the saddle and saddle cloth backward together until the saddle sits in its correct position behind the withers. Attach the saddle pad to the saddle by threading the middle girth strap through the loop provided on the pad.

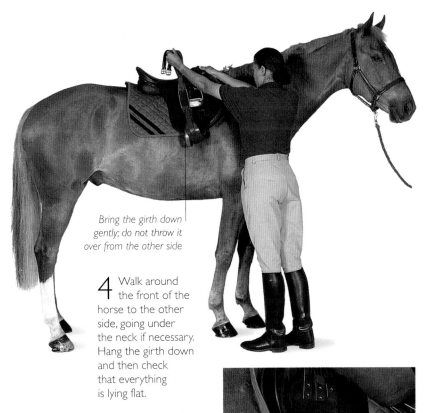

Bring the girth down gently; do not throw it over from the other side

4 Walk around the front of the horse to the other side, going under the neck if necessary. Hang the girth down and then check that everything is lying flat.

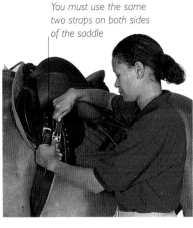

You must use the same two straps on both sides of the saddle

5 Walk back around the horse and fasten the girth. Attach one buckle to the front strap. This strap is fixed to the saddle separately so that if it breaks, the other one will hold the girth, and vice versa. Pull the girth tight without wrinkling the skin.

6 Pull the buckle guards down over the buckles of the girth. This stops the buckles from moving around or digging into your legs while you are riding, and prevents them from rubbing and damaging the saddle.

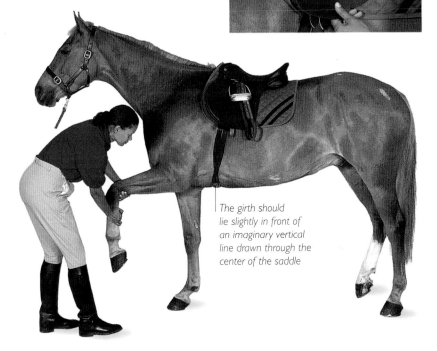

The girth should lie slightly in front of an imaginary vertical line drawn through the center of the saddle

Run the stirrups up the leathers and thread the leathers through them

Removing the saddle
Undo the girth on one side, then cross it over the saddle. Take hold of both saddle and saddle pad and lift them off together, moving them backward slightly as you do so.

7 After you have checked and tightened the girth, pull each foreleg forward to make sure that no skin is wrinkled under the girth. If the horse reacts as you tighten the girth, it may be a bad habit, but it could be because of a back problem or a painful saddle.

PUTTING ON A BRIDLE

Put the bridle on after the saddle. Carry it on one arm by the crownpiece and the reins, with the browband pointing toward your elbow. Make sure you will be able to put it on without having to untangle it or untwist straps. Approach the horse from the front, so that it can see what you have in your hands. Try not to let a metal bit clink as you walk, because some horses will react to the noise. Always have some means of restraint on the horse's head or neck while you are putting on the bridle so that you can stop it from walking off. Do not let the horse escape from you with the bridle hanging half on, because it could easily get a leg caught in the reins.

The stirrups should always be run up until you are ready to mount

1 Untie the horse, then undo the halter, slip it off the horse's muzzle, and fasten it around the neck. Stand on the left side of the horse, take the reins in your right hand, and put them over the horse's head. Alternatively, you could put the reins over the head, then remove the halter.

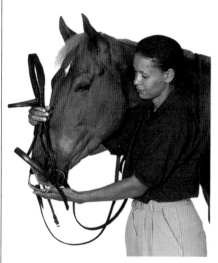

2 Put your right arm under the horse's jaw and hold the cheekpieces of the bridle together in front of its face. Rest the bit on your left hand, just under the muzzle. The noseband will encircle the horse's jaws.

3 Move the bridle gently up the horse's face. When the bit touches the horse's mouth, insert your thumb gently between the lips at the corner, so that it presses slightly on the gum in the gap between the horse's teeth. This should encourage the horse to open its mouth.

5 Check that all the parts of the bridle are lying straight and flat before fastening the buckles. Do the throatlatch up first, so that if the horse pulls away from you, it will not pull the bridle off. It is the throatlatch that keeps the bridle on. Fasten it loosely (see p. 181).

4 Bring the crownpiece up over the horse's ears one at a time, taking care not to let the bit drop out of the horse's mouth. Carefully fit both ears between the browband and the crownpiece, and check that all the horse's forelock is lying free over the browband.

Put the end of each strap through its keeper and runner

6 Finally, fasten the noseband. A cavesson noseband should be fastened loosely and should lie next to the horse's face, underneath the cheekpieces. A drop noseband should be fastened tighter and lie below the bit (see p. 181).

Removing the bridle

When you remove the bridle, first fasten a halter loosely around the horse's neck. Undo the noseband and then the throatlatch on the bridle. Bring the reins up the horse's neck, and take hold of them and the crownpiece in one hand. Pull them all gently over both ears at once, and lower the bridle slowly down the front of the horse's face. The horse will ease the bit out of its mouth, and the noseband will fall away of its own accord. Do not pull the bridle off too quickly and bang the bit against the horse's teeth.

LEAVING A HORSE TACKED UP SAFELY

If you have to leave a horse tacked up, twist the reins loosely and fasten the throatlatch through them. Secure the stirrups so that they cannot swing around. Put a halter on over the bridle and tie the horse up.

Pass the stirrup leathers through the stirrups, and thread the loose ends through the loops

EXTRA EQUIPMENT

The bridle and saddle are the means by which we stay on the horse and control where it goes, but in some cases, extra equipment may be needed. For example, some horses have a shape that makes it difficult for them to wear a saddle without it slipping backward. In such cases, a breastplate or a breastgirth may be necessary. There are also horses who throw their heads around; for these horses, a martingale is used to restrict their head movements. Take care not to use extra items of tack unless you have first checked that they really are necessary: a breastplate is no substitute for a properly fitting saddle, and you should not use a martingale to mask a painful mouth that causes resentment of the bit.

BREASTPLATE

Features and fitting

A breastplate is a fixed loop that passes around the horse's neck, and is anchored to the saddle by a strap on each side, and to the girth by a strap between the legs. At rest, the breastplate should allow four fingers between it and the horse's shoulder. Check that none of the straps is twisted.

BREASTGIRTH

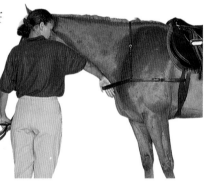

Features and fitting

A breastgirth is a strap that is fixed to the girth on both sides, passing around the breast. A strap over the neck stops it from slipping down around the legs. A breastgirth should lie more or less parallel to the ground and, as with the breast plate, should allow four fingers to fit between it and the horse when at rest.

USING A RUNNING MARTINGALE

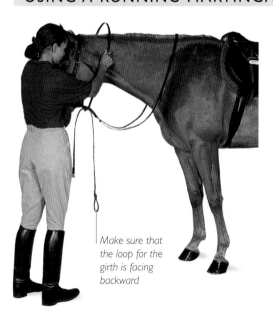

Make sure that the loop for the girth is facing backward

1 A running martingale is a strap that attaches to the girth. It is split in two, with a ring on the end of each part through which the reins are allowed to run freely. It is supported by a neck strap. It helps a rider to control a horse that tends to carry its head too high. When using a running martingale, put the saddle and bridle on first. Pass the neck strap of the martingale over the head and the reins.

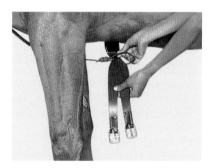

2 Unbuckle the girth, and pass it through the loop on the end of the martingale's girth strap. (This loop has a buckle, which you should use to adjust the length of the martingale— see *step 3*.) Fasten the girth of the saddle again.

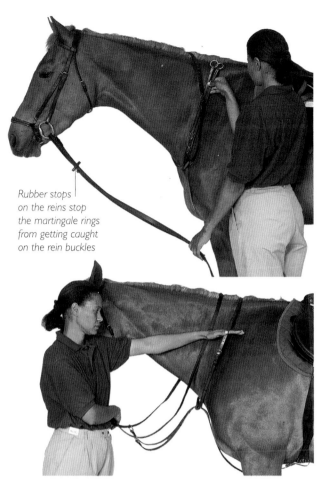

Rubber stops on the reins stop the martingale rings from getting caught on the rein buckles

3 The first time you put on the martingale, check the length of the ringed straps. It is these that apply pressure to the bit via the reins if the horse lifts its head. Adjust the length so that they reach together to the top of the neck near the withers.

4 Separate the reins by undoing the buckle. Thread one rein through each ring, then re-buckle the reins. Make sure that neither the reins nor the martingale straps are twisted.

Use a thick rubber ring, designed for the purpose, to keep the neck strap and martingale together

5 Check that the neck strap allows four fingers between it and the horse's neck. When leading a horse that is wearing a running martingale, do not bring the reins over the head, because you will put pressure on the bars of the horse's mouth. For very short distances, hold both reins about 12 in (30 cm) under the horse's chin. Otherwise, unbuckle the reins and tie up the rings, or use a halter.

USING A STANDING MARTINGALE

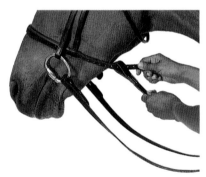

1 A standing martingale has one strap that attaches to the girth and the noseband, and a neck strap. It prevents a horse from lifting its head too high. Fix the martingale to the girth in the same way as a running martingale. Pass the noseband through the loop on the martingale strap and fasten it.

A standing martingale should be used only with a cavesson noseband

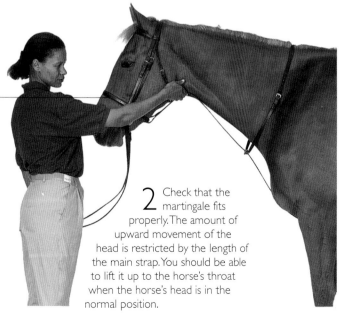

2 Check that the martingale fits properly. The amount of upward movement of the head is restricted by the length of the main strap. You should be able to lift it up to the horse's throat when the horse's head is in the normal position.

LEFT **Bits and bridles** A large variety of bits and bridles are available to a horse owner. Aim to use the simplest tack possible— a horse should be trained to behave as you want rather than forced to do so by harsh bits and complicated tack.

RIGHT **Tack room** Tack should be stored in a dry environment to protect the leather. Never put tack away dirty—it will always be more difficult to clean later. Good storage prolongs the working life of your tack.

BELOW **Strapping up** Either put the saddle on the horse yourself or check it personally before mounting. Watch out that the horse does not breathe in while you fasten the girth—this will result in a loose girth when the horse relaxes.

BOTTOM RIGHT **Attending to blankets** The blankets you use need attention, both on the horse and off it. While a blanket is on the horse, you need to make sure that it does not slip around its legs. When they are not being used, blankets should be kept clean and dry.

CLEANING TACK

Keep tack clean, supple, and in good repair. It is especially important that the bit, girth, and saddle pad are cleaned, otherwise dirt will rub into the horse's skin during riding and cause inflammation and infection. Use saddle soap on leather at least once a week, and clean off dirt after every ride. Check for wear, especially of the stitching, as you clean. If it breaks while you are riding, it could cause an accident and injure both you and the horse. Take the bridle apart for a thorough check once a month, even if you do not ride often. Tack can still deteriorate even when it is not being used.

TACK-CLEANING EQUIPMENT

You should keep all your tack-cleaning equipment together, perhaps in a bucket kept solely for cleaning. Keep it really clean, otherwise it will simply transfer dirt back to the tack. The type of sponge you use is particularly important. You need to be able to squeeze it almost dry. Replace it regularly. There is no point in using one that is falling apart.

BUCKET

SADDLE SOAP

STIFF BRUSH

SPONGE

DAMP CLOTH

POLISHING CLOTH

DRY CLOTH

STABLE RUBBER

METAL POLISH

BRUSH FOR OIL

SADDLE OIL

CLEANING THE BRIDLE

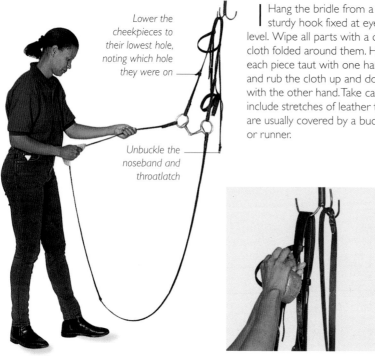

Lower the cheekpieces to their lowest hole, noting which hole they were on

Unbuckle the noseband and throatlatch

1 Hang the bridle from a sturdy hook fixed at eye level. Wipe all parts with a damp cloth folded around them. Hold each piece taut with one hand, and rub the cloth up and down it with the other hand. Take care to include stretches of leather that are usually covered by a buckle or runner.

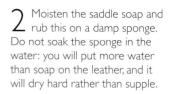

2 Moisten the saddle soap and rub this on a damp sponge. Do not soak the sponge in the water: you will put more water than soap on the leather, and it will dry hard rather than supple.

3 Soap all the leather on both sides by rubbing the sponge up and down. Remember to include the pieces from which the bridle is hanging.

Bit and stirrups

The bit must always be washed after use. Soak it in a bucket of water to wash off dried grass and food. Also soak the stirrup irons to wash off mud. Remove the stirrup leathers first, and then wash the stirrup treads separately if necessary.

Be careful not to put any of the leather in the water—it will damage the leather and any stitching

Polishing metal

Any metalwork that shows can be buffed up with metal polish. Do not use polish on the mouthpiece of the bit. It will taste unpleasant and irritate the horse's mouth.

CLEANING THE SADDLE

1 Remove the girth, the buckle guards, if detachable, and the stirrup leathers. Clean a leather girth and the stirrup leathers in the same way as the bridle. Turn the saddle upside down, and clean the panel and the underside first. Then rest the saddle on a saddle-horse while you do the rest. Start by washing off dirt and grease with a damp cloth.

CLEANING NON-LEATHER GIRTHS

Remove mud and hair with a stiff brush, then soak the girth in soapy water and rinse thoroughly. Do not use detergent, because it can irritate the horse's skin. Clean saddle pads in the same way. Some girths and cloths can be put in a washing machine. They must be completely dry before they are used again.

Brush down in the direction of the grooves

2 Apply saddle soap to all leatherwork with a circular motion. Soap all the crevices between the flaps and straps. Do not soap any cloth or suede areas, but brush them to remove dirt.

3 Oil leatherwork periodically to protect it more, especially the rough underside, because this is the most absorbent. Oil only clean leather. Wipe off excess oil, which could stain your clothes.

STABLE BLANKETS

The top stable door, windows, and air vents should be open year-round in most climates, so a stabled horse, especially one that has been clipped, usually needs to wear a blanket during the winter to keep it warm. Once you have started to use a blanket at night, do not leave it off, even on milder nights, because the horse could get chilled; wait until you can leave it off permanently for the season. Stable blankets have two layers, an outer one for protection and a lining for warmth. The lining should extend over the whole blanket; in cheap blankets, only half the blanket is lined. The outer layer can be made of a variety of materials; the best is linen. There is also a wide range of fastenings, many claiming to hold the blanket in place even if the horse rolls.

PUTTING ON A BLANKET

1 Fold the blanket in half, front to back, with the straps inside. Carry it over your arm, with the front half of the blanket uppermost and the fold away from you. Approach the left side of the horse, and warn it that you are about to put on the blanket by placing your free hand on its shoulder.

2 Throw the folded blanket over the horse's withers. Place it so that the front is just a little farther forward than its final position. Unfold the blanket over the quarters, then pull it back and check that it is lying straight over the back of the horse.

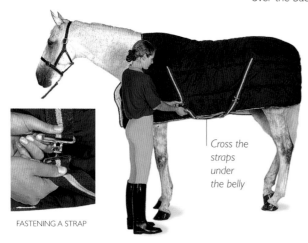

Cross the straps under the belly

FASTENING A STRAP

3 Go around to the other side of the horse to bring down the straps and check that the blanket is flat. Return to the near side to fasten the blanket. Fasten the belly straps first. If the horse escapes, it may panic if the blanket slips and hangs around its neck.

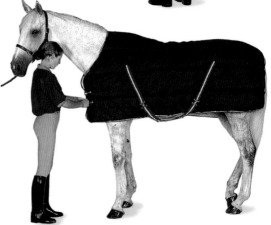

4 Fasten the breast straps. If the blanket is too far forward, pull it back slightly. If it is too far back for the breast straps to be fastened, take it off and start again. Never pull a blanket forward; this rubs the coat hairs the wrong way and causes discomfort.

The correct size

Blankets come in a range of sizes, measured lengthwise. Measure your horse for a blanket from the center of its breastbone along its side to the point of the buttock. A blanket must reach from the withers to the top of the tail. When it is on, you should be able to fit a hand sideways under it at the shoulder and at the breast, without disturbing its position.

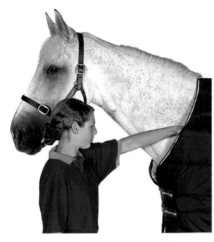

CORRECT FIT AT SHOULDER

The blanket must not be too tight or it will rub the horse

CORRECT FIT AT BREAST

PUTTING ON A LINER AND A SURCINGLE

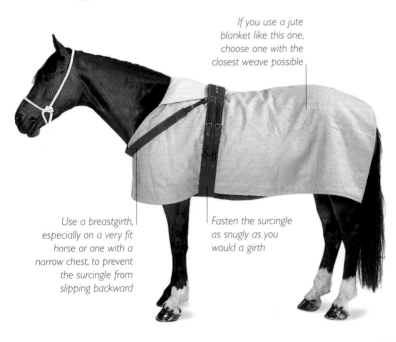

1 If you need to provide extra warmth for a horse, use a liner under the blanket. Place it as far up the horse's neck as possible, with its rear edge reaching the tail. Fold the front corners up to meet on the horse's spine.

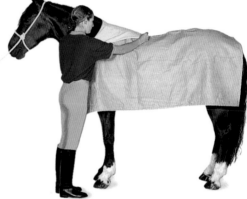

2 Check that the liner is lying flat and hanging evenly on both sides, then put the blanket in place. Be careful to position the blanket correctly without disturbing the liner underneath. Fold the exposed triangle of liner from the neck over on top of the blanket. This helps to stop the liner from slipping.

If you use a jute blanket like this one, choose one with the closest weave possible

Use a breastgirth, especially on a very fit horse or one with a narrow chest, to prevent the surcingle from slipping backward

Fasten the surcingle as snugly as you would a girth

3 When using a blanket with no belly straps, secure it with a surcingle and breastgirth. Fasten the surcingle around the horse just behind the withers. Depending on the style, a surcingle may need extra padding over the spine, such as a piece of sponge placed between it and the blanket.

OTHER BLANKETS

There are a variety of blankets, used mainly to keep a horse warm or as protection from bad weather. Take care when fitting a new blanket, especially a New Zealand: the stiffness of the material or the slight hindrance of movement can upset some horses. Blankets must not be used when dirty. Wash them regularly, including the straps, in a non-irritating laundry detergent, and then rinse and dry them thoroughly.

NEW ZEALAND BLANKET

A New Zealand blanket must be long enough to protect the horse's underside from wind and rain

Main features
The New Zealand blanket is designed to be worn in a field to give protection from wind and cold. Modern versions are light and almost completely waterproof. The fit of this blanket is particularly important, because the material does not mold well to a horse's shape.

Checking a turned-out horse
Keep an eye on a horse that is turned out in a blanket, in case the blanket slips out of place. If it does slip, tie the horse up securely, then take the blanket right off and put it back on again. If you just tug it back into place, you will rub the horse's coat the wrong way.

PROTECTION AGAINST FLIES

Some horses become distracted by flies around their heads. This has been linked to head-shaking behavior, so you may need to use a fly mask to keep flies away from your horse's ears while out riding. Modern, lightweight mesh visors offer coverage from ears to muzzle for sensitive horses, and can be worn in the field to protect against sunburn as well as biting insects.

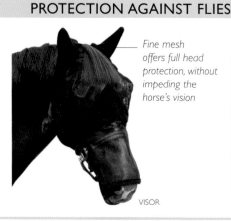

Fine mesh offers full head protection, without impeding the horse's vision

VISOR

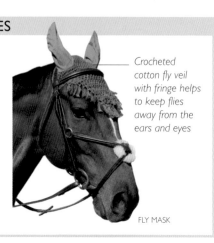

Crocheted cotton fly veil with fringe helps to keep flies away from the ears and eyes

FLY MASK

MORE TYPES OF BLANKET

Waterproof blanket

There are waterproof blankets that are much lighter and more flexible than traditional New Zealand blankets, and provide protection for the head and neck. Some horses resent a head cover at first, so give them time to get used to it before turning them out.

When worn under a light blanket, the mesh allows air pockets to form, providing insulation from the cold

This blanket is shaped to follow the lines of the horse to give a better fit

Anti-sweat sheet

This mesh sheet is used after hard work to provide some warmth against the cooling effect of sweating while still allowing the sweat to evaporate. A anti-sweat sheet, secured with a surcingle, may be used both in the stable and out in the field.

A tail cord, which runs around the back of the hindquarters under the tail, must be used to prevent the sheet from blowing forward

Exercise sheet

Fitted under the saddle, this provides warmth for a clipped horse during slow work. It covers the hindquarters but leaves the shoulders free for movement. An exercise sheet should not be used in fast work, because it will prevent sweat from evaporating and may cause muscles to overheat.

Summer sheet

This is really the summer version of a New Zealand blanket, and is made from lightweight material. The sheet is not waterproof, but it may provide welcome protection from flies and can be used to keep a horse clean. The surcingles, or straps, go from front to back, crossing under the belly, to hold down the light material in the wind.

PROTECTIVE BOOTS

Boots for horses are not fitted over the feet, but are attached to the legs to protect them from injury during exercise, or during turnout in the case of leg protectors. They must be fastened tight enough to prevent chafing, because movement may rub dirt into the skin and start an infection. They should be taken off after work. Various boots are available in different materials. Beware of "scientific" boots that claim to help the horse withstand the stresses of work. Nothing strapped to the leg will do that.

Brushing boots
As the name implies, these boots are worn to prevent brushing (see p. 143). They should be fitted so that the straps are on the outside, and the major protective face is on the inside. They should be worn as one of a pair.

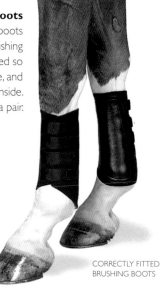

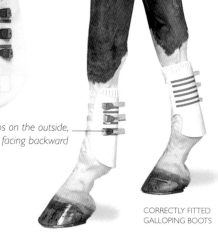

BRUSHING BOOT

CORRECTLY FITTED BRUSHING BOOTS

Galloping boots
These are designed to provide extra protection for the tendons while restricting movement as little as possible. If the horse damages them during fast work, they should be thrown away and a new pair used, because the horse is likely to hit itself again in the same place.

GALLOPING BOOT

The two padded areas should go on either side of the tendons

INSIDE OF GALLOPING BOOT

Straps on the outside, facing backward

CORRECTLY FITTED GALLOPING BOOTS

Bell boots
These boots protect the heel and the lower part of the pastern. Some types are circular and are pulled on over the foot, while others are open and fastened around the pastern with Velcro or a buckle. They are loose-fitting, but must not be too long, which is dangerous because the horse can trip on them. They should just cover the bulb of the heel but not be touching the ground. Remember, they will be nearer the ground in fast work.

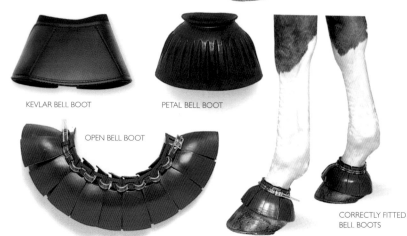

KEVLAR BELL BOOT

PETAL BELL BOOT

OPEN BELL BOOT

CORRECTLY FITTED BELL BOOTS

Fetlock rings

These rings come in different sizes. Large ones are used on an injured leg in the stable. When the horse lies down, the ring lifts the foot and leg off the ground, protecting the pastern, fetlock, and elbow from knocks. Small ones can be worn during exercise on a hind leg, as shown here, to prevent brushing.

FETLOCK RING

CORRECTLY FITTED
FETLOCK RING

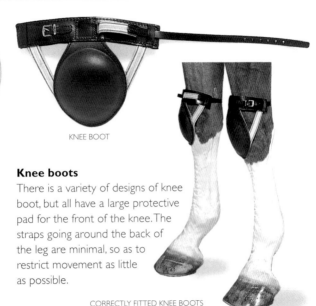

KNEE BOOT

Knee boots

There is a variety of designs of knee boot, but all have a large protective pad for the front of the knee. The straps going around the back of the leg are minimal, so as to restrict movement as little as possible.

CORRECTLY FITTED KNEE BOOTS

Shipping boots

Used only during shipping, these protect the leg from the knee or hock down to the foot. They are used to provide padding, rather than protection from hard knocks sustained at speed, so are made from soft materials.

SHIPPING BOOT FOR
FRONT LEG

CORRECTLY FITTED
FRONT BOOTS

TRAVELLING BOOT FOR
HIND LEG

CORRECTLY FITTED
HIND BOOTS

PUTTING ON SHIPPING BOOTS

1 Wrap the boot around the leg, with the straps on the outside and pointing backward. Place it slightly higher than its final position, with the shaped parts above the joints they are designed to fit. Fasten the middle strap around the leg, to hold the boot in place.

2 Slide the boot downward so that the fetlock and the knee or hock fit into the appropriate parts of the boot, and the top of the hoof is covered. Fasten the lower straps, keeping the pressure even all the way down.

3 Fasten the top straps. The horse will not be doing anything more than a gentle walk, so the boots need to be fastened just tight enough to keep them in place. Finally, check the center strap again. It may now seem too loose.

TAIL AND LEG BANDAGES

There are circumstances other than first aid in which you need to use bandages on a horse. For example, a tail bandage is used to keep the tail clean and prevent the hairs from being rubbed off or caught on something, especially during shipping (*see p. 76*). A bandage can also be used after grooming to encourage the hairs to lie flat (*see p. 67*). Leg bandages are used to provide support, protection from injury, or warmth. They should never be used without some padding between the leg and the bandage. The padding provides extra warmth and helps to keep the pressure even. The method of fastening bandages varies with the make; tapes and Velcro fastenings are common. Keep all the bandages clean by washing carefully and rinsing thoroughly. They must be perfectly dry before you use them again.

BANDAGES AND PADDING

Types of bandages
Tail bandages are fairly thin, and are made of crepe or synthetic material. Exercise bandages are slightly elastic, to enable them to mold to the shape of the legs. Stable bandages are thick, feltlike leg bandages designed to provide warmth rather than fit.

TAIL BANDAGE
3–4 IN (7–10 CM) WIDE

STABLE BANDAGE
4 IN (10 CM) WIDE

EXERCISE BANDAGE
3 IN (7 CM) WIDE

Types of padding
Quilting can become compacted and lose its padding ability with repeated use, but it is easier to shape around the leg than sheet cotton and is more durable. Quilting can be washed to extend its life, but sheet cotton cannot.

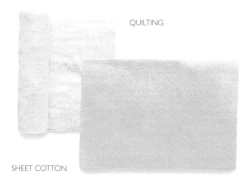

QUILTING

SHEET COTTON

PUTTING ON A TAIL BANDAGE

1 Start bandaging with the straight end forming a point across the base of the tail. Wrap the bandage under and around the tail, keeping it as close to the base as possible.

2 Fold the point over the first circle of bandage and cover it with the second layer. Be sure the bandage is secure at the top, because this will ensure that the finished bandage stays on.

3 Work your way down the tail, overlapping every layer half or two-thirds of the width of the previous layer. Keep the tension firm and even, but not too tight or the bandage will cut off the circulation.

4 Bandage the tail as far down as the tail bones (the dock) extend. This will usually be as far as the groin area at the top of the legs. Then bandage back up the tail.

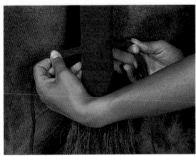

5 The bandage may have two tapes at the end. Separate them, keeping tension on the one pointing away from the bandage or the last layers will come loose.

6 Cross the tapes behind the tail, keeping them flat. Tie them with a bow at the front, being careful to tie them at the same tension as the bandage.

7 Fold a layer of bandage down over the loops and loose ends of the tapes to give a neat finish. This should also stop the tapes from coming undone.

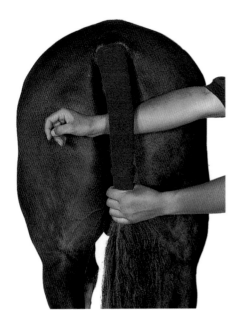

8 Lift the bandaged tail and place an arm underneath it to act as a fulcrum. Gently bend the tail over the arm. This will help it to sit snugly over the horse's buttocks rather than stick straight out behind them.

Removing a tail bandage

Never leave a tail bandage on for more than a few hours, because it can stop the circulation to the tail. When you remove it, untie the tapes, then grasp the sides of the bandage at the top and pull downward with a sharp tug. The tail narrows toward the tip, so the bandage will come off easily.

LEG BANDAGES

Using leg bandages

Stable bandages can be used as support, or to protect veterinary dressings from dirt and from the horse. They can also be used instead of boots (see p. 197) for protection when shipping. Exercise bandages can be used to protect the legs, especially the tendons, from knocks during exercise. Take great care when putting on leg bandages. If they are too tight, they can damage the tendons. If they are too loose, they will fall off and get trapped around the horse's feet.

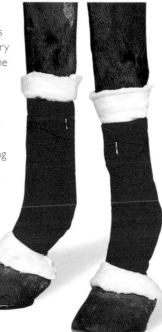

Stable bandage

Always bandage a pair of legs, even if only one is injured, to stop one leg from taking more strain than the other. For shipping, make sure that each bandage extends down over the coronet band.

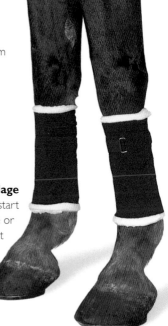

Exercise bandage

The bandages should start just below the knee or hock, and extend to just above the fetlock joint. Ask an expert to help you put them on. Remove them immediately after use.

PUTTING ON A STABLE BANDAGE

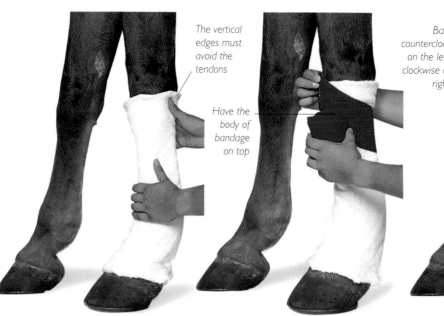

The vertical edges must avoid the tendons

Have the body of bandage on top

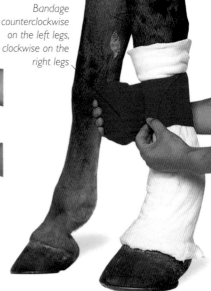

Bandage counterclockwise on the left legs, clockwise on the right legs

1 Wrap padding around the leg, keeping it flat. Overlap it so the outer edge goes counterclockwise on the left legs and clockwise on the right legs.

2 Start at the top. Lay the end of the bandage to form a point at the top, then wrap it around twice, from front to back, in the same direction as the padding.

3 Fold the point down over the turns of bandage, and cover it with another layer to anchor it. Do not pull too hard, or the bandage will move around the leg.

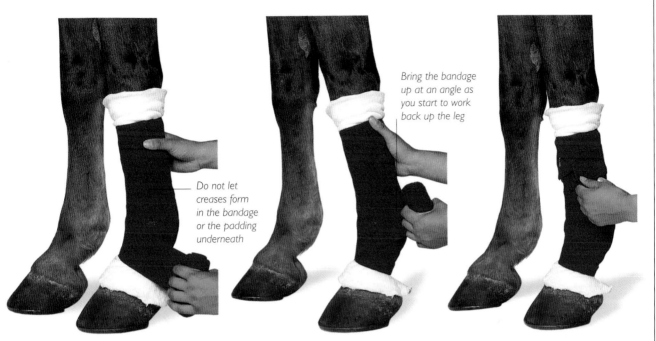

Do not let creases form in the bandage or the padding underneath

Bring the bandage up at an angle as you start to work back up the leg

4 Continue bandaging down the leg, keeping a firm, constant pressure. Overlap each layer about two-thirds of the one above. Take care to maintain the overlaps over the fetlock joint.

5 Work back up the leg. Form a V-shape at the front of the leg between the last layer of bandage going down and the first layer going up. This stops the bandage from moving as the horse moves.

6 Aim to finish the bandage just below the starting point. The fastening may be a Velcro strap or tapes to tie. Try to fasten it on the outside of the leg, so that it does not rub against the other leg.

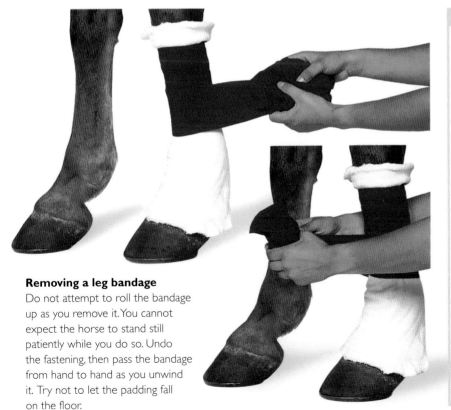

Removing a leg bandage
Do not attempt to roll the bandage up as you remove it. You cannot expect the horse to stand still patiently while you do so. Undo the fastening, then pass the bandage from hand to hand as you unwind it. Try not to let the padding fall on the floor.

ROLLING UP A BANDAGE

You must roll up a bandage properly so that it is the right way around when you use it. Start at the end that has the strap or tapes. Fold it over, then roll the bandage firmly with the fastening on the inside. Try to align the edges neatly.

Start rolling at the end with the strap

CHAPTER EIGHT

HINTS AND TIPS

THE HORSE WORLD IS FULL OF TECHNICAL TERMS. TO

MAKE SURE YOU KNOW WHAT MANY OF THEM MEAN,

THIS SECTION INCLUDES A COMPREHENSIVE GLOSSARY

WHERE THEY ARE BRIEFLY EXPLAINED. THERE ARE

POINTERS ON WHAT TO LOOK FOR WHEN BUYING A

HORSE, TIPS ON HOW TO ORGANIZE YOUR TIME WHEN

YOU OWN A HORSE, AND GUIDELINES FOR CHOOSING

A BOARDING STABLE SHOULD YOU NEED TO. YOU

CANNOT BE EXPECTED TO KNOW EVERYTHING ABOUT

HORSE CARE, SO THE ADDRESSES WILL HELP YOU

FIND OUT MORE. NEVER BE EMBARRASSED TO ASK FOR

HELP; YOUR IGNORANCE MAY HARM THE HORSE.

YEAR-ROUND CARE

The life of a wild horse might seem boring to you, because every day is basically the same, but the horse has evolved with the expectation that every day will be like the others. The domesticated horse must have a regular routine, too, to avoid problems such as colic and azoturia. The best routine is one that you can stick to for 365 days of the year. It has to fit in with weekday activities such as work or school without changing drastically on weekends. If you change it, do so gradually.

Don't forget that it is not just your horse that requires care throughout the year. If you have a paddock, this will also require maintenance. The fences need to be checked regularly—don't wait until your horse has escaped before repairing that weak spot. During the growing season, you will need to be on the lookout for poisonous plants (*see pp. 94–5*). Remember that these will need to be removed at the root rather than simply cut down. The tack will also require attention if you want it to last

for a long time. Any stitching that starts to fray should be replaced at once—the lives of both you and your horse may depend on it. Finally, there is the maintenance of the stable. Vermin control is an obvious matter to attend to, but people often fail to appreciate the fire risk that cobwebs and dust present. Electrical cables and equipment must be checked regularly for the same reason. The charts on these pages will give you detailed ideas about what to do through the seasons.

POSSIBLE ROUTINES FOR KEEPING A HORSE OUTSIDE

DAILY	SUMMER	WINTER
Early	Catch the horse and check for any injuries. Pick out feet, and wipe any discharge from the eyes before it attracts flies. Check water source, or refill a bucket with fresh water. Feed concentrate if necessary.	Catch the horse and check for injury. Check feet for signs of disorders. Check blanket, exchanging for clean, dry one if necessary. Check that water is not frozen. Feed hay, and concentrate if necessary.
Midmorning	Catch the horse for riding. Lightly groom and tack up. On return from riding, untack the horse and wipe down. Pick out feet, put on fly repellent or fringe if necessary, and turn out. Feed if necessary.	Remove blanket, lightly groom, and tack up. Replace blanket after riding, pick out feet, and turn horse out. Feed hay, and concentrate if necessary. Check that boundaries are secure, and remove debris.
Afternoon	Feed concentrate if necessary. Check water source. Check that field boundaries are secure, and remove any debris or large stones. Clean tack.	Catch the horse. Adjust blanket, and check underneath for rubs. Pick out feet and turn out. Feed hay, and concentrate if necessary. Check water supply. Clean tack.
Evening	Catch the horse and check for any signs of lameness or injury. Pick out feet and turn out again. Check water supply. Feed concentrate if necessary.	Catch horse, and check for any signs of lameness or injury. Adjust blanket, and turn out again. Feed hay, and concentrate if necessary. Check water supply.

WEEKLY	MONTHLY	YEARLY
Remove droppings from field. Check field for poisonous plants and remove and burn. Check feed supply. Clean tack thoroughly. Check first-aid kit.	Cut the paddock during the growing season. Check dates of next worming and next visit from farrier. Clean water buckets and troughs.	Arrange dental check and tetanus and other vaccinations. Apply preservative to fencing and shelters. Clear ditches. Follow pasture maintenance procedure.

POSSIBLE ROUTINES FOR KEEPING A HORSE STABLED

DAILY	SUMMER	WINTER
Early	Check horse all over, and pick out feet. Fill haynet, and feed concentrate if necessary. Give fresh water. Muck out stable.	As summer, but also remove and replace blanket and any liner with lighter blanket. Check for rubs. Deal with any ice and snow in the stableyard.
Midmorning	Groom lightly to remove stable stains and make horse comfortable. Tack up and exercise. On return, remove tack and groom thoroughly. Fill haynet, and feed concentrate if necessary. Check water supply.	As summer, but remove any sweat after exercise, and dry thoroughly before replacing blanket.
Afternoon	Remove droppings. Check hay and water. Tack up and exercise. (If not possible, trot horse up and down to stretch its legs and check it for lameness.) Feed concentrate if necessary. Clean tack.	As summer, but check position of blanket, and look for any rubs, if horse is not being ridden.
Evening	Remove any droppings and shake up the bed. Feed concentrate if necessary. Pick out feet. Check water and fill haynet. Make final check of horse last thing and check security of stableyard.	As summer, but replace day blanket with usual night blanket for extra warmth at night.

WEEKLY	MONTHLY	YEARLY
Check feed supply. Clean tack thoroughly. Clean blankets. Remove cobwebs from upper stable walls. Check first-aid kit. Clean stable equipment.	Check bedding supply. Check date of next worming and next shoeing. Check drains and guttering. Clean waterers and mangers.	Arrange manure disposal, tetanus and other vaccinations, and dental check. Check fire extinguishers. Do major maintenance jobs such as painting.

POSSIBLE ROUTINES USING THE COMBINED SYSTEM

DAILY	SUMMER (HORSE IN DURING THE DAY, OUT AT NIGHT)	WINTER (HORSE IN AT NIGHT, OUT DURING THE DAY)
Early	Check horse all over, and pick out feet. Adjust blankets. Fill haynet, and feed concentrate if necessary. Change water, and remove droppings.	As summer, but also remove and replace blanket and any liner with lighter blanket. Check for rubs. Deal with any ice and snow in the stableyard.
Midmorning	Groom horse lightly, tack up, and exercise. On return, untack, rub down, and put on field blanket. Pick out feet, and turn out. Feed hay, and concentrate if necessary. Check water in field.	As summer, but remove any sweat after exercise, and dry thoroughly before replacing blanket.
Afternoon	Muck out stable. Clean tack. Check horse and blanket. Feed hay, and concentrate if necessary. Check field boundaries.	As summer, but check position of blanket, and look for any rubs, if horse is not being ridden.
Evening	Catch horse and bring in. Change rug. Give fresh water, and concentrate if necessary. Fill haynet. Make final check of horse last thing, and check stableyard security.	As summer, but replace day blanket with usual night blanket for extra warmth at night.

BUYING AND KEEPING A HORSE

Before you look for a horse to buy, you must make definite arrangements about where and how you are going to keep it. Apart from anything else, this will affect the type and size of horse that you can have; if you have only a small stable and paddock, you will not be able to accommodate a large horse. You can care for your horse yourself or keep it at a boarding stable. The most expensive way to keep a horse is to have it at "full board." The horse is fed, stabled, groomed, and possibly exercised by the staff. Other forms of livery include "do-it-yourself" and partial board.

VIEWING A HORSE

The horse should move freely around the field

If the horse is in a halter, this may mean it is difficult to catch

In the field
When buying a horse, ask the owner if you can see it loose in the field first. Watch its body language as it approaches both you and other horses, to spot signs of aggression or timidity. Make sure that you are able to catch it easily on your own.

In the stable
See what type of bedding is used and why. If the horse needs different bedding from the other horses, this may indicate respiratory problems. Watch for signs of stable vices such as weaving.

The horse should not resent taking the bit

Tacking up
Tack the horse up yourself before riding it to see how it behaves. Make sure that it stands still and that its back does not sink down when you fasten the girth. An adverse reaction by a horse to being tacked up may mean that you will have problems later.

The vet will check the horse's teeth to assess its age

Veterinary examination
Always ask a vet to check the horse thoroughly before purchase. The examination will cover every aspect of its health, including any defects and how they may affect the work you want the horse to do. The opinion is only really valid on that day for that specific purchaser.

BOARDING A HORSE

A neat stableyard
The overall discipline that results in a neat stableyard may ensure a good, regular routine for your horse. Look around the yard for clues such as a neat manure pile, tack that is clean and in good condition, and well-shod horses.

Choosing a boarding stable
When choosing a boarding stable for your horse, it is more important to learn about the people who work there than about the buildings. Spend some time watching the staff; are they kind to the horses? Do they seem to work efficiently? Is the tack clean and in good condition?

Boarding will be cheaper if you do tasks such as tack cleaning yourself

Grazing facilities
Whether you keep your horse at home or board it, it should have access to grazing land. The paddocks should be safe (see p. 84) and, even in winter, there will ideally be some grass around, if your climate permits. Horses prefer to graze with company rather than alone; make sure that your horse will have amiable, not hostile, companions.

Responsibility for routine tasks
It is important to have set down in writing the services that will be provided by the boarding stable, and which of these will be charged for separately. For example, will you have to clean your own tack? Who will arrange the worming of your horse, and who will pay for the wormer? Equipment such as blankets and grooming kit, which you may have to provide, can also be a significant extra cost.

GLOSSARY

Abscess A localized accumulation of pus.
Action The way in which a horse moves its legs at each gait. The term covers the straightness of the movements, how high the horse lifts its feet off the ground, and the amount of flexion of the joints.
Aged Any horse older than eight years is said to be aged.
Antibiotic A drug that kills bacteria in or on the horse.

Bacteria Microscopic single-celled organisms that live in or on larger creatures such as the horse.
Bars (1) The hard stretches of gum, between the last incisor tooth and the first molar tooth, on which the bit rests. **(2)** The ends of the hoof wall, which extend from the heels toward the center of the sole.
Bone The substance that makes up the skeleton of the horse. It is also used to refer to the circumference of the cannon bone as an indication of the horse's size and potential weight-bearing capacity.
Boxy feet Narrow, upright feet with small frogs and closed heels. Feet with this shape can cause problems, because they do not absorb concussion properly and may put excessive strain on the legs.
Breaking out This is when a horse begins to sweat again after it has already cooled off after exercise.
Breed A variety of horse (or other animal) consisting of a group of individuals that share the same genetic and physical characteristics and pass these on to their offspring.
Bringing up Gradually bringing a horse back into work after a rest at grass, and usually into a stabled lifestyle.
Broken down A term used of a horse that has suffered a severe sprain of a flexor tendon.

Canine tooth This tooth is not always present in horses. When it is present, usually in male horses, it is called the tush and lies behind the incisor teeth.
Cartilage A substance that covers the joint surfaces of bones to form a smooth, moving surface.
Cast (in a stall) A horse is said to be cast when it lies down or rolls in a confined space and is unable to stand up again because it is stuck.
Cast a shoe A horse is said to have cast a shoe when a shoe comes off by accident.
Cereals Grasses that have been developed to provide seeds as food are called cereals. Examples include barley, oats, and wheat.
Clean legs (1) Legs free from blemishes or swellings, such as splints or thickened tendons. **(2)** Legs with little or no feather.

Clinch The end of each horseshoe nail is bent over to hold the nail in place, and the resulting hook is called a clinch.
Coldblood A heavy horse descended from the primitive Forest Horse of northern Europe.
Colored horse A horse whose coat has large, distinct areas of white hair and black or brown hair. (Coats of more than two colors are called "odd-colored".)
Colt A young male horse that has not been castrated.
Commonbred A horse of indeterminate breeding, usually with a low proportion of Thoroughbred blood.
Concentrates The food given to provide high levels of nutrition in a small volume.
Concussion (1) Shock or jarring that affects the feet and legs and is caused by percussion of the foot on hard surfaces.
(2) Unconsciousness or temporary brain injury caused by a blow on the head.
Condition The horse's level of fitness or fatness. A horse in "soft" condition has flabby muscles and possibly extra fat; one in "hard" condition has well-toned muscles and no surplus fat.
Conformation The way a horse is put together.

Dam A horse's mother.
Diastema The technical name for the bars of the mouth.
Dishing Faulty action in which a horse throws its front feet out to each side instead of moving its legs straight.
Dominant gene A gene whose influence is greater than that of similar genes. For instance, among the genes for coat color, gray is dominant over all others.
Draft horse A horse used for pulling heavy loads.
Dumped toe Poor foot shape caused by bad farriery. The foot is rasped so that the toe is cut off short, instead of the shoe being made to fit the foot, or the wall of the hoof being trimmed properly.

Entire A male horse that has not been castrated.

Feather Long, coarse hair on a horse's fetlocks and lower legs.
Fiber Also known as cellulose, this is the tough material that strengthens the leaves and stems of plants. Feeds with a high proportion of fiber, such as grass and hay, are called roughage.
Filly A young female horse (up to four years old) before she has had a foal.

Flehmen A behavioral response in which the horse opens its mouth and curls up its upper lip.
Folic acid A vitamin needed for blood cell formation.
Fungal spores The microscopic particles by which fungi spread through the air. They can trigger allergies in some horses.

Gait A pattern of leg movements. The gaits common to all horses are walk, trot, canter, and gallop. Special gaits particular to certain breeds include the paso, done by the Peruvian Paso, and the tölt, a speciality of the Icelandic pony.
Galls Swellings or sore, rubbed areas caused by badly fitting tack.
Galvayne's groove A groove down the upper-corner incisor teeth, used to give an approximate age for older horses.
Gelding A castrated male horse.
Going The condition of the ground, and the extent to which it affects a horse's movements. (For example, "hard going" is hard ground, and "heavy going" is deep mud that clings to the horse's feet.)
Good keeper A horse that needs only a small amount of food to stay in good health and condition.

Halfbred A horse with one parent that is Thoroughbred and one of a different breed.
Hand A unit of measurement for horses, which is equal to 4 in (10 cm).

Hard mouth A "hard-mouthed" horse is unresponsive to rein aids. This problem is caused by bad, heavy-handed riding, which damages the surfaces of the bars of the mouth, and deadens the nerves in the area.
Heating Describes feed that gives a horse too much energy and makes it excitable.
Heavy horse A very large, heavily built horse developed for its great strength.
Hemoglobin The substance in red blood cells that carries oxygen.
Hierarchy A social grouping of horses, or other animals, in which the members have different levels of importance. The most dominant horses are at the top of the hierarchy, and the most submissive ones are at the bottom.
Hogged mane A mane that has been shorn off down to the neck.
Hotblood A horse of Thoroughbred or Arab breeding.

Incisors The front teeth, used for biting grass and other food.
Infundibulum An indentation exposed on the biting surface of the incisor teeth at certain stages of wear.
In hand A way of leading a horse from the ground (particularly in show classes).
Instinct Automatic behavior that the horse does not have to learn but appears to know from birth.

Keratin A protein that is the main element in hard tissue such as hoof horn.

Lactic acid Substance produced by muscle fibers during exercise. It can cause muscle damage if it is not quickly removed by the circulation.
Ligament Fibrous, cordlike structure that attaches one bone to another.
Light horse A finely built horse bred for speed rather than strength.
Light of bone A term used for a horse with an inadequate bone circumference for its build.
Lunging A way of exercising a horse from the ground. The horse moves around a handler, who controls it with a long rein.

Mare A mature female horse.
Molars Large teeth with broad, flat top surfaces, found at the back of the mouth. They are used for grinding up food.

Nappy Used to describe a horse that will not go in the required direction, usually out of willfulness rather than fear.
Near side The horse's left side.

Off side The horse's right side.

Pace (1) The speed of the horse at a certain gait. In order of speed, the paces are: collected (slowest), working, medium, extended. **(2)** A specific two-beat gait where both legs on the same side move at the same time.
Parasite A living organism that lives on and offanother creature. It feeds off food ingested by the host, or feeds from the animal itself, but gives no benefit in return.
Percussion The impact of a horse's foot as it hits the ground.
Pigment An element within the skin, horn, or hair that gives it its color.
Pony A horse smaller than 14 hh 2 in (147 cm) when fully grown.
Poor keeper A horse that needs a large amount of food to stay in good health or maintain condition.

Profile The shape of the horse's nose when seen from the side. It may be straight, convex (a "Roman nose"), or concave ("dished").
Purebred Another name for a Thoroughbred.
Pus The matter formed by accumulation of bacteria and dead white blood cells when there is a localized infection.

Recessive gene A gene whose influence is weaker than all other similar ones. Its influence is only passed on to offspring if both parents have that gene.
Roughage Long-stemmed plant material, which makes up most of a horse's diet.
Roughing off The process by which a fit horse in hard work is prepared for total rest at grass.

Scope Athletic ability, especially for jumping.
Season Also known as estrus, this is the time during which a mare is able to conceive a foal.
Sire A horse's father.
Sound horse (1) A horse that is not lame. **(2)** At time of sale, a horse without any problems that will affect its usefulness.
Stale To pass urine.
Stallion An uncastrated adult male horse.
Staring coat A coat in which the hairs stick up and look dull.

Tack The equipment worn by a horse, hence the term tacking up.
Tendon A fibrous, cordlike structure that links a muscle to a bone.
True to type Means that the horse has the same physical characteristics as its parents and other typical members of its breed.
Type A group of horses that are not genetically similar and do not breed true to type, but which have a broadly similar body shape.

Vice An undesirable behavioral habit.
Virus Microscopic infectious agent. There are no practical antiviral drugs.

Warmblood A horse whose ancestors include both coldbloods and hotbloods.
White line The junction between the horn of the hoof wall and that of the sole.
Whorl A small circular pattern on a horse's coat, with the hairs radiating outward from the center.
Wind A horse's breathing.
Wisping A form of skin massage in which a wisp or massage pad is brought down hard and repeatedly on a horse's muscles, to tone them and improve circulation.
Wolf tooth A small molar tooth not always present and usually removed to prevent biting problems.

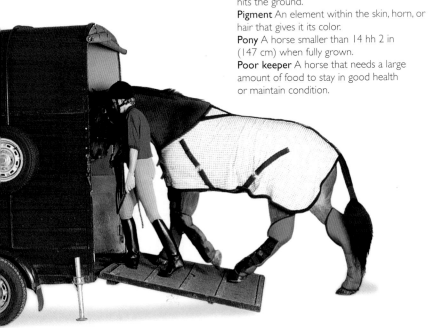

ADDITIONAL INFORMATION

Money-saving tips

The welfare of your horse should come before all other considerations, and certainly before financial matters. The following points, however, should reduce the costs of horse care:

• Consider clubbing together with other horse-owners and keeping all your horses in one place, taking turns to look after the horses and do the chores. This will give you some of the benefits of keeping a horse at livery, without the cost of livery fees.

• Set up a mutual lending arrangement for equipment that is not often used (such as clippers).

• For routine veterinary procedures (such as vaccination) and farrier's visits, get together with other owners so that the vet or farrier can visit you all on the same day. The visiting fees will be cheaper, and it will save the vet or farrier from making several trips to the same area.

• Think hard before you buy anything, to make sure that you need it. If you are not sure, seek expert advice from your vet, farrier, saddler, or riding school instructor. When you buy new feed or equipment, buy the best quality; it will last much longer, and be much better for your horse, than cheaper brands.

• If your horse is stabled, make sure that the bed is deep enough. A thin bed is a false economy. It does not protect the horse from injuring itself on the floor, so the horse may need veterinary treatment or even be unrideable; also, it does not keep a horse warm enough, so you will pay more for feed and rugs.

Time-saving tips

Because you have voluntarily accepted the responsibility of keeping a horse, you owe it to the animal to make its life as pleasant as possible. Having said that, there are some points to bear in mind if your time is limited by work or family commitments:

• A mutual horse-care arrangement will save time as well as money. Make sure that everyone involved agrees beforehand when they can be there for the horses, and you all divide the tasks so that nobody ends up doing too much. In this way, each of the group members can ensure adequate care for their horse without having to be there all day.

• Make a list of every single task that you have to do for your horse, then arrange them in order of priority. Top of the list should be jobs that directly affect the horse: exercise, grooming, mucking out (if stabled), daily check (if living out).

• Plan ahead and allocate sufficient time for tasks that don't have to be done daily – for example, thorough tack cleaning, picking up droppings from grazing land, tidying the yard, and muck heap.

• For infrequent jobs such as worming, use a year planner so that you can see instantly when they have to be done. As soon as the task has been taken care of, note on your planner the next time it has to be done. Every time the vet or farrier comes, make your next routine appointment while they are still with you. Planning ahead in this way will save you from constantly worrying about these tasks, and conversely will also ensure that you do not leave it too long before attending to them.

• If you don't have time to mix your own feeds, don't be fussy about using pre-mixed feeds; these feeds are carefully formulated for different types of horse or pony at various levels of work. (Ask your vet which type or brand would be best for your horse.)

Insurance

As well as cover for your horse, you will need insurance for tack and other equipment, any stables and other buildings that you own, and yourself. Your vet, or a local riding school proprietor, is likely to know which companies process claims with few problems.

• Have your horse and equipment accurately valued.

• Read the policy carefully, preferably with expert help, so you understand exactly what it does and doesn't cover.

• Carry out all correspondence in writing and keep copies of all your letters for your reference.

• Keep your insurance policy number handy in case of sudden accidents or other problems.

Alternatives to owning

If you cannot afford to buy your own horse, consider shared ownership or taking a horse on loan. Joint owners share the actual price of the horse as well as the cost of its upkeep. A horse on loan still belongs to its owner, but the person using it takes care of it and may have to pay most of the costs of keeping it.

• Joint horse-owners should work out beforehand, and put down in writing, who will do which chores at what times. They must also agree on a riding programme that gives each person a fair amount of riding time without over-tiring the horse.

• Before a horse goes out on loan, a legally binding agreement must be drawn up by a solicitor. The agreement should include how long the loan home can have the use of the horse, how the horse will be kept, what may or may not be done with it, and who is responsible for paying for vets' and farriers' visits and for insurance premiums.

• Some horse rescue charities let horses go out on loan, but these animals need expert, caring homes because they may have physical or psychological problems.

• Any owner loaning a horse will probably want to see how you intend to keep it, and how well you are able to ride and handle it.

USEFUL ADDRESSES

UNITED STATES

American Association of Equine Practitioners
4075 Iron Works Parkway,
Lexington, KY 40511
Tel: (859) 233-0147
W www.aaep.org
A professional association of veterinarians who specialize in treating horses.

American Society for the Prevention of Cruelty to Animals (ASPCA)
424 East 92nd Street,
New York, NY 10128-6804
Tel: (800) 582-5979
W www.aspca.org
Nonprofit animal advocacy group and American's oldest humane society. Education information, publications, audio-visual materials, legislative support, and activities nationwide.

United States Department of Agriculture: Animal Health
4700 River Road, Unit 84
Riverdale, MD 20737-1234
Tel: (301) 734-7833
W www.aphis.usda.gov
The federal and state governments' agriculture departments oversee the management of land and livestock, including horses.

United States Department of Agriculture: Education and Outreach
W www.usda.gov
Click education and outreach for local programs.

United States Equestrian Federation (USEF)
4047 Iron Works Parkway
Lexington, KY 40511
Tel: (859) 258-2472
W www.usef.org
The USEF serves as the national governing body for equestrian sport; it trains, selects, and funds the United States Equestrian Team and licenses competitions across the United States.

National 4-H Council
1400 Independence Ave., S.W., Stop 2225
Washington, D.C. 20250-2225
W www.national4-hheadquarters.gov
The four "Hs" are Head, Heart, Hands, Health. Established by the Department of Agriculture to instruct young people in skills such as animal husbandry, community service, and personal development. Check for local branches.

United States Pony Club
4041 Iron Works Parkway,
Lexington, KY 40511-8462
Tel: (859) 254-7669
W www.ponyclub.org
The pony clubs were founded in order to:
• encourage young people to ride and enjoy all types of mounted sports
• provide instruction in riding, horsemanship, and the care of horses
• promote the highest ideals of sportsmanship and citizenship.
There are over six hundred clubs in the United States and branches in 30 countries worldwide. Membership is open to children up to 17 years old and includes non-horse-owners as well as those with their own ponies. Branches hold competitions, instruction rallies, Summer Camps, and organize the Pony Club's tests, which cover riding and horse care.

North American Riding for the Handicapped Association
P.O. Box 33150, Denver, CO 80233
Tel: (800) 369-7433
W www.narha.org
This national organization can refer you to local and state organizations that support this rewarding activity for physically and mentally challenged people.

CANADA

Canadian Equestrian Federation
2685 Queensview Drive, Suite 100,
Ottawa, Ontario, K2B 8K2
Tel: (866) 282-8395
W www.equestrian.ca

Canadian Pony Club
P.O. Box 127, Baldur, Manitoba, R0K 0B0
Tel: 1-888-286-PONY
W www.canadianponyclub.org
The Pony Club has about one hundred and sixty branches in Canada.

Canadian Society for the Prevention of Cruelty to Animals (SPCA)
W www.spca.com

Canadian Therapeutic Riding Association
5420 Hwy. 6 N., Suite 11, R.R. #5,
Guelph, Ontario, N1H 6J2
Tel: (519) 767-0700
W www.cantra.ca

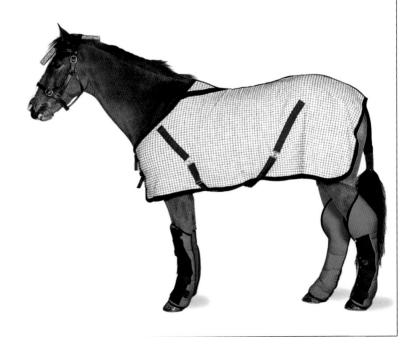

INDEX

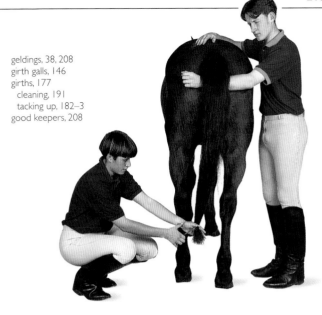

ACKNOWLEDGMENTS

FIRST EDITION
Author's acknowledgments
The author would like to thank the staff of Gillham House Veterinary Group for their help and patience during the preparation of this book.

Publisher's acknowledgments
Dorling Kindersley would like to thank the following people:

Nereide and John Goodman for use of the horses, helpers, and facilities at Wellington Riding Ltd.

Ascot Stables Ltd. for use of the show stable at Old House Farm.

Owners and horses at Wellington Riding Ltd.: Heather Berryman (Rose); Jackie Caldwell (Tikka's Dream); Peter Caldwell (Pendragon); Philippa Earthy (Fergus); Sarah Elmslie (Five & Twenty); Nereide Goodman (Wellington Laska and Wellington Trafalgar); Tessa Lawton (Nivelle); Richard Morrish (Milarochy Bay); Fiona Pavitt (Boothlands Azzaro); Robert Pickles (Wellington Asyllus); Kathleen Ramey (Catherston Dear Edward); Anna Shelton (Kerry); Theresa Hulton (Captain Morgan); Pat Watts (Brandysnap).

At Ascot Stables Ltd.:
Sheila Baigent (Puzzle).

All the staff at Wellington Riding Ltd. for their help and patience, especially Beverley Davies, Alex Ehrmann, and Suzanne Judd.

Ralph Butler, Beverley Davies, Harriet Green, Samuel Harpur, Katie John, Suzanne Judd, Shelly Moores, David Sheerin, Claudia Steele, Colin Vogel for modeling. Emma Butcher, Anna Shelton, and Amanda Webb for assistance. Clive Duffin for farriery.

Mark Runiewicz for the use of his trailer.

Hilary Bird for the index.

Becky Halls for picture research. Rachel Leach for additional picture research.

Dorling Kindersley would also like to thank Cam Equestrian Ltd. and Ride Away for the loan of saddlery, clothing, and equipment; Clayton Equine Safety for the Equipack first-aid pack; B and J Dance and Dengie Crops Ltd. for horse feeds; Fieldguard for rubber matting; Hemcore for hemp bedding.

For 2011 edition: Threshers Barn for providing equipment, Jo Eeley, Aimee Lister, Emma Lister, Linda Self for co-ordinating the photoshoots and providing horse, Luke Silcock for providing horse shoes, Paul Self for additional photography

Picture credits
Key: t top, b bottom, c center,
l left, r right,

Illustrations
All illustrations by Andrew Macdonald except for Joanna Cameron 28c, 29cl, tr; Tony Graham 26, 28bl, cr; Janos Marffy 50; Sean Milne 10; Dan Wright 29cr.

Photography
Additional photography by Peter Anderson, Peter Chadwick, Geoff Dann, Mike Dunning, Andreas Einsiedel, Neil Fletcher, John Glover, Steve Gorton, Anna Hodgson, Colin Keates, Dave King, Bob Langrish, Andrew McRobb, Ray Moller, Gary Ombler, Roger Philips, Tim Ridley, Matthew Ward.

Alamy.com/Mark J.Barrett 55b; Animalcare 109t, c, b; Animal Photography/R.T.Wilbie 122b; Ardea London Ltd/Johan De Meester 5 bcr; Biofotos/Heather Angel 94c; Boehringer Ingelheim Vetmedica Inc. 168t; Bruce Coleman Ltd./Jeff Foott Productions 42b/Flip de Nooyer 95tr/William S. Paton 10cr/Dr. Eckart Pott 10b, 92br/Hans Reinhard 70t/Gunter Ziesler 42c; Corbis/Kevin R.Morris 4tr/Kit Houghton 110t, 189t, bl/Richard Hamilton Smith 95cr/Robert Holmes 4tc/Roger Tidman 95cl/Sylvia Cordaiy Photo Library Ltd 122tr/Christine Hipkiss 189br/James de Bounevialle 156; courtesy Equibrand 130bl, c, 204cr; FLPA/David Hosking 55t; Getty Images/The Image Bank/Jack Ward 38t, 54, Getty Images/Stone 86t, 113cr; Robert Harding Picture Library 5tcr, 94t, 122tl, 188/Jane Legate 5bl; Michael Holford 8–9; Kit Houghton 4br, 5tcl, 6, 20bl, br, 30bl, 32cr, 37tl, cl, 46t, 47bl, br, 63tl, 80t, c, b, 81tr, cl, cr, br, 82, 87tl, 88t, br, 90b, 92t, 108b, 110b, 112t, 118–119, 123tr, 129br, 157t, 171tl, 174–175, 202–203; Derek Knottenbelt/University of Liverpool 138b, 139tl, bl, 140clb, bl, 141t, c, 142cld, 143bl, 144cl, bl, 145t, c, 146t, c, b, 147t, bl, bc, 148br, 149t, c, 153, 154cb, b, 155b; Bob Langrish 1, 2, 5tl, bcl, 22bl, 40, 46b, 47tl, tr, 75bl, 81bl, 87tr, 102, 105t, 108cl, cr, 132, 170, 171tr, tc, cl, cr, 172t, b, 173, 205b, 207tl; Microscopix Photo Library/Andrew Syred 21tr; National Geographic Images Collection 90tl; NHPA/Henry Ausloos 4bc; Only Horses Picture Agency 86b, 129br; Oxford Scientific Films/Christine Steimer 89/Lothar Lenz 5tr/Philip Tull 157b; Harry Smith Horticultural Collection 92cr, bl, bc, 93cr, 94br, 95c, cl; ZEFA 38b, 85tr.

p. 11 Highland pony—*Monarch of Dykes* Countess of Swinton

pp. 12–13 Hack—
Mr. and Mrs. D. Curtis
Riding pony, cob, hunter—
Robert Oliver

p. 14 Dorsal stripe—*Fruich of Dykes* Countess of Swinton
Dun—*Montemere O'Nora*
Nan Thurman

p. 15 Blaze—*Spooks*
Peter Munt
Snip—*Hippolyte*
Haras Nationale de Pau

p. 18 Arab—*Muskhari Silver*
Janet and Anne Connolly, Silver Fox Arabians, West Midlands
Ardennais—*Trojan*
Charlie Pinney, Egrement Farm, Payhembury, Honiton, Devon

p. 50 t—*Noaner*
Istituto Incremento Ippico di Crema

The publishers would like to make it clear that no horses were injured during photography for this book.